BUSINESS AND BUDDHISM

Business and Buddhism explores alternative ways of leading in the aftermath of the Great Recession and the many stories of fraud and greed that emerged. The book explores shifts in business perspectives as more value is placed on soft skills such as emotional intelligence and listening, and introduces the reader to the principles in Buddhist philosophy that can be applied in the workplace.

Buddhist practices are increasingly understood as spiritual, rather than religious, *per se.* In fact, Buddhism is sometimes referred to as a philosophy or psychology. In this book, Marques explores the value of applying the positive psychology of Buddhism to work settings. She outlines the ways in which it offers highly effective solutions to addressing important management and organizational behavior-related issues, but also flags critical areas for caution. For example, Buddhism is non-confrontational and promotes detachment. How can business leaders negotiate these principles in light of the demands of modern-day pressures?

The book includes end-of-chapter questions to promote reflection and critical thinking, and examples of Buddhist leaders in action. It will prove a captivating read for students of organizational behavior, management, leadership, diversity and ethics, as well as business consultants.

Joan Marques serves as director of the BBA program and is assistant professor of management at Woodbury University, USA. She has published in the *Journal of Business Ethics*, the *Journal of Management Development*, and *Business and Society*, and has authored or co-authored nine books on management and leadership topics.

BUSINESS AND BUDDHISM

Joan Marques

NEW YORK AND LONDON

First published 2015
by Routledge
711 Third Avenue, New York, NY 10017

and by Routledge
2 Park Square, Milton Park, Abingdon, Oxon OX14 4RN

Routledge is an imprint of the Taylor & Francis Group, an informa business

© 2015 Taylor & Francis

The right of Joan Marques to be identified as author of this work
has been asserted by her in accordance with sections 77 and 78 of the
Copyright, Designs and Patents Act 1988.

All rights reserved. No part of this book may be reprinted or reproduced
or utilized in any form or by any electronic, mechanical, or other means,
now known or hereafter invented, including photocopying and recording,
or in any information storage or retrieval system, without permission in
writing from the publishers.

Trademark notice: Product or corporate names may be trademarks or
registered trademarks, and are used only for identification and explanation
without intent to infringe.

Library of Congress Cataloging-in-Publication Data
Marques, Joan.
  Business and Buddhism / by Joan Marques. — 1 Edition.
    pages cm
  Includes bibliographical references and index.
1. Entrepreneurship—Religious aspects—Buddhism. 2. Leadership—
Religious aspects—Buddhism. I. Title.
HB615.M378 2015
294.3'373—dc23
2014033786

ISBN: 978-1-138-78604-2 (hbk)
ISBN: 978-1-138-78606-6 (pbk)
ISBN: 978-1-315-76743-7 (ebk)

Typeset in Bembo
by Apex CoVantage, LLC

CONTENTS

Introduction   *vii*

1 The Growth of Business: From Then to Now   1

The History of Trade: A Brief Overview   1
The Corporation   3
The Industrial Revolution   6
Business in the Twentieth Century   9
Summary   12
Questions   14

2 The Twentieth Century in the United States: Setting the Stage   16

Quantum Leaps in Development   16
Summary   25
Questions   27

3 Ambivalent Views Toward Modern-Day Business   30

Business in the Twenieth Century: A Management Overview   30
Change, Growth, and Development   37
The Reputation of Business   39
Summary   39
Questions   41

4 New Insights in a New Millennium   43

The Changing Leadership Climate: Hard Versus Soft Skills   43
Using Soft and Hard Skills in Today's Workforce   47
Summary   51
Questions   52

vi Contents

5 Buddhism: Some Foundational Notes   55

Buddhism: An Interpretation   55
Summary   62
Questions   63

6 Main Vehicles of Buddhism   65

Two Schools, One Buddhism   65
Buddhism in the United States: A Brief Overview   70
The Dalai Lama and Tibetan Buddhism   75
Summary   77
Questions   80

7 The Place of Suffering and Harming in Our Lives   84

Buddhism: Some Basic Concepts   84
Buddhism and Consciousness   96
Summary   102
Questions   105

8 Buddhism and Business: Friends or Foes?   109

A Fertile Climate for Change   109
Buddha Enters the Workplace   112
Summary   125
Questions   127

9 A Closer Look at the Points of Caution   130

A Middle Path for Everything   130
Summary   142
Questions   143

10 Buddhist Business Leaders in Action   146

Three Leaders, One Mindset   146
Common Practices   154
The Seven-Point Mind Training   156
Summary   160
Questions   161

Index   *165*

INTRODUCTION

Business has been around since humankind began, but made enormous strides during the Industrial Revolution, and became more complex in the knowledge era. The ease of starting a business today has dramatically changed its nature and its constituents. Starting a business has never been easier, as much of it can simply be done online. Many contemporary businesses have no formal "brick and mortar" location, and their shoppers purchase everything from the comfort of their own home or office. Concepts about doing business have immensely changed as well: today, everyone who shops online engages in global business, as it is very easy to compare rates, quality, and delivery service in a few clicks. Business performers often find their competitors in all sizes and many countries of the world. It is therefore no secret that business has the potential to enter where very few others can.

Business is treasured and despised at the same time because it can bring change, growth, and development, but it can also suffocate, disrupt, and deprive. In the past century, and more clearly in the first decade of the twenty-first century, we have witnessed many businesses and their leaders making the news in a very negative way. Investigation reveals that many of these businesses have been performing immorally for decades, and got away with doing so because of a strong support system, shrewd leaders and accountants who managed to manipulate information they shared with external auditors, and societies that were simply ignorant of what was going on. Among those unethical performers we find representatives in almost every field of business: from energy companies that manipulated the supply of a direly needed service to increase prices, to drug companies that insisted bringing drugs in the market of which they knew the disastrous side effects beforehand; from automobile concerns that simply decided that saving human lives was not worth a recall of cars with a serious defect, to finance moguls that preyed on their clients' desire to be home owners and set them up for failure.

viii Introduction

Yet, with the changing dynamics in human society, where we get exposed to more information in one month than our forefathers witnessed in an entire life, our awareness increases. As humanity's collective awareness rises through increased global exposure, the emphasis of business is gradually changing from a one-dimensional bottom-line focus, which prevailed in the twentieth century, to a growing multidimensional social and moral responsibility approach in the twenty-first century. The advances are minuscule, and many a setback can be detected along the way, but a trend of elevated awareness is setting in and spreading nonetheless.

Buddhism has been around for more than 2,500 years, starting with its originator Siddhartha Gautama, better known as "the Buddha," who acquired some valuable insights over the course of his life. These insights have been formalized in various "vehicles" or "schools," passed on through the centuries and spread worldwide. The most commonly known schools are Theravada, the old, or smaller vehicle, and Mahayana, the larger vehicle. The two schools agree on foundational insights and teachings such as suffering, impermanence, no-self, karma, nirvana, dependent origination, mindfulness, the Four Noble Truths, and the Noble Eightfold Path. However, they also have their differences, as will be explained in this book. As an example, the Theravada tradition considers awakening to be attainable only by ordained male Buddhist monastics. The Mahayana school, however, adheres to the belief that everybody can become a "bodhisattva" (enlightened being).

Buddhism has always proposed openness and a welcoming approach to people from all walks of life. This principle finds its origin in the Buddha's life, as he disagreed with a number of issues that were quite common in his times, such as the local caste system, the notion that one could only be from one particular group to attain "liberation." He welcomed followers from all ranks of life, and proposed a lifestyle which he called the Middle Way, based on his past experiences that excesses are not constructive to our personal and mental wellbeing. As will be described in the book, the Buddha had experienced an excessively lavish lifestyle, followed by a rigorous ascetic one, only to conclude that neither of the two brought him any insights. He ultimately engaged in deep meditation, also known as Vipassana, and attained enlightenment. Upon attaining enlightenment, he started teaching to people who were interested in his insights, and acquired quite a following, which continues to this day in the worldwide interest in Buddhism.

Buddhism can be perceived in many ways, such as a social model, a religion, a philosophy, or a psychology. In each of its applications, it eludes the query about a higher being, and focuses more on the teaching of virtues such as non-harming and the ending of suffering through a series of steps pertaining to our views, intentions, speech, actions, livelihood, efforts, concentration, and mindfulness.

As business leaders become more informed about the importance of combining hard and soft skills in their relations, they also become aware of the importance of stakeholder inclusion and consideration of the many forms of diversity within the human cohort. This may indicate that we have ultimately reached the point where Buddhist psychology could find broad reception in contemporary workforces. However, while there may be great enthusiasm in applying the positive psychology of Buddhism to work settings, there are some *critical areas* for caution that need to be heeded. For instance, Buddhism is nonconfrontational, promotes detachment, and emphasizes non-harming. Could business leaders therefore really fully adhere to Buddhist-based practices? This book will review the critical pros and cons of implementing Buddhist psychology in management, and provide some serious points to ponder.

1

THE GROWTH OF BUSINESS

From Then to Now

> In this world everything changes except good deeds and bad deeds; these follow you as the shadow follows the body.
>
> Bhikkhu Bodhi

The History of Trade: A Brief Overview

The Early Days

When we want to review business in historical context, we actually have to start with the history of trade. After all, trade is the forerunner of business as we know it today. If we consider matters within that scope, business has been around since human beings have, because they have always done some kind of exchange with one another. As prehistoric nomadic people migrated across the continents of Asia, Africa, Australia, Europe, and the Americas, they gathered fruits, vegetables, and animals, raised their offspring, and gradually developed navigational skills and cultural patterns that distinguished them from one another and enabled them to engage in exchanges.

As time evolved, human beings became interested in more than just the basics for survival. They started appreciating external adornments, paintings and other symbolisms, and about 100,000 years ago, trade started with neighboring communities in order to obtain necessities and desired items such as herbs, animal hides, ornaments, and stones from one another.[1] Over the next centuries, many tribes surrendered their nomadic existence for a more domesticated style of living, which gave way to the need for more rules, regulations, protection measures, and boundary determinations as well as tendencies to saving and storing. Villages were erected, and the notion of a "home base" set in. The previous nomadic herders

2 The Growth of Business

started to experiment with different types of grass to ensure long-term feeding opportunities for their flocks. Their discoveries and inventions became new trading objects with neighboring and nomadic tribes, and the exchange process increased. Over time a task-division system evolved within the villages, with some families specializing in crops, others in cattle, and others in building tools for farming, cooking, or other activities.[2]

As the transition from a day-by-day, unpredictable nomadic lifestyle to a more domesticated one gave way to increased specialization, the need for social interaction and trade at multiple levels increased, as did the need to learn about other communities in order to interact. Basic villages evolved into complete cultures, each with their own areas of expertise. Long-distance trade became the new trend, enabling people to exchange a wide range of products and tangible goods, such as stones, exotic goods, furs, herbs, salt, bronze, iron, and pottery, as well as intangibles such as ideas and knowledge about innovative techniques, causing small villages to expand into larger communities.[3] As early as 10,000 BCE (before common era), there were long-distance caravan networks, and by 8,000 BCE, trade routes had been established in Africa, Asia, and Europe. Goods were transmitted from farmers and artisans to merchants and traders at an ever-increasing pace, and in a similarly increasing variety. Gold, silver, beads, seeds, wine, spices, food preservatives, textiles, wool, opium, pottery, mosaics, livestock, honey, and even furniture and weaponry became popular trade items. Thus, the system evolved, and merchants became very powerful over time due to their ability to communicate across cultures. With this evolution, new areas of professional expertise emerged, such as record keepers, coin producers, gold and silver smiths, and specialists in food and beverage preservation. Merchants developed uniform scales and measurements to facilitate trade between cultures. They also became masters in weather predictions and global navigations.[4]

While much of the above has been proven through archaeological findings, the earliest international trade records only date back to the nineteenth century BCE, when Assyrians, Arabians, Egyptians, Indians, Greeks, Romans, and Chinese were involved in trading spices, silk, gold, silver, ivory, gemstones, incense, aromatics, coffee, and luxury goods.

Trade From the Middle Ages On

It is in the "Middle Ages" (the timespan between 5 CE and 15 CE [common era]) that the closest precursor of business as we know it today can be found. This is the timeframe in which we see the major rise of the entrepreneur, a medieval capitalist who helps determine the speed of Europe's transition from feudalism to capitalism. In her book *Gold & Spices: The Rise of Commerce in the Middle Ages*, Favier describes London, Bruges, Venice, Lubek, and Genoa as energetic, emerging centers of commerce. It is the trade of those days that led to immense wealth, not only within that generation, but into second and third generations as well. The tasks within merchant families varied from informants and correspondents to agents and service specialists. Daring, intelligent traders expanded the world's horizons.[5]

In seventeenth- and eighteenth-century Europe, international trade entered a more systematic stage, which is now referred to as "mercantilism." In mercantilism, the main objective of trade was identified as promoting a favorable trade balance. This meant that nations had to export more than they imported, in order for their trade balance to be considered favorable.[6] In those days, exporting, especially of finished goods, was seen as a desirable trend, and importing goods was seen as undesirable. The idea was that imports should, as much as possible, be limited to only raw materials. In order to manipulate their country's trade balance, mercantilists were constantly pushing their governments to raise taxes on trade. Then something happened that shifted the entire emphasis of what mattered in international trade: The publication of Adam Smith's book, *An Inquiry into the Nature and Causes of the Wealth of Nations*. Smith encouraged people to engage in specialization, theorizing that this would increase productivity and efficiency, thereby producing more goods from the same resources.[7]

Since those times, trade has made great strides, and recent history has brought us reduced trade barriers and increased trade collaborations, generally known as Preferential Trading Agreements (PTAs). Today we have various gradations of PTAs, beginning with the standard PTA, which reduces or eliminates barriers on selected goods between member nations; progressing to the Free Trade Area, in which member nations agree to reduce or eliminate trade barriers on all their goods; followed by the Customs Union, which removes tariff barriers between members and accepts a common tariff against nonmembers; the Common Market, which heads toward full economic integration, entailing free trade of more than just tangible goods among members; the Economic Union, which entails a common market between members and a common trade policy toward nonmembers; the Monetary Union, which moves toward macroeconomic integration between members; the Fiscal Union, in which tax rates are synchronized toward greater mutual support and unity; an Economic and Monetary Union involving a single economic market; and finally, the Complete Economic Integration, involving a single economic market.[8]

The Corporation

It is the desire of people to associate and build lasting groups, which lies at the foundation of today's corporations. This desire is an ancient one, so we have to take a quantum leap back in time to discover the origins of corporations many centuries ago, in the days of Greek, Roman, and Germanic dominance.

In late medieval Europe (between 1300 and 1500), the notion of family became stronger than in previous centuries. Prior to this time, the idea of "family" was largely based on the tribal concept, including immediate as well as distant relatives as part of the household. The new perception of family gave way to economic

4 The Growth of Business

and political corporations: entities that were deliberately created with a predefined interest and structure. The notion of "corporation" in this light should be seen broader than a for-profit entity. It comprised cities, communes, educational institutions, fraternities, guilds, businesses, professional organizations, and more.[9]

The nuclear family, consisting of a pair of adults and their children, won prestige and attraction in those days under influence of the Church. The powerful Church dictated the structure and lifestyle of families and prohibited forms of living that would lead to too much expansion, such as polygamy, divorce, remarriage, and concubinage. Over time, the term "family" became limited to only those within the same household, or at least not too far beyond that.[10] The demise of clans and ancestry-lines and the rise of commercialization, class structures, and state formations, runs parallel with the spread of Christianity.[11]

The corporation complemented the nuclear model of family, and soon turned out to be more attractive and advantageous for the individual than the larger tribal form, even if that was based on kinship. Corporations were created on the basis of an interest, and members were attracted to collaboration toward a predefined purpose. The corporations existed for the advancement of its members, had leaders who were responsible for their growth, and had lifespans that were independent of those of its members. As state and Church started losing authority, corporations gained it. The corporate concept found appeal within local societies, especially because there was no royal permission required to set up a corporation. Besides, corporations provided protection and social safety to their members against governments, pirates, and each other, and did not require kinship from anyone who wanted to be part of it.[12]

By the thirteenth century in Europe, as the corporate phenomenon developed, so did the awareness about the advantages of the nuclear structure. Consequently, families became smaller, marriages were planned for later in life, regulation increased, rights were formulated, brands established, and knowledge expanded. Corporations became so powerful that they started dictating governments' actions.[13] It is due to the emergence of the corporate model that Europe started gaining economic significance in the global forum, ultimately leading to a commercial revolution and a series of expansions and control-based actions such as imperialism, colonization, and industrialization. This all happened because there was an interesting mutualism at play between corporations and rulers of those days. The rulers had the military power but not the organizational savvy that corporations had. Together, however, they formed a perfect team. Tribal societies became easy targets to conquer and control for the powerful European-grown corporations with their iron self-governance. The trend persisted over the centuries, and still does today.

Corporations in the United States

The American Revolution is closely linked to corporate growth. In the last two decades of the eighteenth century (around 1780), state legislatures created a large number of corporations, right at the time when in Europe, the phenomenon of corporations was considered outdated. In fact, France had outlawed them in 1791.[14] In the first three decades of the eighteenth century, it became apparent that the number of U.S. corporations aimed at economic activities such as banking, insurance, construction, and manufacturing, was greater and more dominant than in any other country at the time.[15] When the general government attempted to follow the European tradition of those days in making Congress the only power to incorporate, it was met with fierce opposition. Over the course of the century, Americans remained passionate about creating corporations, a trend that forced legislators to deviate from the European model and take the innovative route. It should also be noted that U.S. corporations were markedly different from the prior English ones, as well as from those that emerged in Britain in the nineteenth century. The U.S. corporation had developed its own culture, based on the American Revolution, which gave birth to it.[16]

The original center of corporate growth in the United States was located in Massachusetts. This development inspired local jurists to develop corporate laws from early on in order to effectively resolve the problems that emerged from the performance of these corporations. Massachusetts' corporate laws, many of which were created in the early nineteenth century, soon became the role model for the rest of the United States. Early U.S. corporations were not, as many think, solely focused on financial profits. In the early years of corporate existence in the United States, more than half of these entities were focused on political influence, and a large part of the others on religion, education, and charity. Those that focused on business performance concentrated on banking, manufacturing, construction, and engineering. This trend of corporate division, albeit dominant in numbers in Massachusetts, could also be found in other parts of the country. Corporations even acquired the right to perform as a person in the late nineteenth century, with all the privileges as such: they could own property, could sue or be sued, could protect themselves, and could live on after their founders had passed on.[17] The way corporations obtained personhood continues to be a topic of debate, sometimes even disbelief, among many who criticize the unbridled power and influence these entities obtained over time. Yet, in the early 1800s, the U.S. Supreme Court started recognizing corporations as having the same rights as natural persons in regards to contract enforcements. Near the end of the century, this idea had expanded to greater depth, when in multiple legal cases the Fourteenth Amendment to the Constitution was cited as justification for granting every person the equal protection of the laws, and applying this notion of personhood to corporations. Since then, this doctrine has been reaffirmed by the Court many times.

The acknowledgement of corporations as persons brought along its share of ethical complexities. One major moral issue that manifested itself, and does so to this day, is the fact that corporations and individual humans compete for critical privileges such as gaining rights, property, influence, and wealth, and for limited resources such as assets, clean air, water, and energy.[18] Another moral problem in

6 The Growth of Business

recognizing corporations as persons is the fact that they cannot make decisions as easily and rapidly as individual humans can, and with the global size of modern corporations in which decision-makers often reside in other continents, this interval has become even larger.[19] Corporations have a longevity advancement over humans as well, because their existence can transcend multiple human lifespans, which humans cannot equal. Then there are the human stockholders of the corporations, who aim to reap profits from their investments, but hold very little responsibility in regards to the general moral performance of the corporation.[20]

The sizes in wealth that corporations can attain is yet another moral dimension to consider. For instance, if Wal-Mart were a country, it would be the 25th largest one. Many contemporary corporations are larger than many countries in the world. Here are some examples based on their 2010 revenues: Yahoo is bigger than Mongolia, Visa bigger than Zimbabwe, Consolidated Edison bigger than the Democratic Republic of the Congo, McDonalds bigger than Latvia, Amazon.com bigger than Kenya, Cisco bigger than Lebanon, Apple bigger than Ecuador, Microsoft bigger than Croatia, Costco bigger than Sudan, Proctor & Gamble bigger than Libya, Wells-Fargo bigger than Angola, Ford bigger than Morocco, Bank of America bigger than Vietnam, General Motor bigger than Bangladesh, General Electric bigger than New Zealand, Fannie Mae bigger than Peru, Chevron bigger than the Czech Republic, Exxon-Mobil bigger than Thailand, and Wal-Mart bigger than Norway.[21]

Indeed, since corporations went public, many of them have expanded beyond gargantuan sizes. Yet, it was not until the nineteenth century that a distinction was formulated between public and private corporations. Up until then, all corporate forms were treated without distinction, and their main purpose was seen as servicing the public wellbeing, regardless whether they were banks, medical facilities, or construction entities: in their purpose statements it was usually included that their actions were geared toward the advancement of society as a whole. But in the nineteenth century the trend of creating associations, which was created in New England, became an increasingly popular trend. Many associations arose, and while their focus was widely divergent, the aspect of profitability for the leaders became one of their main goals. One of the often offered reasons for this love for corporation formation in the United States may have been the fact that corporations provided greater means, influence, and action power than average individuals would be able to muster on their own. The shift to corporations aimed at capital generation in the midst of the nation's growth may therefore be considered a logical one.[22]

The Industrial Revolution

As the eighteenth century was approaching its last few decades, business was entering a new era where hand production was replaced with machine processing. Chemical manufacturing, iron production processes, and steam power, among others, became the drivers behind enhanced output and greater efficiency.

There were actually two critical surges within the Industrial Revolution. The first running from about 1760 to around 1840, igniting in England and spreading to Western Europe and the United States. The second revolution was marked by a further surge of technology and economic boom and started in the middle of the nineteenth century.

The reasons for the emergence of the Industrial Revolution in England are interesting: the country was able to pay its citizens high wages because of its immense economic success in the international arena. Britain expanded commercially and imperialistically. Due to the high wages that were paid in that country in comparison to other nations, and to the low energy prices in Britain in those days, British firms developed technologies to substitute capital and energy for labor. In addition, the high wages enabled people in Britain to seek more education and training, which in turn delivered higher literacy rates, greater craft skills, improved engineering talents, and more innovative and creative minds. Hence, Britain's leadership in the Industrial Revolution was established.[23]

With the new magnitude in production that the Industrial Revolution brought, rapid growth in productivity and living standards become noticeable. The second part of this revolution, after 1840, brought modern transportation means and advanced communication, along with improved packaging technology, instigating a trend of mass production and expansive distribution systems.[24] Particularly the last part of this era was driven by an implementation of ideas and discoveries of great thinkers such as Descartes, Galileo, and Bacon. Thanks to improved techniques on almost all fronts of performance, production could be increased at lower costs and with higher revenues.[25]

The Industrial Revolution made a number of century-old standards, behaviors, and paradigms obsolete, and galvanized radical changes in the most essential areas of human performance of those days: agriculture, textile, mining, transportation, economic policies, manufacturing, and social structures.[26]

Agricultural changes entailed an increased yield of wool and cotton production, as well as food crops, thanks to new insights, which led to improved techniques. For instance, farmers learned to restore the fertility of their soil faster, and ensure richer harvests. As a result, there was also more food for herds, which ensured more livestock, and thus, more meat delivery. Increased breeding, insect control, better farming methods, and development of new crops were some additional causes of increased production. The increased production ensured feeding factory workers, who could thus perform more adequately and help expand the English economy.[27]

Textile used to be produced in individual households by women and children. It was a time-consuming, tedious chore that consisted of many layers of performance, from sorting to cleaning and dying, carding and combing, weaving and processing. The Industrial Revolution brought mechanization, and with that, more rapid, increased production, and more consistency in the quality of fabrics.[28] Over time, machines became more advanced, and able to perform multiple tasks

8 The Growth of Business

in one procedure. The domestic preparation of textile was replaced by a factory approach, where women and children were employed at lower wages than men in poorly ventilated conditions without much regulation, and textile production increased tremendously.

Mining has always been a risky undertaking. If already perceived as such during the twentieth century, imagine the risks of this labor in the eighteenth and nineteenth century. Coal mining required physical power, and children were preferred for this job, due to their smaller size. When, during the Industrial Revolution, ponies and carts on rails were used, production increased. Gradually, progress was made in this area as well, and ventilation in tunnels improved, transportation improved, both underground and at the surface, and less hazardous ways were developed to remove coal seams and illuminate the tunnels.[29]

The advancement in transportation has had a huge impact on progress during the Industrial Revolution. Thanks to innovative transport means, products, finished and raw, could find their way to their destinations quicker, as could food and people. Canals and rivers had been utilized well in recent centuries, but when the railways entered the picture, everything shifted into higher gear, especially when engineers managed to apply the steam engine.[30] Several attempts were made in the decades prior to the steam locomotive, but some were too heavy, others too slow. Once settled in properly, however, railways were built and then expanded to enable this innovative way of transporting humans and goods.

The Industrial Revolution also affected longevity of human life. As life became safer, the food supply became more consistent, plagues were reduced, wages increased, and housing conditions improved, mortality rates decreased, and birth rates increased.[31] The Industrial Revolution also affected human settling: increasingly, people dwelled near the factories where they worked, thus creating towns around these factories. Factory owners facilitated this trend as it guaranteed a steady workforce in their premises.

It may not even have been the change in production and distribution processes itself, but rather the changes in social behavior and living standards that deserve the label "revolution." Old habits were replaced by new, more convenient ones; manufacturers' investments tripled, and annual productivity increased to almost six times its previous size. On the consumer's side, incomes increased, and populations started to enlarge. In fact, the Industrial Revolution is particularly known for the increase of per-capita economic growth it instigated in capitalist economies, marking a new milestone in human history.

And while productivity was on the rise, production costs decreased, thanks to those advanced, efficient, and effective machines. Due to the new extent of productions, corporate leaders had to find creative ways to sell more of their products and increase demand in order to sell their increased inventory. This means that new habits needed to be created. Yet, demand can only grow to the extent of available markets, and at the end of the nineteenth century, many manufacturing companies found themselves in a situation where they had to join forces in order to keep themselves afloat. This led to a number of mergers and acquisitions in the early twentieth century.[32]

Business in the Twentieth Century

As the twentieth century advanced, corporations continued their expansions through mergers and acquisitions, and we see manufacturing as well as trading entities spreading beyond local borders. In particular, the trading firms were often family businesses, even though their sizes would not lead us to think they were. The reason why trading firms could maintain family ownership so long was because they were not as dependent on long-term credits as manufacturing firms were. They could survive with short-term loans and were not in such great need of capital as those in the manufacturing industry. Thus, family ownership was not merely a beginning stage for many of the major trading businesses in the past two centuries; sometimes it lasted for many decades. An important reason why family ownership was maintained in these firms is the fact that family leadership often focused more on sustained relationships than on short-term profits. Long-term relationships also guaranteed reduced transaction costs, which was an advantage to the business. Also, a family business was able to make less popular decisions, and sometimes less economic advantageous ones, in order to uphold its principles.[33]

However, when perceived from a more general viewpoint, it becomes apparent that the twentieth century business climate was influenced by a number of significant developments, varying from world wars to ending colonial relationships, and shifts from prior colonial or developing nations, such as the BRIC countries (Brazil, Russia, India, and China) into aggressively emerging economies.

One of the major colonial powerhouses, the British Empire, experienced a steady decline in size in this century. As the empire faced the challenge of losing its geographically dispersed resources (colonies), government and business in the United Kingdom collaborated more closely in their determination of international legislation and execution strategies. Colonies that were acting up against corporate management were straightened out by governmental, financial, and judicial leaders from the motherland. British banks, oil companies, and other business entities often performed as agents of the empire in colonial nations.[34]

Even after the formal colonial reign was over, a power relationship was maintained in former colonies, either by supporting local governments that were in favor of the former colonizer, or by ensuring major dependency from British-originating corporate employers in the former colonies through so-called development funds with strict allocation directives in favor of corporations from the former colonizer. This was not merely a British tendency, but a strategy that was widely used by all former colonizers.

The twentieth century business climate also changed due to a transfer in the manufacturing climate: industrialized nations focused more on service provisions, and left the repetitive manufacturing chores to emerging economies.

10 The Growth of Business

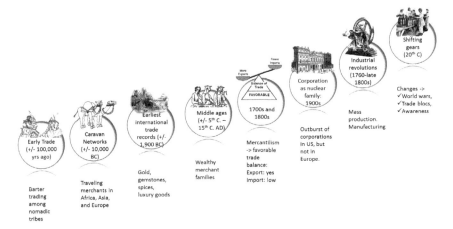

FIGURE 1.1 Snapshot of trade development

Cross-national agreements in different sizes and with different degrees of unity were established, as mentioned in an earlier section of this chapter. European countries formed the European Union, in the Americas we saw various efforts for regional economic integration represented in organizations such as NAFTA (USA, Canada, and Mexico); the Caribbean Community and Common Market (CARICOM) and the Central American Common Market (CACM), both in Central America; and the Andean Community (CAN) and the Southern Common Market (MERCOSUR) in South America. In Asia, albeit with lesser success than Europe and the Americas, the Association of Southeast Asian Nations (ASEAN) was formed in 1967, and the Asia Pacific Economic Cooperation (APEC) in 1989. Africa harbors the Southern Africa Development Community (SADC), the Common Market for Eastern and Southern Africa (COMESA), the Economic and Monetary Community of Central Africa, the West African Economic and Monetary Union (WAEMU), and the African Union, formerly the Organization of African Unity (OAU). Figure 1.1 provides an overview of trade development as it has been discussed in this chapter.

Management in the Twentieth Century

When we consider the way corporations have been managed in the twentieth century, an interesting world of awareness opens up. From the turn of the nineteenth to the twentieth century on, theorists have been working on a formulation of ways to improve efficiency and effectiveness in work environments. While the eighteenth and nineteenth century were marked by major advances in industrialization, the twentieth century was marked by an ever-increasing speed of output and performance. As a result, corporate leaders were pressured to rapidly turn around failing companies and demonstrate profits. Time became more of the essence than anything else.

Scientific management has taken the lead as the popular way of implementing efficient and productive approaches in work environments in the twentieth century. Frederic Winslow Taylor, to be discussed in more depth in the next chapter, published a book on scientific management in 1911, a work that was inspired by the industrial age that was at its height around that time. Enthusiasts of Taylor's theory even spoke of "Taylorism" in those days, emphasizing their admiration of this management thinker's invention. Taylor's theory, as we will see in chapter 3, had great benefits for corporate leaders, but completely disregarded the feelings of the "tools" in the process, who were human beings.[35]

As the 1920s came around, the auto industry was booming, and Alfred Sloan introduced a model of delegation of responsibilities at General Motors. As a result of this model, corporations started developing layers with shared and well-defined managerial responsibility and clear reporting lines.[36]

As the twenties advanced, the Hawthorne Experiments, cosponsored by the National Research Council, found that employees are motivated by much more than just their salaries. They prefer attention to their emotional needs as well. The findings of these studies encouraged more group decision making in corporations.[37]

In the late 1930s, an even more human resource oriented stream emerged, thanks to Mary Parker Follett, a U.S. social worker, management consultant, and pioneer in the fields of organizational theory and organizational behavior. Follett's ideas about collaboration, influence, and employee involvement were critical in the development of organizational studies and human relations in work environments. Around that same time, David Packard and Bill Hewlett promoted "Management by Wandering Around (MBWA)" as a way of maintaining daily connections and more direct lines between managers and employees.[38]

The 1950s brought the wisdom of W. Edwards Deming, who laid the foundation for every worker and department to take individual responsibility for the quality delivered. Deming had more success with his theory in Japan, and only when the Japanese started to outperform the U.S. auto makers, did the United States seriously consider Deming's concepts.[39]

In general, some of the better known management trends that emerged throughout the century were scientific management, administrative theory, bureaucratic theory, human relations, and human resources. Some of these theories, especially those in the latter part of the twentieth century, considered the wellbeing of the workforce, but most of them were mainly concerned with process enhancements and shareholders' pockets. Especially in capitalist systems such as the United States, economic drivers were considered the most critical pillar of work processes, so even fairness rulings were mainly considered from the viewpoint of benefiting the larger group (utilitarianism) instead of doing the right thing.[40]

In the last few decades of the twentieth century, the concept of change emerged as one of the most powerful concepts in business. Workforce members were

12 The Growth of Business

made aware that change was the only constant, and that it was occurring at an ever-increasing pace. Every member and every aspect of the corporate chain was subject to speed: speed in innovating to surpass competitors, speed in output to expand market share, and speed in profit generation to keep shareholders satisfied. The quicker a manager could demonstrate an upward trend in the corporation's performance, the more heroic he was considered to be.[41]

In the next chapter, we will review some of the dominant management trends of the twentieth century, and then move to some of the most prominent perceptions that exist about business.

Summary

In this chapter, we presented:

- A general historical overview of trade as the forerunner of business today, starting with the evolutionary interests of nomadic people from mere primary needs to adornments, paintings, clothing, and other external features, and moving into their evolution toward domestication, including the shifts this brought in lifestyles and outputs. Merchants became experts in buying and selling wares from one tribal community to others, and distinctive areas of expertise emerged between tribes as well as within.
- Trade in the Middle Ages, epitomized by an increased manifestation of merchant families and a mindset of mercantilism, in which the main objective of trade was identified to maintain a favorable trade balance. Exports, especially of finished goods, were considered favorable, and imports unfavorable. These times were also influenced by Adam Smith's notion of specialization in order to increase productivity.
- The corporation in its initial form, as it emerged in medieval Europe. With the increased influence of the Church, the nuclear family won prominence and the tribal notion started losing importance. Early corporations were not necessarily "for profit" entities, but could be anything: a city, a commune, a fraternity, church, or school. Corporations were created on basis of an interest, existed for the advancement of their members, had leaders who were responsible for their growth, and had lifespans that were independent of those of their members.
- Corporations in the United States, which started emerging during the American Revolution and have been forming since. The original center of corporate growth in the United States was located in Massachusetts, which subsequently also became the place where corporate laws were initiated. In the eighteenth century, the United States had more corporations than any other country. Americans remained passionate about creating corporations, and the U.S. corporation developed its own culture, based on the American Revolution, which gave birth to it.

The Growth of Business **13**

- The Industrial Revolution, which had two major stages, one from around 1760 to around 1840, igniting in England and spreading to Western Europe and the United States, and one starting in the middle of the nineteenth century. While there was a revolutionary trend in manufacturing output and speed, the greatest revolution happened within societies where people changed their buying habits, and populations increased.
    - Leadership of the Industrial Revolution should be attributed to England: due to the high wages that were paid in that country in comparison to other nations, and due to the low prices for energy that were customary in Britain in those days, British firms developed technologies to substitute capital and energy for labor.
    - The Industrial Revolution galvanized radical changes in the most essential areas of human performance of those days: agriculture, textile, mining, transportation, economic policies, manufacturing, and social structures.
        - Agricultural changes entailed an increased yield of wool and cotton production, as well as food crops, thanks to new insights, which led to improved techniques.
        - Textile production shifted from a tedious, time-consuming, domestic activity to mechanized factory labor, resulting in more rapid, increased production, and more consistency in the quality of fabrics.
        - Coal mining progressed with the use of ponies and carts on rails, improved ventilation in tunnels, and less hazardous ways to remove coal seams and illuminate the tunnels.
        - Transportation innovations such as the application of the steam engine and railway system enhanced movement of products, finished and raw, as well as food and people.
    - The Industrial Revolution affected longevity of human life: mortality rates decreased and birth rates increased.
    - The Industrial Revolution affected human settling: new towns rose around factories.
- Business in the twentieth century, which became more versatile and could be considered from different angles. One such consideration is manufacturing versus trading firms. These two types of businesses had different needs and were therefore led in different ways. While manufacturing firms were more concerned with a constant capital flow to safeguard production, trading firms could afford to focus on long-term performance. These firms were therefore often family-based. The twentieth century, marked as it was by wars, anticolonialism movements, and a quest for new horizons, forced former colonial powers such as the United Kingdom to look for other means of safeguarding their corporations. An increased number of trade unions emerged in the second half of the century, in order to safeguard business performances, and the rise of emerging economic powers further challenged the business climate.

14 The Growth of Business

- Management in the twentieth century, marked by a mosaic of theories, such as scientific management, administrative theory, bureaucratic theory, human relations, and human resources. Some of these theories, especially those in the latter part of the twentieth century, considered the wellbeing of the workforce, but most of them were mainly concerned with process enhancements and shareholders' pockets. In the last few decades of the twentieth century, change emerged into one of the most powerful concepts in business.

Questions

1. When considering this chapter overall, we could conclude that humanity, as we know it today, is not very old. Which of the original tendencies described in the first part of the chapter have you seen, and where? Please describe.
2. The chapter discusses Preferential Trading Agreements (PTAs) in two sections. Select one PTA, either from the enumeration of organizations mentioned, or one not listed in the chapter, and engage in some online research about this organization. Formulate an overview of this PTA in about 300 words. Prepare to share.
3. Britain is labeled as the leader of the Industrial Revolution in this chapter. Please explain in your own words why that is. Do you agree with the assertions made in the chapter?
4. Business in the twentieth century experienced its share of ups and downs as a result of the volatile global climate of the days. One challenging fact that was mentioned was the end of colonialism. As an example, the United Kingdom was mentioned. How did the end of colonialism affect U.K. corporations, and what are some of the new strategies that were implemented?
5. Management in the twentieth century is briefly described near the end of the chapter. It is stated there that, especially in capitalist systems, the wellbeing of workforces was not prioritized. Do you agree or disagree with this statement? Please explain.

Notes

1 Chora, G. S. (July 9, 2009). Ancient Trade and Civilization. *Aurlaea, the Poetics of Design.* Retrieved on September 29, 2013 from www.aurlaea.com/article-177-ancient_trade_and_civilization.html
2 Ibid.
3 Ibid.
4 Ibid.
5 Favier, J. (July 1998). *Gold & Spices: The Rise of Commerce in the Middle Ages.* Holmes & Meier Publishers, New York, NY.
6 Irwin, D. A. (November 26, 2001). A Brief History of International Trade Policy. *Library of Economics and Liberty.* Retrieved on September 29, 2013 from www.econlib.org/library/Columns/Irwintrade.html
7 Ibid.

The Growth of Business **15**

8 Stages of Economic Integration. (2013). *Economics Online*. Retrieved on September 12, 2013 from www.economicsonline.co.uk/Global_economics/Economic_integration.html

9 Greif, A. (2006). Family Structure, Institutions, and Growth: The Origins and implications of Western Corporations. *The American Economic Review, 96*(2), 308–312.

10 Ibid.

11 Korotayev, A. V. (2003). Unilineal Descent Organization and Deep Christianization: A Cross-Cultural Comparison. *Cross-Cultural Research, 37*(1), 133–157.

12 Greif, A. (2006). Family Structure, Institutions, and Growth: The Origins and Implications of Western Corporations. *The American Economic Review, 96*(2), 308–312.

13 Ibid.

14 Maier, P. (January 1993). The Revolutionary Origins of the American Corporation. *The William and Mary Quarterly, 50*(1), 51–84.

15 Ibid.

16 Ibid.

17 Ibid.

18 Beets, S. (2011). Critical Events in the Ethics of U.S. Corporation History. *Journal of Business Ethics, 102*(2), 193–219.

19 Ibid.

20 Ibid.

21 Trivett, V. (June 27, 2011). 25 US Mega Corporations: Where They Rank if They Were Countries. *Business Insider*. Retrieved on April 13, 2014 from www.businessinsider.com/25-corporations-bigger-tan-countries-2011–6?op=1

22 Maier, P. (January 1993). The Revolutionary Origins of the American Corporation. *The William and Mary Quarterly, 50*(1), 51–84.

23 Allen, R. C. (2011). Why the Industrial Revolution was British: Commerce, Induced Invention, and the Scientific revolution. *Economic History Review, 64*(2), 357–384.

24 Jensen, M. C. (1993). The Modern Industrial Revolution, Exit, and the Failure of Internal Control Systems. *The Journal of Finance, 48*(3), 831–880.

25 Montagna, J. A. (1981). The Industrial Revolution, in *An Interdisciplinary Approach to British Studies, 1981 Volume II*. Yale-New Haven Teachers Institute. Retrieved on April 24, 2014 from www.yale.edu/ynhti/curriculum/units/1981/2/81.02.06.x.html

26 Ibid.

27 Ibid.

28 Ibid.

29 Ibid.

30 Ibid.

31 Ibid.

32 Jensen, M. C. (1993). The Modern Industrial Revolution, Exit, and the Failure of Internal Control Systems. *The Journal of Finance, 48*(3), 831–880.

33 Dejung, C. (2013). Worldwide Ties: The Role of Family Business in Global Trade in the Nineteenth and Twentieth Centuries. *Business History, 55*(6), 1001–1018.

34 White, N. J. (2000). The Business and the Politics of Decolonization: The British Experience in the Twentieth Century. *Economic History Review, 53*(3), 546–564.

35 Tanz, J. (October 1, 2003). A Brief History of Management. *Fortune Small Business*. Retrieved on April 29, 2014 from http://money.cnn.com/magazines/fsb/fsb_archive/2003/10/01/353427/

36 Ibid.

37 Ibid.

38 Ibid.

39 Ibid.

40 Van Buren III, H. J. (2007). Fairness and the Main Management Theories of the Twentieth Century: A Historical Review, 1900–1965. *Journal of Business Ethics, 82*, 633–644.

41 Ibid.

2

THE TWENTIETH CENTURY IN THE UNITED STATES

Setting the Stage

No great work has ever been accomplished without going mad—that is, when expressed in modern terms, without breaking through the ordinary level of consciousness and letting loose the hidden powers lying further below. These powers may be devilish sometimes, but there's no doubt that they're superhuman and work wonders. When the unconscious is tapped, it rises above individual limitations. And, this is where the Samurai training joins hands with Zen.

D. T. Suzuki

Quantum Leaps in Development

Since the main focus of this book is on the American ideological and business landscape, we will first provide a brief overview of the twentieth century as it was experienced in this country.

1900–1909: A Manufacturing Era

In the first decade of the twentieth century there were about 75 million Americans in the United States, and perspectives about basic human freedom were still in their infancy: women were not allowed to smoke in public, and there were fewer than 10,000 cars in the entire country. The average worker earned about $13 per week for a total of 59 hours of labor.[1] While philanthropists such as Rockefeller, Phelps-Stokes, and others advocated for education opportunities for African Americans, large parts of the nation, particularly in the South, and to a lesser degree the North, insisted in the existing norm of racial segregation in education.[2] However, the twentieth century turned out to be one where technology, science, and inventions would progress at an accelerated rate, far beyond any other century before. Airplanes, automobiles, and radio were still in their infancy, but there was a steady urge to bring all these novelties to fruition. The first decade of the twentieth century presented inventions such as the Zeppelin, a rigid-frame airship; escalators; vacuum cleaners; air conditioners; neon light; lie detector tests, also called polygraph machines; corn flakes; synthetic plastic; manned helicopters; cellophane; and instant coffee.[3] Consequently, materialism and consumerism made their grand entrance into American daily life.

One major problem of the day was child labor. In the early twentieth century, the United States needed a large labor force to operate the factories that were so important to the manufacturing industry. Many of the cotton mills in North and South Carolina, Georgia, Massachusetts, Vermont, Missouri, and other states harbored underage workers who could not then receive proper education due to their long and tiring work schedules. In the states of Washington, New York, and Delaware, child labor manifested itself in the form of underage newspaper vendors. In Pennsylvania, Tennessee, and Virginia, boys of 12 to 14 years could be found working in coalmines, and in Indiana, Florida, Rhode Island, Mississippi, and Louisiana, there were kids as young as 6 or 7 years old working in glasswork, tobacco, shrimp picking, and all kinds of canning factories. Children of similar young ages could be found in field and farm work in states such as Massachusetts, Connecticut, Oklahoma, Colorado, and Baltimore. Children could be found almost everywhere working as full-time employees, from San Francisco to New York, and from Boston to Washington, DC. Aside from the earlier mentioned professions, they also performed as salesmen, bootblacks, bowling alley servants, postal telegraphs, or coal shovels.[4]

Fortunately, general awareness about the importance of health rose as well during this decade, and legal safety measures were established for food processing and toward the environment, thus gradually leading to an improvement of the circumstances for children. The positive change in people's perspectives could be attributed to the newly acquired luxury of radio broadcasts, as well as transportation, by automobiles, ships, and trains.[5]

1910–1919: Economic Struggles and a World War

The second decade of the twentieth century brought major changes as well. Issues that we are struggling with today were first manifested in this decade: there was a great influx of immigrants, poverty soared, and battles between employees and employers were rampant. In addition, work safety as well as child labor remained major concerns.[6]

The U.S. population had increased by about one-third, to 92.5 million people. The average annual salary had increased to about $750, and national debt was about $1.15 billion. In spite of the Sherman Antitrust Act of 1890, the business

18 The Twentieth Century

landscape was still covered in monopolies. Children were still hired to work in factories, mills, and mines, not only for long work hours, but also in unsafe and unhealthy conditions. Concern for the wellbeing of children finally led to some legal actions, and while there was still no federal law against child labor, every state had passed a minimum age law by 1915. This age varied depending on the tasks a child was involved in: minimum 16 years to work in any formal occupation; between 12 and 14 years as a caddy on the golf course; and between 14 and 16 years in work that would not interfere with school attendance.

Nonetheless, large numbers of children were underfed, and education was still considered secondary to work. Less than 10% of youngsters graduated from high school, and African Americans were facing increasingly worsening treatment.[7]

In 1914 World War I broke out, and U.S. industry boomed: the nation grew to be the most industrialized country of those days, with soaring automobile and tobacco production, and immense social change. The American culture was considered popular, and gained following in multiple parts of the world. This was also the era in which the Titanic sunk (1912), causing the loss of more than 1,500 lives. Parachute jumping was successfully introduced, and the Girl Scouts of America was formed.[8]

As trendsetters of modernization, a number of interesting U.S.-based inventions were reported. Motion picture came into being, thanks to Edison, and movie cameras evolved into motorized versions, replacing the hand-cranked ones. Fashion was making headway with the invention of bras and zippers. The gas mask came into being as a useful, durable safety measure. Radio tuners that could receive multiple stations made their debut, and so did stainless steel, short wave radio, and pop-up toasters.[9]

1920–1929: Booming Years

In the 1920s, the U.S. population grew to about 106.5 million people, with an unemployment rate of just over 5%.[10] In 1921, immigration laws placed a rigid cap on the number of foreigners allowed into the country, in an attempt to call a halt to the overcrowding of cities and rising wages. There was a general sense of fear and intolerance projected onto Eastern European and Asian immigrants.[11] Nonetheless, the decade was generally known as a booming one. World War I was over, and the postwar recession was history. There was a massive increase in spending, and corporations showed major profits as a result of the increased spending on credit rather than savings.[12] Inventions were the prestigious fad of the day, and numerous people considered themselves inventors, patenting everything they could, and earning patent attorneys a fortune. Among the more impressive inventions of this decade were the adhesive bandage (Band-Aid®), the first robot, insulin, traffic signals, the television, a complete electronic TV system, quartz clocks, penicillin, bubble gum, electric shavers, and car radios.[13]

The inventions were not limited to consumer goods, but stretched also revolutionized production methods, resulting in increased profits for manufacturers, as well as increased wages.

In contrast to the booming era in the United States, those living and working in Europe were faced with massive hyperinflation, which wrecked the middle class and instigated political and economic mayhem. In the United States, however, there were about 15,000 millionaires in 1927, and at least one billionaire. The number of financial transactions was unparalleled with an excessive use of cash, forcing the government to print more dollars at a faster rate. Since there was such prosperity overall, salaries of executives distended to extreme levels, widening the gap between affluent and poor.[14] Average annual salaries increased to about $1,236, and illiteracy decreased to 6% of the population.[15] A Ford automobile cost about $290.00. Women acquired the right to vote. However, on October 24, 1929, the stock market crashed and the nation descended into panic mode. Banks closed their doors, and a depression started that would run throughout most of the 1930s.

1930–1939: The Great Depression and World War II

As the thirties commenced, the Great Depression soared. The American Dream turned into a nightmare and opportunity turned into despair. Unemployment was widespread and reached upwards of 20%, with 13 to 15 million job searchers moving from town to town in search of employment. Industrial production, the main source of income in the nation, had come to a near standstill. For those who still worked, wages dropped. As one of the many consequences of Black Tuesday (October 29, 1929, when the market lost around $9 billion of its worth), stock prices fell to about 10% of their previous value. The high levels of credits used in the roaring twenties for purchases of homes and cars now caused massive foreclosures and repossessions. Since export markets had been steadily dwindling after the World War I, food prices collapsed as well. In addition to this, farmers were confronted with unmatched drought and dust storms, and many lost their land.[16]

The American people had come to question the very foundation of their nation's ideologies: democracy, capitalism, and individualism. Many packed their sparse belongings and moved to California, where life seemed to provide greater promise. Family incomes dropped by about 40%. Advancement was placed on hold. Survival was the term of the decade. While the United States managed to maintain a democratic regime, other countries, such as Germany and Italy, fell to dictatorships.[17]

In the U.S. political arena, the Republican President Hoover, who insisted that the social malaise was not the Government's responsibility to solve, lost in a landslide to Democratic candidate Roosevelt. Roosevelt got a nationwide bank holiday approved by Congress, and managed to prompt a reform in banking and the stock market. His efforts led to protection of home mortgages and stabilization in industrial and agricultural production, as well as the creation of major public, federally funded works, that provided work and income to millions. He created

20 The Twentieth Century

the Works Progress Administration (WPA), a permanent jobs program, which ran from 1935 to 1943, and employed almost 9 million people. The Social Security Act came into effect, securing pensions for senior citizens.[18]

Near the end of the decade (1939), World War II formally started when Germany invaded Poland, although this transgression was preceded by Japan's invasion of China in 1937. When the United States entered the war in 1941, this involvement provided a new focus for the WPA, and many people found employment in the armed forces and as civilian workers in army camps.[19]

In spite of the volatile economic climate, however, human intellect continued to thrive, introducing society to novelties such as scotch tape, frozen food processes, jet engines, electron microscopes, zoom lenses, parking meters, stereo records, drive-in movie theaters, road-reflectors, nylon, canned beer, radar, photocopiers, and ballpoint pens.[20]

1940–1949: New Developments and the Baby Boom

The Japanese attacked Pearl Harbor in 1941, thus forcing the United States into World War II, which defined the 1940s. America's economy re-emerged into a thriving war industry, with factories fully producing, and unemployment vanishing, even though it would take the stock market another decade (1954) before it would return to pre-Depression levels.[21]

Meanwhile, immigration increased again: many European artists and academics entered the country to escape Hitler's Holocaust, bringing with them many new ideas. The wartime production enabled women to enter the workplace en masse, as their husbands were needed in the war. African Americans also found their way into the mainstream workplace, due to the high need for workers. Thanks to the changed circumstances of these days, perspectives on equality, mutual tolerance, abilities, and trends changed immensely, affecting clothes, toys, eating habits, and social structures. With the GI Bill instated, in 1944, more men could now get a college education.[22]

Health care made a giant leap of progress when, in 1941, penicillin was successfully used as an antibiotic, ensuring fewer fatalities from war wounds among the troops, and increasing survival rates for surgeries.[23] Franklin Delano Roosevelt, the U.S. President at the time, died in 1945, and in that same year President Harry Truman ordered the atomic bombs to be dropped on Hiroshima and Nagasaki as a horrific, yet effective, way to end the war.

After the long absence, many men returned home to their wives, and there followed a massive population surge, known as the Baby Boom. The effects of this boom are still being felt today, as the "Boomers" enter retirement age.

The decade that led the world to the middle of the century brought forth some interesting inventions, such as the color television system, the jeep, the software-controlled computer, synthetic rubber, kidney dialysis machine, the atomic bomb, the microwave oven, the mobile phone (only to be sold commercially another four decades later), the transistor (semiconductor device), Velcro, and cake mix.[24]

1950–1959: Family Values Revived

At the dawn of the fifth decade, World War II was recent history, and the American population grew to about 151 million people. The unemployment rate was barely more than 2%, and the average salary had risen to almost $3 per hour. The workforce consisted roughly of 71% men and 29% women.[25] The postwar energy levels were high and American industry expanded to meet peacetime needs. Americans were especially focusing on purchasing goods they could not find during the war, which resulted in production and job expansion in corporations, from manufacturing to transportation, and from mining and constructions to utilities.

Transcontinental television was introduced to the masses with a speech by President Truman. This was a decade of increased awareness in human equality, and laws for immigration became more lenient through the removal of racial and ethnic barriers. In 1954, the U.S. Supreme Court ruled that racial segregation was unconstitutional in public schools. Yet, African Americans had a long way ahead to receive equal rights. In Montgomery, Alabama in 1955, Rosa Parks made history when she refused to give up her seat on a public bus to a white man.[26]

Healthcare continued to make positive strides as Dr. Jonas Salk developed a vaccine for polio. Nationwide infrastructure continued to develop, and in 1956, the Federal Highway Act was signed, commencing the interstate highway system. Interest in space reached new heights when the first U.S. satellite, Explorer I, successfully orbited the earth, while national air travel was introduced through a jet-airline passenger service. The nation expanded geographically as well with the inclusion of Alaska and Hawaii as the 49th and 50th U.S. states.[27]

The 1950s was also the decade of major television enticement. The medium had been invented earlier, but the idea that family values could be restored in a postwar climate and the immense drop in price of television sets, thanks to the mass production of these units, may have been the fertile soil for television viewing to become the main family activity in this decade. Television broadcasts also became the primary news and information source during this time.

Some inventions that enhanced societal performance were: the invention of the credit card to replace the old store credit accounts, the creation of super glue, the introduction of power steering, video tape recorders, diet soft drinks, radial tires, black box flight recorders for airplanes, transistor radios, oral contraceptive pills, nonstick (Teflon®) pans, the first McDonalds was opened (in 1954), computer modems, lasers, internal pacemakers, and microchips.[28]

1960–1969: Radical Changes

As the baby boom was ending, the U.S. population grew to almost 178 million people. The unemployment rate lingered at about 2%, and the nation's debt grew to $286.3 billion. The average salary was now around $4.75 per hour, with minimum wage being set at $1.[29] The sixties were marked by youthfulness, as

22 The Twentieth Century

70 million baby boomers became teenagers and young adults. The abundant presence of youngsters made the sixties entirely different from the rather conservative fifties: the United States was changing culturally, and more openness and tolerance were demanded. Change became a defining element of the days, and critical pillars of society were transformed, from education to values, and from laws to entertainment.[30] The powerful young generation had its own mindset and refused to live in the shadows of prior generations. The baby boomers voiced their opinions in colleges and public forums, and had their own stance about the Vietnam War, one of the most volatile social debates of the day.

Another equally pressing matter in the sixties was the civil rights movement, which commenced successfully in spite of major opposition, and was joined by whites as well, specifically Jews. People from many minority ethnic groups including African Americans, Hispanic Americans, and American Indians, emerged from the margins of society, demanding equal rights. Women's movements also became more active and the term "glass ceiling" was coined. Abortion and artificial insemination became legal.[31]

The wind of change in the sixties also affected the landscape of religion. Prayer was rendered unconstitutional in public schools, and large clusters of youngsters exchanged their traditional Protestant-based religions for Eastern ones, with Transcendental Meditation and Zen Buddhism growing in popularity. Crime and drug experimentation soared as expressions of defying authority. In political aspects the government's anti-Cuba movement and the assassination of President John F. Kennedy were the issues of the decade. Other assassinations that made headlines in this decade were the murders of Malcolm X, Martin Luther King, and Robert F. Kennedy.[32]

Smoking was openly condemned as a health hazard, and the first artificial heart was implanted. The decade was wrapped up by Neil Armstrong's and Buzz Aldrin's historical walk on the moon in the successful Apollo XI spaceflight.[33]

The sixties brought us its fair share of inventions, such as valium, nondairy creamer, the audio cassette, the first computer video game, silicone breast implants, the video disk, permanent-press fabric, soft contact lenses, NutraSweet, the compact disk, Electronic Fuel injection for cars, the handheld calculator, the computer mouse, the Arpanet (first internet), and the ATM.

1970–1979: Rights and Racial Integration

As the Vietnam War dragged on into the 1970s, the U.S. population increased to almost 205 million people. Unemployment was kept a little under 2%, and national debt had risen to $382 billion. The average salary was around $7.56 per hour.[34]

The general trends of the sixties continued in the seventies, with government disenchantment, civil rights advances, women's increased prominence, environmental awareness, and space exploration as some of the contemporary highlights.

On college and university campuses the antiwar movement was clearly visible. Racial integration, now formalized, was settling in, but not without upheavals from segregationists. Women and gays continued to demand their equal rights.[35]

In 1973 the U.S. military participation in the Vietnam War ended. Immigration increased when a law that favored Western European immigrants was modified, so that now citizens of developing nations were also allowed to move to the United States in search of a better life. Women were now better represented in the workplace, but also became sole breadwinners in many instances as divorce rates increased. Several cities such as Los Angeles, Detroit, and Atlanta elected their first African American mayors.[36]

In the area of general progress, the 1970s can be seen as the birth decade of the practical computer thanks to the invention of the floppy disk and the microprocessor. The seventies also brought us other fascinating novelties such as the food processor, the word processor, gene splicing, the Ethernet (local computer network), sticky (Post-It®) notes, liposuction, the laser printer, the ink-jet printer, the artificial heart, cell phones, the Walkman, and roller blades.

1980–1989: Wealth Accumulation and Consumerism

With a U.S. population of about 227 million, a national debt surging to $2 trillion, and average salary rising to $15.76 per hour, the eighties established their own character, which was starkly different from the change-driven and rebellious sixties and seventies.[37] The baby boomers had now reached adulthood, and their youthful radicalism had mellowed, gradually converting into a passion for wealth accumulation. The nation saw numerous hostile takeovers, leveraged buyouts, and mega-mergers, leading to a new generation of billionaires. Consumerism was skyrocketing, and life was typified by video games, aerobics, minivans, camcorders, and talk shows.[38]

The face and understanding of "war" was changing as President Reagan declared war on drugs. AIDS was the huge scare of the day, claiming the lives of many prominent Americans, among them actor Rock Hudson, playwright Charles Ludlam, and attorney Geoffrey Bowers, who became the inspiration for the 1993 movie *Philadelphia*. Unemployment was on the rise again, and as the decade came to an end, the Berlin Wall came down, signaling the end of Communism. Increasing numbers of Americans gravitated to personal computers at home, office, and school.[39]

Results of the strides made in previous decades were now manifesting themselves, as the 80s saw the first woman Supreme Court Justice (Sandra Day O'Connor), the first woman presidential candidate (Geraldine Ferraro), and the first black candidate (Jesse Jackson). Crime rates kept increasing, and prisons overflowed. The structure of the American family kept changing also, with more single parents, more unmarried couples with children, more two-earner families, more women with college degrees, and fewer children per family.[40]

24 The Twentieth Century

The eighties gave birth to many new multinational corporations, delivering a growth rate of 3.2% per year, the highest rate for such a timespan in U.S. history, caused by a combination of economic, financial, legislative, and regulatory factors, and the birth of a new expression: "corporate greed.".[41] Other inventions attributed to the 1980s are, MS-DOS, the IBM-PC, genetic engineering of the human growth hormone, the Apple Lisa, soft bifocal contact lenses, the CD-ROM, the Apple Macintosh, Windows program by Microsoft, synthetic skin, the disposable camera, disposable contact lenses, digital cellular phones, and high-definition television.[42]

1990–1999: Global Communication

In the final decade of the twentieth century, the U.S. population had reached about 281.5 million people. Unemployment was a little more than 2%, and national debt reached a height of $3.83 trillion. The average salary was around $13.37 per hour, and minimum wage was set at $5.15 per hour.[43]

The 1990s opened the doors to instant global connection through the World Wide Web, which was invented in 1992.[44] Not just U.S. society, but the entire global community was increasingly encouraged to communicate in a different way. Email became the main source of communication, and consumerism refocused itself with this major vehicle at its disposal: online shopping, gaming, and personal as well as professional connecting become the new norm. In 1989, 15% of American households had a computer, and by 2000, this number had increased to 51%.[45]

The 1990s brought another stream of war involvement for the United States, starting with the Gulf War. Aside from this war, the United States, under President George H. W. Bush (Bush Senior), also sent troops to Somalia, Haiti, Bosnia, and Yugoslavia. Internal issues of this decade varied from immense corporate mergers to health care, social security reform, and gun control issues. Democratic President Clinton was accused of sexual misconduct by more than one woman. The United States struggled with numerous internal troubles that were broadcast globally, varying from the O. J. Simpson trial to the bombing of the Alfred P. Murrah Federal Building in Oklahoma City by army veteran Timothy McVeigh, and the Columbine High School shooting in Littleton, Colorado.[46]

On a more positive note, the economy was booming, which led to record low unemployment. The stock market soared like never before, as online buying and trading increased. More Americans traveled than ever before, and consumerism was high. Education rates were promising: about 84% of the population completed high school.[47]

The 90s were the birthplace of genetic engineering, cloning, and stem cell research. This was not only the era of the World Wide Web, as mentioned above, but also of a number of other astounding inventions such as the digital answering machine, the Pentium processor, Java computer language, DVD (Digital Versatile

FIGURE 2.1 The United States in the twentieth century

Disc or Digital Video Disc), Web TV, and Viagra. Figure 2.1 depicts the spirit of the decades in the twentieth century.

Summary

In this chapter, we presented:

- The first decade of the twentieth century (1900–1909) in America as a manufacturing era, still inundated by major discrepancies in equal rights for women and non-whites. Racial segregation and child labor were widespread. Materialism and consumerism were on the rise. Some major inventions were the Zeppelin, air conditioners, and manned helicopters.
- The second decade of the twentieth century (1910–1919) as an era of economic struggles and the First World War. There was a great influx of immigrants, poverty soared, and battles between employees and employers were rampant. Children were still working long hours in unsafe and unhealthy conditions. World War I brought industry growth in the United States. Among the inventions of the era were the motion picture, the gas mask, and short wave radio.
- The third decade of the twentieth century (1920–1929) as a booming time with massive spending, and great corporate profits as a result. Inventions were the prestigious fad of the day, and numerous people considered themselves inventors. Among the more impressive inventions of this decade were the adhesive bandage (Band-Aid®), the first robot, insulin, traffic signals, the television, and car radios. On October 24, 1929, the stock market crashed.

26 The Twentieth Century

- The fourth decade of the twentieth century (1930–1939) as the one of the Great Depression and World War II. Unemployment was widespread and reached heights past 20%. Stock prices fell to about 10% of their previous value. Family incomes dropped by about 40%. President Roosevelt created the Works Progress Administration (WPA), a permanent jobs program. In 1939, the World War II started. Some critical inventions of the decade were jet engines, stereo records, and drive-in movie theaters.
- The fifth decade of the twentieth century (1940–1949) as one of new developments and the creation of the baby boom generation. The U.S. economy re-emerged into a thriving industry fueled by World War II. Unemployment vanished, and immigration increased again. Thanks to the GI Bill, which passed in 1944, more men could now get a college education. Atomic bombs were dropped on Hiroshima and Nagasaki. After the war ended there was a population surge known as the baby boom. Some interesting inventions of the era were the color television system, the kidney dialysis machine, and the microwave oven.
- The sixth decade of the twentieth century (1950–1959) as one in which family values were revived. The postwar energy levels were high and American industry expanded to meet peacetime needs. This was a decade of increased awareness in human equality, and laws for immigration became more lenient through the removal of racial and ethnic barriers. Rosa Parks made history when she refused to sacrifice her seat on a public bus in Montgomery, Alabama. Alaska and Hawaii became the 49th and 50th U.S. states. Some major inventions were radial tires, black box flight recorders for airplanes, and transistor radios.
- The seventh decade of the twentieth century (1960–1969) as one of radical changes. The sixties were marked by youthfulness, as 70 million baby boomers became teenagers and young adults. The United States was changing culturally, and more openness and tolerance were demanded. The Vietnam War and the civil rights movement were major events of the decade. Many members of the younger generation exchanged their traditional Protestant-based religion for Eastern ones, with Transcendental Meditation and Zen Buddhism becoming popular. Some important inventions of the decade were the audio cassette, silicone breast implants, the video disk, and the handheld calculator.
- The eight decade of the twentieth century (1970–1979) as one of rights and racial integration. The general trends of the sixties continued in the seventies, with government disenchantment, civil right advances, women's increased prominence, environmental awareness, and space exploration as some of the contemporary highlights. Immigration increased, and women were better represented in the workplace. Some importance inventions were the floppy disk, the microprocessor, and the artificial heart.
- The ninth decade of the twentieth century (1980–1989) as one of wealth accumulation and consumerism. The baby boomers had reached adulthood,

and their youthful radicalism made place for a passion for wealth accumulation. The nation saw numerous hostile takeovers, leveraged buyouts, and mega-mergers, leading to a new generation of billionaires. Consumerism was skyrocketing. The first woman Supreme Court Justice, the first woman presidential candidate, and the first black candidate emerged in this decade. Corporate greed became a widespread term. Some major inventions were MS-DOS, genetic engineering of the human growth hormone, and the Windows program by Microsoft.

- The 10th and final decade of the twentieth century (1990–1999) as one of instant global connection through the World Wide Web, which was invented in 1992. The entire global community was increasingly encouraged to communicate in a different way. The 1990s brought the Gulf War, and troops were also sent to Somalia, Haiti, Bosnia, and Yugoslavia. The economy was booming, which led to record low unemployment. Major inventions were genetic engineering, cloning, and stem cell research.

Questions

1. Perusing the ten described decades of the twentieth century in the United States, which one do you consider most interesting? Why?
2. In the sixties, the baby boomers became young adults. Change was the norm. Many exchanged their religious believes from Protestant to Transcendental Meditation and Zen Buddhism. Read up on Zen Buddhism and explain what it is.
3. In the fifties, Rosa Parks refused to give up her seat in a public bus. Was she setting a new trend or just following the law? Please review and explain.
4. The baby boomers are now entering retirement stage. Please engage in some research and formulate two advantages and two disadvantages of this generation's exit from the workplace.
5. List, of each decade discussed in this chapter, the one invention that interests you most. Explain in your list why you are so interested or impressed by this invention.

Notes

1 Whitley, P. (2008). 1900–1909. *American Cultural History*. Lone Star College-Kingwood Library, Kingwood, TX. Retrieved on April 17, 2014 from http://wwwappskc.lonestar.edu/popculture/decade00.html
2 Ibid.
3 Bellis, M. (2014). 20th Century Timeline 1900–1999: 20th Century—the technology, science, and inventions. Retrieved on April 17, 2014 from http://inventors.about.com/od/timelines/a/twentieth.htm
4 *The History Place: Child Labor in America*. With photographs of Lewis W. Hine. Retrieved on April 17, 2014 from www.historyplace.com/unitedstates/childlabor/

28 The Twentieth Century

5 Whitley, P. (2008). 1900–1909. *American Cultural History*. Lone Star College-Kingwood Library, Kingwood, TX. Retrieved on April 17, 2014 from http://wwwappskc.lonestar.edu/popculture/decade00.html

6 Whitley, P. (2008). 1910–1919. *American Cultural History*. Lone Star College-Kingwood Library, Kingwood, TX. Retrieved on April 17, 2014 from http://wwwappskc.lonestar.edu/popculture/decade10.html

7 Ibid.

8 Ibid.

9 Bellis, M. (2014). 20th Century Timeline 1900–1999: 20th Century—the technology, science, and inventions. Retrieved on April 17, 2014 from http://inventors.about.com/od/timelines/a/twentieth_2.htm

10 Whitley, P. (1999). 1920–1929. *American Cultural History*. Lone Star College-Kingwood Library, Kingwood, TX. Retrieved on April 17, 2014 from http://wwwappskc.lonestar.edu/popculture/decade20.html

11 Illinois State Museum (December 31, 1996). *Timeline 1920–1950*. Retrieved on April 18, 2014 from http://exhibits.museum.state.il.us/exhibits/athome/1920/timeline/index.html

12 Scott, R. (2012). *Business and Economy: From Boom times to Depression*. Retrieved on April 18, 2014 from www.1920–30.com/business/

13 Bellis, M. (2014). 20th Century Timeline 1900–1999: 20th Century—the technology, science, and inventions. Retrieved on April 17, 2014 from http://inventors.about.com/od/timelines/a/twentieth_3.htm

14 Ibid.

15 Whitley, P. (1999). 1920–1929. *American Cultural History*. Lone Star College-Kingwood Library, Kingwood, TX. Retrieved on April 17, 2014 from http://wwwappskc.lonestar.edu/popculture/decade20.html

16 Taylor, N. (April 18, 2014). A Short History of the Great Depression. *The New York Times*. Retrieved on April 18, 2014 from http://topics.nytimes.com/top/reference/timestopics/subjects/g/great_depression_1930s/

17 Sutton, B. (1999). 1930–1939. *American Cultural History*. Lone Star College-Kingwood Library, Kingwood, TX. Retrieved on April 18, 2014 from http://wwwappskc.lonestar.edu/popculture/decade90.html

18 Taylor, N. (April 18, 2014). A Short History of the Great Depression. *The New York Times*. Retrieved on April 18, 2014 from http://topics.nytimes.com/top/reference/timestopics/subjects/g/great_depression_1930s/

19 Ibid.

20 Bellis, M. (2014). 20th Century Timeline 1900–1999: 20th Century—the technology, science, and inventions. Retrieved on April 18, 2014 from http://inventors.about.com/od/timelines/a/twentieth_4.htm

21 Taylor, N. (April 18, 2014). A Short History of the Great Depression. *The New York Times*. Retrieved on April 18, 2014 from http://topics.nytimes.com/top/reference/timestopics/subjects/g/great_depression_1930s/

22 Goodwin, S. (1999). 1940–1949. *American Cultural History*. Lone Star College-Kingwood Library, Kingwood, TX. Retrieved on April 19, 2014 from http://wwwappskc.lonestar.edu/popculture/decade40.html

23 Goodwin, S. (1999). 1940–1949. *American Cultural History*. Lone Star College-Kingwood Library, Kingwood, TX. Retrieved on April 19, 2014 from http://wwwappskc.lonestar.edu/popculture/decade40.html

24 Bellis, M. (2014). 20th Century Timeline 1900–1999: 20th Century—the technology, science, and inventions. Retrieved on April 19, 2014 from http://inventors.about.com/od/timelines/a/twentieth_5.htm

The Twentieth Century **29**

25 Bradley, B. (1998). 1950–1959. *American Cultural History*. Lone Star College-Kingwood Library, Kingwood, TX. Retrieved on April 19, 2014 from http://wwwappskc.lonestar.edu/popculture/decade50.html

26 Ibid.

27 Ibid.

28 Bellis, M. (2014). 20th Century Timeline 1900–1999: 20th Century—the technology, science, and inventions. Retrieved on April 18, 2014 from http://inventors.about.com/od/timelines/a/modern.htm

29 Goodwin, S. & Bradley, B. (1999). 1960–1969. *American Cultural History*. Lone Star College-Kingwood Library, Kingwood, TX. Retrieved on April 18, 2014 from http://wwwappskc.lonestar.edu/popculture/decade60.html

30 Ibid.

31 Ibid.

32 Ibid.

33 Ibid.

34 Gillis, C. (2010). 1970–1979. *American Cultural History*. Lone Star College-Kingwood Library, Kingwood, TX. Retrieved on April 18, 2014 from http://wwwappskc.lonestar.edu/popculture/decade70.html

35 Ibid.

36 Ibid.

37 Whitley, P. (2008). 1980–1989. *American Cultural History*. Lone Star College-Kingwood Library, Kingwood, TX. Retrieved on April 18, 2014 from http://wwwappskc.lonestar.edu/popculture/decade80.html

38 Ibid.

39 Ibid.

40 Ibid.

41 Bellis, M. (2014). 20th Century Timeline 1900–1999: 20th Century—the technology, science, and inventions. Retrieved on April 19, 2014 from http://inventors.about.com/od/timelines/a/modern_4.htm

42 Bellis, M. (2014). 20th Century Timeline 1900–1999: 20th Century—the technology, science, and inventions. Retrieved on April 19, 2014 from http://inventors.about.com/od/timelines/a/modern_4.htm

43 Whitley, P., Bradley, B., Sutton, B., & Goodwin, S. (2011). 1990–1999. *American Cultural History*. Lone Star College-Kingwood Library, Kingwood, TX. Retrieved on April 19, 2014 from http://wwwappskc.lonestar.edu/popculture/decade90.html

44 Ibid.

45 Ibid.

46 Ibid.

47 Ibid.

3

AMBIVALENT VIEWS TOWARD MODERN-DAY BUSINESS

The situation the Earth is in today has been created by unmindful production and unmindful consumption. We consume to forget our worries and our anxieties. Tranquilizing ourselves with over-consumption is not the way.

Thich Nhat Hanh

Business in the Twentieth Century: A Management Overview

Management, as a field of study, may have only come into prominence in the late nineteenth century, but the trend itself could be considered as old as human civilization. After all, there were supervisors and workers ever since the days of ancient Egypt, when pyramids and other structures were built. Some critics feel, however, that those historic work processes were mainly conducted under coercive, slavery-like conditions, oftentimes without any type of compensation. With the Industrial Revolution, humankind reached a stage where a more systematic approach was needed to ensure proper alignment of material and human resources. When considered in that regard, the theoretical foundation of management only starts around the turn of the nineteenth to the twentieth century.

The Scientific Approach

As the activity of managing corporations became a more frequent phenomenon in society, the need for structure emerged. Around the turn of the century, in a time when manufacturing was still a major aspect of business in the United States, some critical minds started contemplating how to enhance efficiency in work processes.

One of those critical minds was Frederick W. Taylor. Taylor remains at the top of the list of those who have contributed to the history of management thought.[1] He was a mechanical engineer, which may explain why he was so interested in motion studies and efficiency. He wanted to ensure a more economical use of resources in manufacturing processes. His "scientific management" theory focused on efficient performance of tasks, matching the most appropriate worker for the task at hand, and developing a reward system that would result in optimal performance, a triangular approach of effort, performance, and reward.[2]

Taylor felt that individual evaluation and rewards would lead to greater passion and input than group-based rewards. His intention was for managers to select the proper employee for a job, based on performance measurement through timing.

In the early years of the twentieth century, Taylor was considered a major force in the management field, surrounding himself with a team of loyal followers, who all made a name for themselves in the field of management consulting: Carl Barth, Henry Gantt, Horace Hathaway, Sanford Thompson, and Morris Cooke.[3] The Taylor team was a rather closed circuit of self-declared management experts, who felt that any outsider would be unable to perform as a proper consultant of the scientific management system. Frank Gilbreth, an independent contractor and builder and a member of the Society for the Promotion of Engineering, was a major admirer of Taylor's work, but had a hard time being accepted as a member of Taylor's inner circle, in spite of his achievements as an engineer. Even though Taylor later granted Gilbreth opportunities to present his Scientific Management theory at various venues, he remained skeptical about Gilbreth's capabilities. When Gilbreth developed the Micromotion technique, which was far more advanced and precise than Taylor's stopwatch-based methodology, Taylor's response was rather lukewarm.[4] Gilbreth subsequently left the building trade and devoted all his time and energy to management consulting, thus becoming an immediate competitor to the Taylor team. What followed was a time of bitter accusations and reciprocal jealousy: Taylor belittled Gilbreth, and Gilbreth criticized Taylor and his team, thus converting from a great fan to a ruthless critic, who described Taylor's system as being void of any human respect. Frederick Taylor died in 1915, and by then, World War I had started. After the war, the Frank Gilbreth and his wife Lilian, also an engineer, became strong public critics of Taylor's stop-watch management study, labeling it unethical, wasteful, and inaccurate.[5] By the time Frank Gilbreth died in 1924, an initial step was set on the path to reconciliation with the Taylor group. After his death, his wife Lilian continued his work and invested significant effort to raise awareness about Frank Gilbreth's contribution to the Scientific Theory.[6]

In the decades after the 1920s, Taylor's theory has met with increased criticism, because it perceivably led to partiality and exploitation. This was not necessarily due to Taylor's theory, but more to the way it was implemented. As may have become clear by now, Scientific Management mainly focuses on the responsibility of managers, who, by virtue of their position, are superior to their workers,

32 Ambivalent Views

whose only "rights" are to perform and earn a wage. Managers were expected to structure the work and determine what type of rewards they would grant to employees.[7] The theory was criticized in later days as exploitative to workers, and over time, the theory of scientific management gained a poor reputation on basis of this manipulative implementation by managers.

Taylor and others, such as the Gilbreths, who devoted their time and expertise to including engineering techniques in work performance, may have assumed that employee compensation would be determined on an individual basis, with consideration of the difficulty of the task and the employee's output. "The principal object of management, according to Taylor, should be to secure the maximum prosperity for the employer, coupled with the maximum prosperity for each employee."[8] Unfortunately, this assumption did not materialize, and the scientific approach ultimately led to strikes in several production factories after the first decade of the twentieth century.

One justified criticism of scientific management is that it was not concerned with the feelings of employees. It focused on managerial decision making and not on employee concerns.[9]

Administrative Theory

In many cases when management is first presented as a learning topic, the abbreviation POLC (Planning, Organizing, Leading, and Controlling) gets introduced. This foursome is now widely known as the four pillars or functions of management, and they come straight from the administrative theory. Henri Fayol, an engineer just like Taylor, was the main founder of this theory and thus became one of the most influential contributors to modern concepts of management.

Fayol developed his management theory at a later stage in life, when he had already completed a successful career in business. He had managed a company with 10,000 employees, the Commentry-Fourchambault company, in the 28 years prior to developing his management theory. Fayol did not develop his theory to become wealthy, because he was already rather affluent at that time. He did come from humble beginnings, however, and may have found his drive to contribute to the knowledge of management from that angle. One of his drives may very well have been one of social acceptance by utilizing his intellectual skills.[10] Over the course of his life, he engaged in many research projects and published several papers on mineshaft design and safety. In addition, he conducted experiments on mining problems and hazards, which were presented to engineering students. His research was oftentimes based on field research and experiments, and this was also the approach he used when starting his research on management.[11]

Fayol's initial idea of the management functions was more comprehensive than POLC. He included six steps in the process: 1) Forecasting and planning, 2) Organizing, 3) Commanding or Directing, 4) Coordinating, 5) Developing output, and 6) Controlling.

Aside from the above, Fayol's most well-known contributions to management theory include his classification of organizational tasks into technical, commercial, financial, security, accounting, or management, and his promotion of 14 managerial principles, which are division of labor, authority, discipline, unity of command, unity of direction, subordination of the individual to the common good, remuneration, centralization, the scalar chain, order, equity, stability, initiative, and esprit de corps.[12]

Fayol was not alone in his beliefs. Two other major proponents of Administrative Theory were Luther Gulick and Lyndall Urwick. Thanks to Fayol's theoretical underpinnings, Gulick's work became highly influential in public administration. Urwick used Fayol's concepts to introduce a functional approach to management.[13] The collective approach from Fayol, Gulick and Urwick was seen as a responsible deviation from Taylor's. The name "Administration Theory" was derived from the fact that it was geared to administrators and the tasks they have to execute in the workplace: POLC. Fayol and his allies were trying to focus on the administration at all levels of organizations.[14]

Thinkers like Fayol, Gulick, and Urwick aimed at establishing universal structures to enhance efficiency in workplaces. The common theme in their theory with Taylor's was the intention to manage individuals. Just like Taylor, the Administrative Theory was not concerned about social or human constraints but mainly on economic needs, which promptly ignited criticism from later management theorists. In the Administrative Theory managers were, again, treated as the sole determinants in the work process, leaving room, as in Scientific Theory, for manipulation and partiality.[15]

Bureaucratic Theory

The man who is mostly credited with developing the bureaucratic theory is Max Weber, a German sociologist, philosopher, and political economist whose ideas influenced social theory, social research, and the entire discipline of sociology. While the term "bureaucracy" has acquired a negative connotation of slow processes and inefficiency, the concept was not designed with that effect in mind. The reason for Weber to develop the bureaucratic theory was because he wanted to create a system with clear reporting lines, so that managers would have less power and influence outside their immediate area of responsibility. His intention was to create a system with legitimate authority and impersonal rules.[16]

Fairness for all in processes and procedures was Weber's aim, captured in a strict hierarchy with clear reporting lines. The rules and documents that came with this strict reporting process were intended to safeguard the element of fairness, and minimize the influence of politics. Unfortunately, it has been proven that the organic nature of human beings is averse to rules that are too rigid and too numerous. Due to its many strict rules, progress in any action slowed down tremendously, and irritated stakeholders.

34 Ambivalent Views

Behavioral and Human Relations Theories

A name that has gained increasing prominence over the past decades, especially when discussing behavioral thoughts in management, is Mary Parker Follett. As a social worker, Follett was particularly interested in workplace-related issues. She was the first who dared to bring up the perspective of seeing employees as active members in the work process, and she believed in group dynamics. Follett also advocated involving employees in thought processes, so that they could positively contribute to better workflows and feel more appreciated.[17]

Mary Parker Follett was a well-educated woman, with a degree from Radcliffe College in economics, government, law, and philosophy. She was a successful writer and speaker in her time. Follet's work on management was posthumously published by Lyndall Urwick, who compiled her lectures and published them as the book entitled *Dynamic Administration: The Collected Papers of Mary Parker Follett.*

Follett was one of the first people to describe conflict as potentially constructive rather than automatically dysfunctional. In the context of human interaction at work, she proposed a third option aside from domination or compromise: integration. Follett felt that working "with" people instead of "supervising" them would work so much better. She also felt that control was best approached via collective self-control including, lateral and vertical co-ordination of controls. Similarly, she did not feel that control should be implemented top-down, but rather as a steady and recurring part of the production process. She advocated facilitation rather than command.

Another critical contributor in the behavioral realm of management is the "Hawthorne effect," based on a research project from Elton Mayo, a Harvard Business School professor, and his associates, done in the late 1920s and early 1930s. The Hawthorne effect claimed that employee performance increased through psychological stimuli. It suggested that when certain employees are positively singled out and treated as more important, either through better accommodation (office, lights, surroundings) or better treatment (work schedule, breaks, leadership), their productivity levels will rise.[18]

There have been mixed reactions in the decades after the Hawthorne studies, some claiming that circumstantial factors of the days (the Great Depression and workers' increased fear for losing jobs) may have influenced the findings. The studies did bring some important insights to the forefront, such as a) the fact that it is hard to predict precise outcomes, even when providing special accommodation, because human beings and their situations differ; b) interpersonal relationships between employees among each other, and among employees and their managers, contributed to the degree of performance; c) the norms defined by working groups determine workers' notions about their workload and, hence, their productivity levels; and d) workplaces are social systems, consisting of interdependent parts.[19]

As can be concluded from the above, behavioral theories differ from scientific, administrative, and bureaucratic theories in that it focuses more on the employee side of work performance rather than the management side. Contradictory to the other theories, behavioral theories don't see informal relationships between employees as a negative, but rather as a positive influence to work performance. Indeed, when people have a trust relationship among each other, they are more willing to assist each other and ensure better overall performance.

Subsequent human resources theorists, such as Chris Argyris, Frederick Herzberg, Douglas McGregor, and Victor Vroom took the behavioral aspect to the next level by pointing out that employees should not be treated as a means to an end, as was implied in all theories before. As an example, McGregor's theory X and Y discussed that employees' behaviors are oftentimes a response to their managers' approach. In other words, the X-manager, who thinks that employees are lazy and unproductive, will find them to behave exactly as expected, while the Y-manager, who considers employees willing and able to do their task, will also find them to behave as expected. It's a self-fulfilling prophecy. Similarly, employees will seek a connection between their efforts and their rewards, and will start withholding their input if they feel that they are taken advantage of.[20]

While there are other important names in the behavioral and human resource movement, we will review here only two highly sensible and influential thoughts:

1. Abraham Maslow's Motivation Theory, based on human needs. Maslow developed a widely known triangle, in which he laid out the various degrees of human needs, based on their social circumstances. He divided the human needs into five levels: 1) physiological, such as hunger and thirst, 2) safety, pertaining to a sense of stability and security, 3) belongingness needs, entailing meaningful relationships, 4) esteem needs, to nurture self-confidence, and 5) self-actualization, pertaining to fulfillment of the desire to prove oneself. Maslow warned that, in most cases, a higher level need can only be satisfied when the lower needs are met.

2. Frederick Herzberg's Motivation–Hygiene Theory, implies that there are different factors at play that cause dissatisfaction (hygiene factors) than those that help achieve satisfaction (motivators). It needs to be emphasized here that the opposite to *dissatisfaction*, in Herzberg's theory, is *no-dissatisfaction*, and the opposite to *satisfaction* is *no satisfaction*. The origins of both categories can be found in the motivators (intrinsic factors) and hygiene (extrinsic or surrounding) factors. Motivators trigger satisfaction or no satisfaction, while hygiene factors trigger dissatisfaction or no-dissatisfaction. Examples of hygiene factors, those that contribute to dissatisfaction or no-dissatisfaction, are working conditions, income levels, job security, supervision, and the work environment. Examples of the motivators, those that contribute to satisfaction or dissatisfaction, are the work itself, a sense of achievement, and recognition.[21] Herzberg's recommendation was to make sure the hygiene factors are reasonably met, but to focus more strongly on the motivators, as they will boost employees' morale, and hence, their performance.

36 Ambivalent Views

When reviewing the management theories above, the following emerges:

- In the scientific approach, employees' voices were not even considered a factor.
- In the administrative and the bureaucratic approaches a responsible foundation was built, yet it was still highly focused on managerial control and partiality than on employees.
- In the behavioral and human resource movements, the consideration of workers became more prominent, because the realization of employees having informal relationships and powerful group mentalities had sunk in.

Of course, the development of all these management theories did not necessarily mean that they were abundantly implemented in work environments. (Figure 3.1 provides an overview of four important management theories in the twentieth century.) What has become clear is that various organizations apply different standards and approaches to their workforces depending on the locations where they operate and the local living standards. As a result, employees of the same company in a developing country may experience an entirely different treatment and reward system than those in industrialized nations. Let us now review this in some more detail.

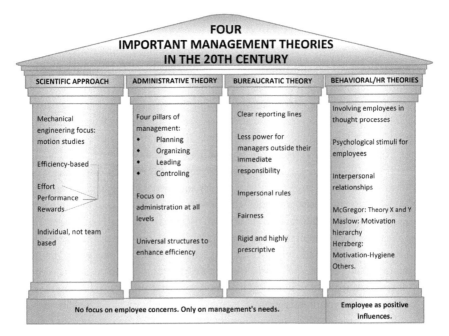

FIGURE 3.1 Four important theories of management in the twentieth century

Change, Growth, and Development

Business is often credited with bringing change, growth, and development, but we should consider that these phenomena can have positive or negative effects on a society. It is rightfully stated that business goes where others cannot. Even though people are aware of business corporations' potential dual impact on their environment, they usually embrace these corporations, because of the employment and opportunities they bring. Indeed, whatever a company's intentions really are, the fact that it establishes an operational unit in any city, state, or country, brings activity and oftentimes has a snowball effect, because it encourages other businesses to follow. So, development is an almost logical consequence of a business establishment, even if that may not be the business organizations' primary intention.

The Good Side

As indicated in the introduction of this section, corporations often bring progress in communities, whether that is their intention or not. They build factories or offices; bring employment opportunities by hiring local folks, and often also by using the services of local distribution networks; and they most likely purchase local resources. Then there are the factors of taxes, which such a corporation has to pay to the local government; infrastructure, which they have to develop or modernize when starting or expanding their operations; and other organizations, suppliers, competitors, or complementary product creators, which follow those that made the first move.

All of these factors bring development into a city, on the short term, and sometimes also in the long term. Over time, living standards may start rising, and locals may get encouraged to start their own entrepreneurial venues in which they may develop derivatives or come up with groundbreaking alternatives. Depending on the location, a corporation may also instigate development for the community as a whole, for instance, through increased living standards, through increased choices it offers, through its influence on the local education system, and by encouraging people to rethink old, useless habits through cultural influence. Gradually, an entire society can change, thanks to the establishment of one business corporation.

The Bad Side

There is no good without bad. Some people even say that we need the bad to continue appreciating the good. Yet, some bad developments are of such a magnitude that recovery from them happens slowly, and is sometimes even impossible. The first negative effect from business entities in any location is the waste, especially of an industrial nature. Pollution, depletion of natural resources, abuse of local workers, and the development of major dumping grounds are only some of the disastrous effects that business corporations can bring with them.

38 Ambivalent Views

Many business organizations that should know better display these behaviors today. In these cases, we see the same company that performs like a role model in the United States or Western Europe take grave advantage of people in some South American, African, or Asian countries. It is important to underscore here that change, growth, and development are not always beneficial.

Some types of change can bring more setbacks than advancement, for instance, when people who used to live peacefully together in a village now become each other's archenemies, simply due to the establishment of a corporation, which may cause some to benefit more than others. An example is the ethnic conflict in the Niger Delta,[22] which arose in the early 1990s as a result of tensions between foreign oil corporations (Shell and Chevron), and some Niger Delta minority ethnic groups. The fact that the latter, particularly the Ogoni and the Ijaw, felt exploited, created an unhealthy climate of ethnic and political unrest, which is still happening at the time of this writing. The fierce competition for oil wealth, which was the foundation of this friction, gave rise to such violence between ethnic groups that the entire region had to be militarized. The civil unrest in the Niger Delta may also serve as a good example of growth in a direction that should be curtailed. The powerful multinational corporations have become closely involved in the military's actions to manhandle, and even kill, local people who protest at the hazards caused by the oil companies.[23]

Some growth may occur in directions that should be curtailed, for instance, when the growth is manifested in the numbers of people with asthma, or cancer, due to industrial vapors, or when genetically modified crops are brought to areas where health conscious, natural trends were maintained for the longest time. A health-based example is the asbestos case that has led to numerous litigations in the twentieth century. Asbestos is a mineral substance, used for several purposes, but was most commonly used as electrical insulation for hotplate wiring and for building insulation. The most prominent asbestos producing company in the United States was the Johns–Manville Corporation. Even though evidence about the health issues related to asbestos surfaced as early as 1918,[24] it took several years before it was openly admitted that asbestos was a health hazard that could lead to asbestosis, lung cancer, and malignant mesothelioma. The Johns–Manville Corporation faced thousands of lawsuits between 1960 and 1990, and this huge corporation filed for Chapter 11 bankruptcy protection in 1982. In 1988 it emerged from the protection, and is still flourishing today.

Some developments may bring more destruction than advancement, such as factories that produce such toxic waste that entire communities start suffering. A classic example is corporate giant Monsanto's decade-long dumping of highly toxic PCBs in Anniston, Alabama.[25] For almost 40 years Monsanto discharged its toxic waste from industrial coolants into a creek in Anniston. As it turns out, Monsanto executives knew since the mid-sixties that fish in that creek were dying within 10 seconds due to the extreme toxicity of their waste dumps, but they decided to keep the information hidden. The local population was literally dirt poor and was unable to fight back. When the unethical, repulsive acts of Monsanto were exposed, the company invested only $40 million in clean up practices, and granted about $80 million in legal settlements.[26]

The Reputation of Business

When considering these factors, we can see why business, as a phenomenon, is often accused of suffocating local trends, disrupting local economies, depleting resources, and, as a consequence, tarnishing cultural values. While some corporate leaders are trying to increase the socially responsible performance of the entities they lead, others ignorantly or deliberately continue with destructive procedures. In many countries and states it is still less expensive to be reactive in regards to the environment than it is to be proactive. In other words, a corporation may learn that a fine for toxic waste will cost them a fraction of what they would pay to reduce their toxic waste overall. History has presented us many of these cases, especially in the oil industry, where the fine of an oil spill or explosion on basis of insufficient safety measure result in a penalty that does not even amount to a month's revenue for that company. Still, many of these corporations appeal the fines and end up paying a fraction of the initial amount, and do so over a long period of time. This is often a direct consequence of the eagerness from governments to have major business corporations operating on their soil. The revenues seem attractive, so there is hope that problems will remain minimized.

Summary

In this chapter we presented:

1. A Management Overview for the twentieth century, reviewing the five main management theories or clusters that emerged:
    1. The Scientific Approach, spearheaded by Frederick Taylor, which focused on efficient performance of tasks, matching the most appropriate worker for the task at hand, and developing a reward system that would result in optimal performance, a triangular approach of effort, performance and reward.
    2. Administrative Theory, most prominently represented by Henri Fayol, and introducing to us the four main management tasks, Planning, Organizing, Leading and Controlling (POLC).
    3. Bureaucratic Theory, mainly developed by Max Weber and aimed at creating a system with clear reporting lines, so that managers would have less power and influence outside their immediate area of responsibility. His intention was to create a system with legitimate authority and impersonal rules.
    4. Behavioral Theories, and

40 Ambivalent Views

5. Human Relations Theories, both of which aim to shift the emphasis toward more employee inclusion. Mary Parker Follett and Elton Mayo are names that are often mentioned when discussing these two theories. The theories that were developed within these two clusters attempted to encourage corporate leaders to involve employees in thought processes, so that they could positively contribute to better workflows and feel more appreciated. The perspective was presented of workplaces as social systems, consisting of interdependent parts.

While the theories clearly demonstrate an awareness trend in which the focus shifted from sole managerial importance to consideration of employees, there are still many corporations that fail to fully implement behavioral and human relations management theories.

2. Change, growth, and development as a series of consequences from business performance. However, these consequences should be viewed from a dual perspective:

1. The Good Side, in which we should consider that corporations can bring progress in communities, whether that is their intention or not. They build factories or offices; bring employment opportunities by hiring local folks; purchase local resources; pay taxes to the local government; improve infrastructure when starting or expanding their operations; and often also bring other organizations, suppliers, competitors, or complementary product creators, which follow those that made the first move.

2. The Bad Side, in which we should remain aware that business entities often cause enormous waste, can bring serious pollution, can cause depletion of natural resources, and abuse local workers. Examples were given of:
   - Change that brings setbacks rather than advancement, such as the ethnic conflict in the Niger Delta between local minority groups and major oil corporations;
   - Growth that occurs in directions that should be curtailed, such as in the Johns-Manville case, where a major corporation was aware early on of the health hazards that asbestos caused, but kept its productions going.
   - Developments that bring more destruction than advancement, such as in the case of the Monsanto Corporation that discharged its toxic waste from industrial coolants into a creek in Anniston, Alabama for almost 40 years, and invested very little in clean up practices and legal settlements.

3. The Reputation of Business, which is still ambivalent, due to the short-term profit focus of many past corporate leaders, leading to questionable practices and a preference for financial advancement rather than wellness of living beings and the environment.

Questions

1. In the first paragraph of the chapter, it is stated that management can be considered an ancient practice, even though its formal theories are a little over a century old. Do you prefer to see management as an ancient practice or as a fairly recent one? Please explain your reasons.
2. Which of the management theories discussed in this chapter appeals most to you? Why?
3. Abraham Maslow's hierarchy of needs is discussed in this chapter, even though it is not exactly a management theory. Why do you think it was included?
4. Please review Frederick Herzberg's Motivation–Hygiene Theory, and then share your opinion about it. Do you consider it strong or weak? Please explain your answer.
5. Under the heading "The Bad Side" in the section "Change, Growth, and Development," several examples are given of large corporations that abused their power and brought death and destruction by doing so. Please select one of the cases and conduct research on a possible update. Explain in about 300 words where this case currently stands.

Notes

1 Wren, D. A. (2011). The Centennial of Frederick W. Taylor's *The Principles of Scientific Management*: A Retrospective Commentary. *Journal of Business & Management, 17*(1), 11–22.
2 Van Buren III, H. J. (2007). Fairness and the Main Management Theories of the Twentieth Century: A Historical Review, 1900–1965. *Journal of Business Ethics, 82,* 633–644.
3 Nadworny, M. J. (1957). Frederick Taylor and Frank Gilbreth: Competition in Scientific Management. *Business History Review, 31*(1), 23–34.
4 Ibid.
5 Ibid.
6 Ibid.
7 Van Buren III, H. J. (2007). Fairness and the Main Management Theories of the Twentieth Century: A Historical Review, 1900–1965. *Journal of Business Ethics, 82,* 633–644.
8 Petersen, P. B. (1991). Scientific Management: An Opposing Point of View by Management in 1911. *Academy of Management Best Papers Proceedings,* p. 137.
9 Van Buren III, H. J. (2007). Fairness and the Main Management Theories of the Twentieth Century: A Historical Review, 1900–1965. *Journal of Business Ethics, 82,* 633–644.
10 Peaucelle, J., & Guthrie, C. (2012). The Private Life of Henri Fayol and His Motivation to Build a Management Science. *Journal of Management History, 18*(4), 469–487.
11 Parker, L. D., & Ritson, P. (2005). Fads, Stereotypes and Management Gurus: Fayol and Follett Today. *Management Decision, 43*(10), 1335–1357.
12 Ibid.
13 Wren, D. A., Bedeian, A. G., & Breeze, J. G. (2002). The Foundations of Henri Fayol's Administrative Theory. *Management Decision, 40*(9), 906–918.
14 Gordon, P. J. (1963). Transcend the Current Debate on Administrative Theory. *Academy of Management Journal, 6*(4), 290–302.
15 Van Buren III, H. J. (2007). Fairness and the Main Management Theories of the Twentieth Century: A Historical Review, 1900–1965. *Journal of Business Ethics, 82,* 633–644.
16 Ibid.

42 Ambivalent Views

17 Hartman, S. W. (n.d.). Management Theory. Retrieved on October 10, 2013 from http://iris.nyit.edu/~shartman/mba0120/chapter2.htm
18 Franke, R. H. & Kaul, J. D. (1978). The Hawthorne Experiments: First Statistical Interpretation. *American Sociological Review, 43*, 623–643.
19 *Hawthorne Effect* (2013). Updated September 24, 2010. Created July 13, 1995. Retrieved on October 10, 2013 from www.nwlink.com/~donclark/hrd/history/hawthorne.html
20 Van Buren III, H. J. (2007). Fairness and the Main Management Theories of the Twentieth Century: A Historical Review, 1900–1965. *Journal of Business Ethics, 82*, 633–644.
21 Hartman, S. W. (n.d.). Management Theory. Retrieved on October 10, 2013 from http://iris.nyit.edu/~shartman/mba0120/chapter2.htm
22 Hook, J. & Ganguly, R. (2000). Multinational Corporations and Ethnic Conflict: Theory and Experience. *Nationalism and Ethnic Politics, 6*(1), 48–71.
23 Shah, A. (2002). Corporate Interests and Actions can Harm the Environment. *Global Issues: Social, Political, Economic and Environmental Issues That Affect Us All*. Retrieved on October 11, 2013 from www.globalissues.org/article/55/corporations-and-the-enviro nment#Corporateinterestsandactionscanharmtheenvironment
24 A History of the Deadly Dust. (2000). *Multinational Monitor, 21*(9), 20.
25 Grunwald, M. (January 1, 2002). Monsanto Hid Decades of Pollution PCBs Drenched Ala. Town, But No One Was Ever Told. *The Washington Post*. Retrieved on October 11, 2013 from www.commondreams.org/headlines02/0101–02.htm
26 Ibid.

4

NEW INSIGHTS IN A NEW MILLENNIUM

Our prime purpose in this life is to help others. And if you can't help them, at least don't hurt them.

His Holiness The Dalai Lama

The Changing Leadership Climate: Hard Versus Soft Skills

Employees in today's workplaces have come a long way in their ideas about leadership. If we compare the qualities that were considered critical for leaders in the twentieth century with the ones that matter most now, a world of difference is revealed. There are numerous reasons that could be listed as foundational in this shift, but one of the most important ones is experience. Especially in the first decade of the twenty-first century, it became obvious that the emphasis that had been laid on leaders' qualities in the recent past led to disastrous outcomes, exemplified by Enron, Tyco, WorldCom, Arthur Andersen, and the like. All these corporations were led by people who were smart, assertive, extroverted, and charismatic, but not very concerned with the wellbeing of their employees and the communities they served. In fact, these leaders were so focused on the bottom line, that they took the worst advantage possible of society, and left many stakeholders in grueling economic hardship once they went under.

Fortunately, every road leads somewhere, and there is no bad experience that, in the end, does not lead to something good. Emerging from the rubble of these devastating corporate demises was a shift in employees' paradigms. Working people started wondering why some skills had categorically been shunned in workplaces, and whether it was not time to reevaluate the behaviors leaders should nurture in order to keep their workplaces afloat, while, at the same time,

44 New Insights in a New Millennium

ensuring employee satisfaction. The fact that the Industrial Revolution had run its course, and had gradually shifted into a Knowledge Revolution, was also a major cornerstone in the shift of workplace values and leaders' qualities that are now considered essential. "The shift from an industrial economy to an information society and an office economy means that many jobs now place an emphasis on integrity, communication, and flexibility.".[1] The notion of "wealth" as an accumulation of material or monetary assets has decreased. In its place arises an understanding and appreciation of the wealth of knowledge, in other words: mind of matter.[2] While not discernible everywhere yet, the exchange of intellectual output is rapidly surpassing the exchange of goods and services in importance.[3] As this trend is accelerating, those who contribute to the output process in workplaces, the employees, call for a more balanced set of leadership skills.

Defining Soft and Hard Skills

A closer look at the definition of soft skills clarifies that they encompass behaviors of motivation, empathy, self-regulation, and social skills.[4] Thus, soft skills focus more on interpersonal relationships.[5] "Soft skills are character traits that enhance a person's interactions, job performance, and career prospects.".[6] Hard skills, sometimes also referred to as "tough skills," harbor traits such as intelligence, analytical/technical skills, determination, rigor, and vision.[7] More precisely, "hard skills include the technical or administrative procedures that can be quantified and measured."[8]

The balance employees are calling for makes perfect sense: we still need the hard skills, but they should not be the only set of qualities a leader harbors. Today, more than ever, it is imperative that leaders understand the art of combining their shrewd business behavior with decent inter-human sensitivity. Yet, communicating this to leaders is not as easy as one might expect, because many business schools, where these leaders have studied, are even slower in adopting soft skills in their curricula than workplaces have been in including them in their list of desired behaviors. What many corporate coaches see happening is that leaders, who pride themselves in their astuteness, intellect, and rationale, oftentimes disregard soft skills as inappropriate for work environments.[9] When confronted with the flaws in their performance, these leaders will blame everyone—the coach, their workforce, the instruments used to measure their effectiveness—except their own skewed behavior.

As can be expected, some leaders are more receptive to the idea of using soft skills in their approaches than others. It turns out that especially those leaders in strong number-crunching or mathematical environments, such as in engineering, have a hard time coming to terms with using soft skills.[10] Leadership coaches advise that these leaders should be nudged in a very careful way into the blended mode of decision making. Sensitive as they are about their reputation

New Insights in a New Millennium **45**

and performance, they should receive guidance in private, and in a step-by-step format. Another group of leaders that has displayed problems with using soft skills is physicians. Coaches find themselves in the delicate position of guiding these leaders into a mindset of less reliance on credentials and more focus on emotional intelligence; less emphasis on intellect alone, and more inclusion of intuition; more accountability, and less fault-finding in others; more focus on authenticity and less on technical competency.[11]

The rise of soft skills in leadership should not be underestimated. This is not a temporary phase that will dwindle in a few years, nor is it a tendency that will be limited to smaller firms or non-profit entities. Also, it is not limited to just one geographical area of the world. A study conducted among workforce members of 11 large European Multinational Corporations revealed that these employees considered soft skills imperative to good leadership.[12] Among the desirable leadership skills they mentioned were integrity, care, ethical behavior, communication with others, long-term focus, open-mindedness, responsibility that surpasses the boundaries of the corporation, systemic thinking, embracing diversity, respect for local and global wellbeing, meaningful interaction, and emotional awareness.[13] In another study, 57 business executives agreed that integrity and communication were some of the most critical soft skills needed in today's workplaces.[14]

Against the backdrop of the many corporate scandals in the first decade of the twenty-first century, it should come as no surprise that corporate workers particularly look for greater trust relationships in their workplaces. Trust is a major soft skill that has been more of a background factor in the aggressive, asset-focused business dealings of the twentieth century. Yet, after having dropped to an all-time low, as shown in the scandalous business strategies of the not-so-distant past, trust is now rapidly moving to the center of solid organizational performance. Trust influences how others perceive our product or service, our leadership, knowledge, or partnership.[15] In workplaces without trust, such as the ones that have been (or are still) performing with a bottom-line focus, we see that lower and mid-level managers mistrust top leaders and refrain from sharing their real opinions because they are afraid of retaliation; employees mistrust information from top management, as it may be driven by selfish motives, such as greed, and all stakeholders mistrust corporate leaders on account of their exorbitant salaries, which demonstrate blatant disregard for fairness.[16]

Trust is often harmed through poor communication. Many leaders have come to take it for granted that communication is fine as long as they give orders. They fail to leave room for participation from employees through constructive information sharing. Employees are the ones who communicate with customers, and hear the stories about what competitors are offering. Employees' opinions should therefore eagerly be solicited instead of silenced. Listening to employees makes them more enthusiastic about their work as well, as it gives them a sense of ownership.

46 New Insights in a New Millennium

Soft Skill–Based Leadership Styles

Respectful Leadership. In Germany, three studies were conducted involving a total of 1,066 employees from multiple work environments. The intention was to find out what employees considered "respectful" leadership. A total of 19 categories surfaced, among which were trust, responsibility, consideration of needs, appreciation, granting responsibility, equality focus, accessibility, acceptance, and openness to suggestions.[17]

Transformational Leadership. Another study done among 252 employees in a total of 25 different departments of a food plant yielded that transformational leadership is highly preferred. Indeed, leaders who care to consider transformational leadership, an in-depth, transforming relationship between the leader and the employees, are finding that behavior of and connectedness with employees improves, which has a positive effect on quality.[18]

Engaged Leadership. When 731 workforce members were asked what they thought of the relationship between leadership quality, work attitudes, and wellbeing in connection to job performance, they responded that they were more willing to perform for a leader who engaged with them, were loyal, supporting, coaching, mentoring, and vision sharing.[19] It turned out that these employees were less concerned with the leaders' track record and capabilities. To them, the current interaction mattered most. The strength of engaged leadership was actually proven in other studies as well. In a major non-profit institution, 191 employees agreed that they had a greater desire to collaborate and perform when they had good relationships with their leaders.[20]

Awakened Leadership. The concept of Awakened Leadership entails flexibility from leaders to adapt to various work environments, employee groups, and social settings. Awakened leaders understand the essence of collaboration and leading by example. In their leadership performance they involve internal and external stakeholders, align organizational objectives with stakeholders' wellbeing, communicate regularly to keep all parties involved in organizational directions, respect personal values, nurture integrity, practice compassion, ensure ethical performance, tirelessly work to exceed their own limitations, serve others, and regularly scrutinize their own motives.[21]

Authentic Leadership. Authentic leadership, just like the four above, also nourishes a soft skill–approach by focusing on the human aspect first. As is the case with awakened leadership, the description of authentic leadership also recommends regular self-reflection so that blind spots can be detected and eliminated, accepting oneself, staying true to values and principles, empowering people to lead, maintaining a support team, and nurturing emotional intelligence.[22]

The common factor in the five leadership styles above is soft skills. Many of the behaviors and terms used in the above descriptions would have been considered misplaced in professional settings during the twentieth century. Fortunately, that is no longer the case. The researchers have investigated among the professionals of the workforce, and the verdict is in. The next step is to spread the movement.

What makes this perspective on soft skills particularly interesting is the fact that it ties in very well with the Buddhist approach, as we will discover in upcoming chapters. Constructive interpersonal relationships are an embedded part of Buddhist thinking, since this psychology assumes equal value and a transcended sense of connection between the practitioner and others. In fact, some Buddhist thinkers adhere to the notion that there are no "others," but only extended versions of what could be considered the entirety of one wholesome existence, consisting of all living beings. When perceiving existence in that regard, there are no important differences in ranks or rights, as all species are seen as equally valuable.

This mindset, then, also facilitates notions of respect and trust, because the ultimate goal and highest concern in being and performing is to do well, not just at the individual level, but in a collective sense.

Buddhist behavior, especially in the workplace, could therefore be classified as a manifestation of soft skills, because it is mainly concerned with the wellbeing of stakeholders, not only those within the workplace, but also those who are affected by what the group does. As will be explained in later chapters, Buddhists center their actions and performances on Four Noble Truths, which instill a set of critical mindsets into the practitioner, namely, that suffering exists, that it has a cause, that it can be ended, and that there is a path to end suffering, which they refer to as The Noble Eightfold Path. On this path there are eight considerations that help the practitioner perceive things in a holistic light; keep track of the reasons behind possible actions; refrain from deliberately saying things that could harm others; guard behaviors and their effects onto others; consider the source of income and make sure it does not have a harmful effect on others; remain constructive in thinking, acting, and intending; understand the many reasons there are for gratitude; and remain focused on what is important.

Using Soft and Hard Skills in Today's Workforce

As indicated in the section above, hard skills are usually easy to observe, quantify, and measure because they are technical and administrative in nature, while soft skills are more difficult to pin down because they relate to human interactions such as communicating, listening, cooperating, solving problems, contributing in meetings, and resolving conflict. A critical footnote to this distinction is that hard skills are useful in entry-level positions and in basic performance, but that soft skills become more important when we are in leadership and management positions. As we start engaging in formal leadership, self-management, conflict resolution, communication with stakeholders, and emotional intelligence, soft skills become increasingly important.[23]

In the past few years, there have been some mistaken mindsets about soft skills. For instance, that soft skills are hereditary, so if you are not born with them, you will have a hard time applying them. This is untrue. Soft skills are mostly developed as we experience life. They increase through observing others, reading, practice, and training. Another misconception is that soft skills are the same as good communication skills. This, too, is incorrect. While communication is a superb supplement and tool in practicing soft skills, there is much more to the skills than communicating. Along with proper communication, soft skills also include the ability to negotiate, find common ground, listen, and think critically. Similarly, soft skills are not merely synonymous with listening, are not gender specific, are not physically noticeable, and are not just the privilege or duty of the supporting staff in a workplace.[24]

Stakeholder Inclusion

An important point to be made in favor of soft skills is that its advantages exceed the internal boundaries of any workplace. When top managers and employees communicate well and clearly, when there is a climate of trust, when there is an atmosphere of friendliness and optimism, and particularly when these traits are nourished by the Human Resources department, a workplace will become more attuned to achieving a triple bottom line. The triple bottom line pertains to an organization's commitment to people, planet, and profit. Such an organization is therefore equally involved in contributing to the community and to giving back, as it is to making profit. The leaders of such an organization are also aware of the fact that the quality of internal communication and the nourishment of soft skills are important to sustainability because they enhance the internal team spirit toward making it happen.[25]

A great example of a corporation that prioritizes soft skills in its employee selection and retention processes is Zappos. This online retail shoe and apparel company has shown that focusing on soft skills and employee happiness yields great returns in more than just the financial realm. Zappos is a popular place to work: the company has made Fortune's top 100 list of best companies to work for at least four consecutive years. In 2014, Zappos ranked 38 on this list. To ensure low employee turnover, the hiring process at Zappos is rigorous. Applicants go through in-depth interviews and training, where both their hard and soft skills are evaluated. Once hired, trained, and established in their work areas, however, they enjoy many fun practices that keep the job interesting, an open floor plan that encourages interaction and collaboration, and a sense of team spirit and mutual support. Employees are not micro-managed, but trusted to do their work diligently. They may take breaks whenever they feel like it, and engage in some gaming in the workplace. Does it make them lazy or less productive? Quite the contrary! They produce more, because they are not on a constant watch.[26]

As a critical point to ponder, soft skills seem to be rather hard to find among younger applicants, especially in the American manufacturing industry. A recent survey conducted by the consultancy Deloitte yielded the concerning reality that more than 600,000 jobs in U.S. manufacturing remained unfilled due to skills shortage.[27] The problem is a bit more complicated than training alone. While aspiring employees can be trained in science, technology, engineering, and math

(STEM), the American manufacturing landscape of today requires more than that. Employees of today need to be computer savvy, solve complex problems, and able to deal with complex tasks. Here is where the need for soft skills becomes an issue. Another survey conducted in 2012 demonstrated that about 20% of employers felt that lack of soft skills was the key reason for not hiring applicants.[28] The interpersonal skills, the enthusiasm and motivation were just not there. Furthermore, within the communication requirements, basic writing skills were also lacking. More than half of the organizations that participated in the survey complained that these skills, which were considered steady among older workers, were a bottleneck for the younger ones.[29]

Diversity

Today's work environments are more diverse than ever before. Not just in gender, but also in age, education, culture and background, ethnicity, religion, and ideologies, among others. Diversity in workplaces will only continue to increase, which is promising in many regards, but also presents an ongoing challenge. As a wider range of cultures and backgrounds get to collaborate toward a common goal, greater tolerance levels will be necessary.[30] Tolerance can only be achieved when soft skills are practiced: good communication, trust, the will to perform as a team, and the proper degree of emotional intelligence to get along constructively. In diverse workplaces, it may take longer before a common stance is achieved, but once this happens, the results are deeper and richer than in a homogeneous workplace, where the mindsets are less diverse, and where, oftentimes, fewer options are considered.

As was mentioned above in the case of Zappos, companies also find that, in the long run, diversity works better for their business. There are multiple reasons at the core of this: employees learn to get along with members from other ethnicities, ages, cultural backgrounds, or gender, which increases understanding and tolerance levels; solutions from diverse work environments to emerging problems are usually better considered and more unique than from homogeneous ones due to the broader representation base of employees, and customers like to see someone they can relate to in the organizations they do business with. The above-mentioned increased output levels is also a factor. Yet, diversity should not merely be implemented for those reasons, but because it is just the right thing to do, because all human beings are equal, and none of us would like to be rejected on the basis of our external traits, so we should be open to granting everyone a fair chance. In addition, we should understand that working in diverse environments enlarges our mental horizons, so we can advance greatly by exposing ourselves to diverse settings. Companies with diverse workforces reinvent themselves more easily, because they have so many different levels of insight within their employee base.

The initiative to create a truly successful, diverse workplace should, ideally, be taken by top management. Once the trend is set at that level, stakeholder buy-in will happen more rapidly and enthusiastically because top management will most likely ensure that diversity is implemented at every level, from personnel hiring to compiling the steering boards. This means that the workforce will be configured and groomed on the basis of diversity, and overall acceptance of this trend will be a natural trend rather than a reactive process. Many corporations still apply diversity for wrong or reactive reasons. An example of a wrong reason is that diversity may be required by their government, so the company leaders feel forced to implement it. An example of a reactive reason may be that the company's leaders realize that a diverse workforce draws more customers. Drawing more customers is a great thing, but it should be a *consequence* and not the *main reason* for implementing diversity. Leaders who only implement diversity for customer increase may not really believe in the trend, and will most likely only allow it up to mid-level management. Yet, if diversity only reaches lower and mid-levels of management, and the corporate top remains highly homogeneous, success will start waning, because perspectives are limited to one particular cultural, age, or religious view, thus excluding others. As a result, the company's reputation will be questioned, and those who cannot identify with the company's direction, or learn about the company's reluctance toward attracting diverse groups, will cease patronizing it. Examples of major corporations that have made grave errors in diversity implementation are Wal-Mart and the Coca-Cola Company. Wal-Mart has faced multiple lawsuits from women groups, who claim that males have much better chances to succeed in the company. Coca-Cola has faced many lawsuits as well, but their recurring problem has been racial discrimination.[31]

Figure 4.1 presents an overview of the impact of soft skills and hard skills in an organization. While both factors are important, soft skills have proven over time to be the determining aspect in longitudinal organizational success, due to their interpersonal focus.

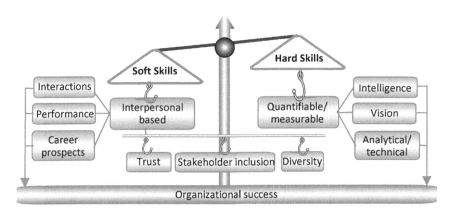

FIGURE 4.1 The impact of soft and hard skills on organizational success

While companies can always reinvent themselves, it should be stated that it takes a while to turn a reputation around. So, why let it get to that point? Diversity is the right thing to do, means good business, and is a logical element of soft skill inclusion in a workplace.

Summary

In this chapter we presented:

- A general overview of hard and soft skills, with inclusion of some of the reasons why soft skills have increasingly come to the forefront in recent years. Initiated by the shift from industrial to knowledge era, and further spurred by the many corporate scandals in the early twenty-first century, the collective view on soft skills has converted from unbefitting to essential in the workplace. The notion of wealth is gradually transforming from accumulation of money and material assets to appreciation for the wealth of knowledge.
- Definitions
  - Of soft skills as those that encompass behaviors of motivation, empathy, self-regulation, and social skills. Soft skills focus more on interpersonal relationships, and enhance our interactions, job performance, and career prospects.
  - Of hard skills as those that harbor traits such as intelligence, analytical/technical skills, determination, rigor, and vision. Hard skills include the technical or administrative procedures that can be quantified and measured.
- The importance to develop and maintain both soft and hard skills in order to perform well in work settings. Today, more than ever, it is imperative that leaders understand the art of combining their shrewd business behavior with decent inter-human sensitivity.
- The difficulty some leaders and managers have with accepting soft skills as being important in the workplace in general, and for themselves specifically. These leaders should be nudged in a very careful way into the blended mode of decision making. Having adhered to only hard skills for the larger part of their career, they should receive guidance in private, and in a step-by-step format.
- The rise of soft skills is only increasing, and doing so at a global level. On multiple continents and in various industries, employees as well as leaders now acknowledge the importance in workplaces of integrity, care, ethical behavior, communication with others, long-term focus, open-mindedness, an expanded sense of responsibility, systemic thinking, diversity, respect for local and global wellbeing, meaningful interaction, and emotional awareness.
- Soft skill based leadership styles such as:
  - Respectful Leadership, which nurtures work climates of trust, responsibility, consideration of needs, appreciation, granting responsibility, equality focus, accessibility, acceptance, and openness to suggestions.

52 New Insights in a New Millennium

- Transformational Leadership, in which an in-depth, transforming relationship is developed between leader and employees, leading to improved connectedness and performance.
- Engaged Leadership, in which leaders are supporting, coaching, mentoring, and vision sharing, and employees perform to a higher degree and with more enthusiasm in return.
- Awakened Leadership, where leaders are flexible in their adaptation to various work environments, employee groups, and social settings, and where behaviors of stakeholder inclusion, regular communication, mutual respect, and a focus on integrity, compassion, ethical performance, and understanding are the norm.
- Authentic Leadership, which also recommends regular self-reflection, truth to values and principles, empowerment, team spirit, and emotional intelligence.
- A deeper look at the use of soft and hard skills in workplaces, and how each set carries its own areas of applicability:
  - Hard skills are useful in entry-level positions and in basic performance.
  - Soft skills become more important when we have progressed on the career ladder to leadership and management positions.
- Stakeholder inclusion, which is essential for successful and long term organizational performance. By applying soft skills in workplaces, not only the internal stakeholders (employees, shareholders, and management) feel involved, but external stakeholders (customers, the community, and the environment as a whole) benefit as well.
- The difficulty of discovering some critical soft skills in younger generation employees, resulting in a large number of unfilled job positions in the U.S. manufacturing industry.
- Diversity in all its facets, as a growing trend in workplaces worldwide, requiring more tolerance among coworkers. Tolerance can only be achieved when soft skills are practiced: good communication, trust, the will to perform as a team, and the proper degree of emotional intelligence to get along constructively.

Questions

1. Soft skills and hard skills are described as equally important in workplaces. Please explain in about 300 words why this is the case.
2. Which soft skills do you harbor? Which hard skills do you harbor? How do you see them being beneficial in your current or future career?
3. The chapter explains that trust is a critical soft skill, and that poor communication harms the trust levels in a workplace. Please provide your understanding of why this could be the case.

4. Why do some leaders have problems accepting soft skills in their workplaces and in their own behavior?
5. How are diversity and soft skills related to each other? Please explain.

Notes

1 Robles, M. M. (2012). Executive Perceptions of the Top 10 Soft Skills Needed in Today's Workplace. *Business Communication Quarterly, 75*(4), 453.
2 Gilder, G. (1990). *Microcosm: The Quantum Revolution in Economics and Technology*. Simon and Schuster, New York.
3 Rifkin, J. (2000). *The Age of Access*. Penguin Putnam, New York.
4 Goleman, D. (2000). Leadership That Gets Results. *Harvard Business Review*, March–April, 78–90.
5 Dixon, J., Belnap, C., Albrecht, C., & Lee, K. (2010). The Importance of Soft Skills. *Corporate Finance Review, 14*(6), 35–38.
6 Parsons, T. L. (2008). *Definition: Soft skills*. Retrieved on October 17, 2013 from http://searchcio.techtarget.com/definition/soft-skills
7 Goleman, D. (2000). Leadership That Gets Results. *Harvard Business Review*, March–April, 78–90.
8 Dixon, J., Belnap, C., Albrecht, C., & Lee, K. (2010). The Importance of Soft Skills. *Corporate Finance Review, 14*(6), 35.
9 Newell, D. (2002). The Smarter They Are the Harder They Fail. *Career Development International, 7*(5), 288–291.
10 Nyman, M. (2006). Want to Be a Topflight Leader? Hone Your People-Skills. *Chemical Engineering, 113*(8), 63–65.
11 Gaillour, F. R. (2004). Want to Be CEO? Focus on Finesse. *Physician Executive, 30*(4), 14–16.
12 Hind, P., Wilson, A., & Lenssen, G. (2009). Developing Leaders for Sustainable Business. *Corporate Governance, 9*(1), 7–20.
13 Ibid.
14 Robles, M. M. (2012). Executive Perceptions of the Top 10 Soft Skills Needed in Today's Workplace. *Business Communication Quarterly, 75*(4), 453–465.
15 Maccoby, M. (2002). Do You Know if You Are Trusted? *Research Technology Management, 45*(4), 59–60.
16 Ibid.
17 van Quaquebeke, N. & Eckloff, T. (2010). Defining Respectful Leadership: What it Is, how it can Be Measured, and Another Glimpse at What it Is Related to. *Journal of Business Ethics, 91*(3), 343–358.
18 Luria, G. (2008). Controlling for Quality: Climate, Leadership, and Behavior. *The Quality Management Journal, 15*(1), 27–40.
19 Alimo-Metcalfe, B., Alban-Metcalfe, J., Bradley, M., & Samele, C. (2008). The Impact of Engaging Leadership on Performance, Attitudes to WORK and wellbeing at Work. *Journal of Health Organization and Management, 22*(6), 586–598.
20 Cadwallader, S. & Busch, P. (2008). Want to, Need to, Ought to: Employee Commitment to Organizational Change. *Journal of Organizational Change Management, 21*(1), 32–52.
21 Marques, J. (2007). *The Awakened Leader: One Simple Leadership Style That Works Every Time Everywhere*. Personhood Press, Fawnskin, CA.
22 George, B. & Sims, P. (2007). *True North*. Jossey-Bass, San Francisco, CA.
23 Laker, D. R. & Powell, J. L. (2011). The Differences Between Hard and Soft Skills and Their Relative Impact on Training Transfer. *Human Resource Development Quarterly, 22*(1), 111–122.

24 Rao, M.S. (2012). Myths and Truths about Soft Skills. *T+D, 66*(5), 48–51.
25 Singh, A. (2013). Achieving Sustainability Through Internal Communication and Soft Skills. *IUP Journal Of Soft Skills, 7*(1), 21–26.
26 Gillespie, L. V. (2012). Targeting Soft Skills Yields Hard Returns for Employers. *Employee Benefit News, 26*(5), 18–20.
27 Schulz, N. (September 20, 2012). Hard Unemployment Truths About 'Soft' Skills. *Wall Street Journal—Eastern Edition.* A15.
28 Ibid.
29 Ibid.
30 Marques, J. F. (2007). Implementing Workplace Diversity and Values: What it Means, What it Brings. *Performance Improvement, 46*(9), 5–7.
31 Ibid.

5

BUDDHISM

Some Foundational Notes

> Without accepting the fact that everything changes, we cannot find perfect composure. But unfortunately, although it is true, it is difficult for us to accept it. Because we cannot accept the truth of transience, we suffer.
>
> Shunryu Suzuki

Buddhism: An Interpretation

Buddhism may be considered one of the most fascinating mass-ideologies we know. Different people view it in different ways. Some see it as a religion, just like Christianity, Islam, Hinduism, and others. Some think of it as a philosophy, because it prescribes notions of existence, values, and mindsets. Within the philosophical realm, Buddhism is often labeled as an ethical system. None of the above is untrue, because Buddhism could, indeed, be discussed as such. However, in this book, Buddhism will be approached as a psychology, which is described as the science or study of the mind and behavior.[1] Put in a more digestible way: we will review Buddhism as a way of living.

Siddhartha: The Early Years

The man we came to know as "the Buddha" was named Siddhartha Gautama, and lived from about 563 or 566 BCE to about 486 BCE.[2] Most research scholars claim that the place of his birth was what we now know as Lumbini, Nepal,[3] yet, there are some sources that refute this and claim that he was born in India.[4,5]

Siddhartha's family was rather affluent. His father, Śuddhodana,[6] was the leader of the Shakya clan, and his mother, a Koliyan princess, was called Maya.[7] Koli

56 Buddhism

people are an ethnic tribe. The word "Maya" has multiple meanings in Sanskrit and Pali, the dominant languages of the area where Siddhartha lived. One of these meanings is "illusion." There may be a possible explanation for using the name "Maya" when referring to the mother of Siddhartha, because, as the story goes, Maya died one week after Siddhartha's birth, so to him, she was an illusion. Maya gave birth to her baby boy under a grove of trees, and named him Siddhartha, which means "he who has attained his goals."[8]

After Maya's passing, the baby was admitted to the care of Maya's younger sister, Mahapayapati, who raised him as if he were her own child. He was very intelligent, but also highly protected, per his father's orders. Shortly after Siddhartha's birth, a well-respected hermit by the name of Asita[9] came to see the little one. Asita was moved by the little boy's radiance and beauty, and predicted that he would either become a sage, a holy man, or a great leader. Śuddhodana, who wanted his son to become his successor, decided to eliminate as many external influences as possible that could drive Siddhartha to sagehood or to the austere life of a holy man. For many years the young boy was kept in royal isolation, but as childhood transmuted into adolescence, this became an almost impossible chore.

Siddhartha: The Young Prince

Wanting to ensure the continuation of his family, Śuddhodana decided that it was time for a wife for his son. It was customary in those days that people got married around the age of 16. Historical reviews of Siddhartha's pre-enlightened life provide inconsistent information about the person he married. Some sources claim that Siddhartha had two wives, others even mention three. This may not have been improbable due to the polygamous nature of relationships in Siddhartha's time, as well as the culture and standing in which he lived.

Gopa

One source[10] provides a very colorful and imaginative description of Siddhartha's marriage. It explains that, through dialogues with Siddhartha, the king had become aware that the young prince was not excessively eager to submerge to physical pleasures, and that mere beauty would not be a determinant in choice for a life partner. Siddhartha was much more interested in a companion who was wise and not blinded by wealth and earthly belongings.

> She whom I shall marry will be in the bloom of youth; she whom I shall marry will have the flower of beauty; yet her youth will not make her vain, nor will her beauty make her proud. She whom I shall marry will have a sister's affection, a mother's tenderness, for all living creatures. She will be sweet and truthful, and she will not know envy. Never, not even in her dreams, will she think of any other man but her husband. She will never

use haughty language; her manner will be unassuming; she will be as meek as a slave. She will not covet that which belongs to others; she will make no inconsiderate demands, and she will be satisfied with her lot. She will care nothing for wines, and sweets will not tempt her. She will be insensible to music and perfume; she will be indifferent to plays and festivals. She will be kind to my attendants and to her maidens. She will be the first to awaken and the last to fall asleep. She whom I shall marry will be pure in body, in speech and in thought.[11]

Śuddhodana sent out his most trusted advisors to find a girl that would meet the requirements, and finally, one emerged. She was also a member of the Shakya clan, and her name was Gopa. To test her character, the king invited her, along with many other beautiful women, to meet his radiant son. Siddhartha had a present for each girl who stepped forward, but Gopa waited till last and by that time, Siddhartha had no presents left. He took his ring off his finger and offered that to her, but she refused. This was a pleasant surprise to him, who promptly acquired interest in the young woman.[12]

Amazingly, Gopa's father was not very eager to have his pure and wise daughter marry a prince as pampered as he perceived Siddhartha to be. Śuddhodana was extremely disturbed when he heard this news, but coercion was not part of his practices anymore, thanks to the influences of his beloved wife Maya, while she was still alive, and the gentle character of his wise son. At first he did not dare to tell Siddhartha about the assertions of Gopa's father, but when his son insisted, he broke down and told him everything. Siddhartha thought this to be rather funny, and took it as a constructive challenge to prove himself. He had an invitation sent out to the best performers in mental and physical activities, and measured his performance to theirs. Invariably, he won, and Gopa as well as her father were in awe of his qualities.[13]

Siddhartha and Gopa married, and had a son whom they named Rahula. Śuddhodana was happy for many reasons. He now had assurance for the continuation of his name, and it seemed that his son would submit to family life from here on.

Yasodhara

The story above is not confirmed by other sources, who claim that Yasodhara[14] was Siddhartha's wife. As the story is told, Siddhartha's father, King Śuddhodana, and Yasodhara's father, King Suppabuddha, were brothers, making Yasodhara Siddhartha's first cousin. Marrying cousins was considered common practice in those days and circles.[15]

According to this version, the unhappy father of the bride was Śuddhodana's younger brother, King Suppabuddha. His aversion about a possible marriage between his daughter and Siddhartha stemmed from his awareness of the old

58 Buddhism

predictions for Siddhartha's life as one who would ultimately abandon his family to become a sage. Yasodhara and Siddhartha shared the same age, and even the same birthday, so they were astrological twins. The story of their first encounter is similar to the one told about Gopa: Śuddhodana had organized a great feast to which all the beautiful women of the country were invited. They all received beautiful gifts from Siddhartha, but did not win his heart. Yasodhara came in last, when there were no gifts left. The difference in this story is that Siddhartha did not give her his ring, but a pearl necklace he was wearing, thus choosing her as his bride.

Similar to the previous story, however, Yasodhara's father also wanted Siddhartha to prove himself as a worthy husband, and the young prince engaged in competition with the best of the country, demonstrating excellence in archery, riding, and swordmanship, and ultimately swaying King Suppabuddha to agree to the marriage. A more traditional religious view claims that the marriage between Siddhartha and Yasodhara was meant to be, because their bond had started many lives ago, when it was predicted that Siddhartha would become a Buddha, and Yasodhara decided that she wanted to be by his side at that time.[16]

Yasodhara bore Siddhartha a son, who was named Rahula by his grandfather, King Śuddhodana. The explanation for this name is that Siddhartha, upon hearing about the birth of his son, uttered the word "Rahu," which means "obstacle," as he saw the birth of a son as an obstacle to his lifestyle.[17]

Siddhartha's Realization About Life

Having lived in three luxurious palaces for most of his young life, and deliberately surrounded by healthy and vibrant folks, Siddhartha was initially rather clueless about many facts of life. He had never seen an old person, never been confronted with illness, and never been made aware of death. Yet, as he matured, he became curious and restless. He wanted to see what was beyond the walls of the palaces in which his father had kept him guarded so carefully. So, he expressed his desire to undertake a trip outside the palace, and his father, fearful of what he might see, took all the precautions he could. He gave orders to free the village from all suffering and old people before allowing his son and his companions to ride out. Still, Siddhartha witnessed an old man, barely able to move forth, weakened by his age, and with a skin full of wrinkles. He asked his guard if this would to become his fate one day as well, and the guard had to admit that it was.

Soon enough, Siddhartha witnessed a sick person on the side of the road, unable to walk, and in severe pain. He asked his guard if this could also become his fate, and again the guard had to admit that illness may overcome all human beings, including Siddhartha. On another ride Siddhartha saw people carrying a dead body, and he asked his guard if death would also be his fate. Once again, the guard had no other option but to tell him the truth.

Now realizing that he had been kept in ignorance of the processes of life, Siddhartha became repulsed by the shallow life of luxury and obliviousness that had been his so far. He started meditating, and decided to turn away from his luscious lifestyle. He wanted to set out and discover some existential answers, so he became an ascetic. Some sources claim that he left behind his palace and luxurious lifestyle on the night his son Rahula was born.[18]

For the next seven years, Siddhartha dwelled in secluded places with other ascetics, and exposed himself to severe physical deprivation. This was quite a contrast with the princely life he had lived in the first part of his life. In the first year after leaving the palace, Siddhartha dwelled among a group of ascetics in a large forest. He observed their habits of sleeping under trees and bushes, and depriving their bodies from all nutrients, taking only the barest of nourishment to stay alive. He came to the conclusion that this was not a fulfilling way of living. He contemplated on the extreme austerity of these hermits, living a life a suffering, and sternly withholding themselves from any form of pleasure in life. He considered their whereabouts, and realized that their lifestyle would not end the cycle of life, because extreme virtue in one life cycle is rewarded by exactly the opposite in the next.[19]

Upon this realization, Siddhartha turned down an offer to become a teacher of the hermits, and said farewell to his hermit friends. He moved to a neighboring town called Rajagriha, and started begging for alms parts of the day, while meditating the rest of the time. He received several offers to end his homeless, begging lifestyle, even by the local king, who had heard about the radiant beggar and rode out to meet him. Siddhartha was kind, but refused to become a guest or even a shareholder in the king's palace, explaining to him that he had abandoned the most lavish of lifestyles to become what he was today. He clarified to the king that he had abandoned all desires from his life, as he had come to understand that they only enslave their beholders. Desires are the source of all misery and suffering, and oftentimes lead to dependency of the most fickle of things. Siddhartha compared surrendering to desires like drinking salt water: one only becomes thirstier. He explained that the only salvation from such thirst was to turn away from it, which was exactly what he had done.[20]

After this encounter, Siddhartha moved on and adopted a solitary, austere lifestyle, barely eating, and mainly meditating. Over time, he gathered a small group of followers, who engaged in the same austere lifestyle of begging barely what was needed to stay alive, and further meditating to find the answers to the mystery of life. Siddhartha weakened significantly in those years, and finally realized that he was not doing anyone a service by starving himself the way he did. He gradually started accepting more food, and regained his strength and beauty over time. His disciples were not happy with this decision and turned away from him.

Becoming Buddha

Siddhartha was now in his mid-thirties. He decided to set himself down and clear his mind from impure thoughts such as temptation, covetousness, and destruction.

60 Buddhism

As he sat down, he started meditating. The meditation he engaged in was an old form that had been practiced before his days, but had been abandoned for quite some time. It is now widely known as Vipassana or "insight meditation." Thanks to the Buddha's re-introduction of this meditation technique in the years after his enlightenment, Vipassana has become a widespread vehicle to attain and expand mindfulness, and will be further explained in chapter 7.

Through his practice of Vipassana, Siddhartha gained insight in the interdependence of all things, and the fact that our ego is just an illusion.[21] It was after this experience that he declared himself to be a Buddha. There is a well-known story to depict Siddhartha's first encounter after becoming enlightened. As the Buddha emerged from his meditation, he walked on a road and came across a man, who was struck by his radiance and asked him if he was a god. The Buddha said, "no," and the man asked if he was a saint, and again the Buddha said, "no." The man asked him if he was a prince, and the Buddha denied that as well. In the end, the man asked the Buddha is he was a man, and again, the Buddha said, "no." Finally, the man asked him, "well, then what are you?" upon which the Buddha stated, "I am awake."[22]

For the next 45 years of his life, the Buddha wandered from place to place in the Ganges valley area, and taught his insights, his *Dhamma* (which is the Pali way of using the word "Dharma," the Sanskrit pronunciation), to everyone who cared to listen. He was often surrounded by followers, who were attracted by his message. Siddhartha, the Buddha, lived to his 80s. At the time of his death, Buddhism was well established as a religion in central India.[23] Figure 5.1 depicts a small fraction of the many lessons Siddhartha learned on his path toward enlightenment.

Influence on His Family

As sources report, Yasodhara, most frequently mentioned as the wife of the Buddha during his years as the young prince Siddhartha, became a nun in later life. She even became an *Arahant. Arahant* is a Pali term, equal to *Arhat* (Sanskrit). An *Arahant* is a person who overcomes the cycle of life and death (*Samsara*), and will therefore no longer be reborn. *Arahants* live saintly lives and have attained enlightenment. According to the sources, Yasodhara had supernatural powers and insights, and could remember thousands of life cycles prior to her current life. She passed away before the Buddha, at age 78.[24]

As for the Buddha's son, Rahula, he saw his father for the first time when he was seven years old, and his father was living the life of an ascetic. The little boy was so enamored with his father that he approached him and expressed his admiration. Siddhartha ordained little Rahula as a novice monk, very much to the grief of his father, King Śuddhodana, who now saw his hope for a serious heir to his throne vanishing. Young Rahula was an eager and quick learner, and, while he had two steady teachers, he also received some important life lessons from his father.

FIGURE 5.1 Some of the lessons Siddhartha Gautama learned in pre-Buddha years

A very important one was about telling the truth. The Buddha explained to Rahula that the respect others have for lying people is as insignificant as the almost invisible amount of water left in a container after it is emptied. Similarly, their personal honor is as minute as this amount of water. Upon turning the container upside down and then back up, he explained that the character of dishonest people is as empty as the empty container.[25]

In the same graphic way, he taught him the virtues of reflection, deep thinking, and the hollowness of vanity. Growing up, Rahula realized how handsome he looked and how well his father looked, but his father explained to him that physical features are of a fickle nature, because they don't stay with us, and they don't represent our deeper selves. Over the years, they leave us, so they are ultimately not ours. Rahula meditated on this lecture of impermanence, and soon also became an *Arahant*. He, too, passed away before the Buddha.[26]

62 Buddhism

Summary

In this chapter we presented:

- A brief foundation about the way Buddhism will be interpreted in this book: not as a religion or a doctrine, even though these perspectives are widely observed, but as a psychology or a way of living.
- The life of a young man named Siddhartha Gautama, who lived from about 563 or 566 BCE to about 486 BCE. He was born in Lumbini, Nepal, or in India, as the son of Śuddhodana, the leader or king of the Shakya clan, and Maya, a Koliyan princess. The name Siddhartha means "he who has attained his goals." Early on it was predicted that the young prince would become a great leader of people or a holy men, and his father wanted to prevent the latter from happening, so he created a very protected life for his son, living in three palaces during, but never leaving them.
- The years of Siddhartha as a young man, married at age 16, either to Gopa, Yasodhara, or both. In both stories, the father of the chosen bride is not happy with Siddhartha as a possible son-in-law, either because of his overprotected life, or because of the prediction that he will soon abandon his lavish lifestyle. Even at his tender age, Siddhartha was not looking for the most beautiful of potential brides, but the one who would see past his vast wealth and good looks. Siddhartha's wife bore him a son, who was called Rahula.
- The gradual realization of Siddhartha that his life had thus far been overprotected and his growing curiosity about the world out there. He started undertaking trips outside his palace, and saw an old person, a sick person, and a dead body, thus realizing that life would not always remain as it currently was. This strengthened his decision to abandon his lavish lifestyle and go out to seek the truth.
- The seven years of Siddhartha as an ascetic in the forest, in which he deprived his body from everything but the very basic needs to stay alive. He did so until he came to the realization that the severe deprivation he was exposing himself to was only weakening his body, but not leading to any higher level of awareness, and definitely not to an end of the cycle of life and death.
- Siddhartha as a homeless person, begging for alms, and refusing all the generous offers for food, comfort, companionship, or luxury. He adopted a solitary, austere lifestyle, barely eating, and mainly meditating. He gathered a small group of followers, but ultimately realized once again that he was merely weakening himself with this lifestyle and not gaining any higher insights. He started eating more, regained his strength, but lost his ascetic followers.
- Siddhartha's decision to engage in Vipassana meditation to attain insight and free himself from the cycle of death and rebirth, known as *Samsara*. Being in his mid- to late thirties when he gained enlightenment, he went on to preach his insights for the next 45 years to many, and gathered a large group of fol-

lowers. Among those who followed him was his son, Rahula, who also became a monk, and reached *Arahant* status.

Questions

1. Does the notion of Buddhism as a psychology (rather than a religion or a philosophy) make any difference to the core of understanding this phenomenon for you? Please share your reasoning.
2. According to the story of Siddhartha's early life, his father, Śuddhodana, restricted him to three palaces in order to remain protected. What was Śuddhodana's reason for restricting his son this way? Did he achieve his goal(s)? Please substantiate your answer.
3. As a young man, Siddhartha abandoned his family and lavish lifestyle to "seek the truth." What was the immediate cause of this decision, and do you feel that it was a justified one? Please elaborate.
4. At several times in his pre-enlightened life, Siddhartha engaged in an ascetic lifestyle, only to renounce it later as too extreme on his path to attain enlightenment. What specific insights did Siddhartha's engagement in the ascetic lifestyle bring to him?
5. The Buddha taught his young son Rahula some important virtues, as mentioned in the chapter. Please select two of these virtues and reflect on them.

Notes

1 *Psychology* (2012). Retrieved on October 18, 2013 from www.merriam-webster.com/dictionary/psychology
2 Gethin, R. (1998). *The Foundations of Buddhism.* Oxford University Press, Oxford, UK.
3 UNESCO World Heritage Center (2013). Lumbini, the Birthplace of the Lord Buddha, retrieved on November 2, 2013 from http://whc.unesco.org/en/list/666
4 "Buddha. Biography" (2013). Retrieved on November 2, 2013 from www.biography.com/people/buddha-9230587
5 "*Historians generally agree. . .*" (2013). Northern Arizona University. Retrieved on November 2, 2013 from http://jan.ucc.nau.edu/jsa3/362/notes/Buddhism1.htm
6 Harold, A. F. (1922). King Suddhodana and Queen Maya. *The Life of Buddha* (tr. by Paul C Blum). Retrieved on November 2, 2013 from www.sacred-texts.com/bud/lob/lob03.htm
7 Ibid.
8 Boeree, C. G. (2007). Siddhartha Gautama Buddha. Retrieved on November 8, 2013 from www-psych.stanford.edu/~knutson/aaa/boeree04.pdf
9 Harold, A. F. (1922). King Suddhodana and Queen Maya. *The Life of Buddha* (tr. by Paul C Blum). Retrieved on November 2, 2013 from www.sacred-texts.com/bud/lob/lob03.htm
10 Harold, A. F. (1922). King Suddhodana and Queen Maya. *The Life of Buddha* (tr. by Paul C Blum). Retrieved on November 8, 2013 from www.sacred-texts.com/bud/lob/lob09.htm
11 Ibid, pp. 29–30.
12 Ibid.

64 Buddhism

13 Ibid.
14 Boeree, C.G. (2007). Siddhartha Gautama Buddha. Retrieved on November 8, 2013 from www-psych.stanford.edu/~knutson/aaa/boeree04.pdf; *Buddhist Studies.* (2008). Retrieved on November 8, 2013 from www.buddhanet.net/e-learning/buddhistworld/buddha.htm; Aemilius (July 14, 2010). Wives of Siddhartha Gautama. *Dharmawheel: A Buddhist Discussion on Mahayana and Vajrayana Buddhism.* Retrieved on November 8, 2013 from www.dharmawheel.net/viewtopic.php?f=41&t=1739
15 Abeysekera, R. (May 13, 2000). Relatives and Disciples of the Buddha: Immediate Family of the Buddha. *BudhaSasana, A Buddhist Page by Binh Anson.* Retrieved on November 8, 2013 from www.buddhanet.net/budsas/ebud/rdbud/rdbud-01.htm
16 Ibid.
17 Ibid.
18 Ibid.
19 Harold, A.F. (1922). King Suddhodana and Queen Maya. *The Life of Buddha* (tr. by Paul C Blum). Retrieved on November 2, 2013 from www.sacred-texts.com/bud/lob/lob17.htm
20 Ibid.
21 Snelling, J. (1991). *The Buddhist Handbook: The Complete Guide to Buddhist Schools, Teaching, Practice, and History.* Inner Traditions International, Rochester, VT.
22 Kornfield, J. (1996). *Teachings of the Buddha.* Shambhala, Boston, MA.
23 Bercholz, S. & Kohn, S. C. (1993). *An Introduction to the Buddha and his Teachings.* Barnes & Noble, New York.
24 Abeysekera, R. (May 13, 2000). Relatives and Disciples of the Buddha: Immediate Family of the Buddha. *BudhaSasana, A Buddhist Page by Binh Anson.* Retrieved on November 8, 2013 from www.buddhanet.net/budsas/ebud/rdbud/rdbud-01.htm
25 Ibid.
26 Ibid.

6

MAIN VEHICLES OF BUDDHISM

When we see beyond self, we no longer cling to happiness. And when we stop clinging, we can begin to be happy.

Ajahn Chah

Two Schools, One Buddhism

Many Buddhist scholars don't perceive Buddhism as a religion but rather as a philosophy, a science, a psychology, or a way of living. And their notions make sense because Buddhism's foundational principle is to focus on our own minds. Rather than relying on a supreme being, Buddhism aims to consider practical matters, such as how to lead a righteous life, how to keep our minds awake, and how to remain healthy and serene.[1] Buddhism presents a particular worldview and way of living that enhances our personal understanding, happiness, and wholesome development.[2] It primarily focuses on an understanding of the operation of causes, conditions, and effects.[3] The Buddha is not worshipped as a god but revered as an awakened teacher.

During his life, the Buddha disagreed with a number of issues that were quite common, such as the local caste system, the notion that one could only be from one particular group to attain "liberation." He welcomed followers from all ranks of life, and proposed a lifestyle that he called the Middle Way, based on his past experiences that excesses are not constructive to our personal and mental wellbeing.[4] As explained in chapter 5, he experienced an excessively lavish lifestyle, followed by a rigorous ascetic one, and neither of the two brought him any insights.

Over the centuries, several interpretations emerged from the Buddha's teachings, resulting in diverging schools of thought. The two main schools that exist today are Theravada and Mahayana. These two schools should be seen as different expressions of the Buddha's teaching. As will be explained in this chapter, both schools or vehicles adhere to the same foundational concepts, and while they may sometimes engage in healthy debates, there is no hostility between followers of the two vehicles.[5]

Theravada

Theravada Buddhism, also referred to as "The Teachings of the Elders," is considered the more conventional of the two schools. It is considered the early Buddhist vehicle, and is more individualistic-based in its teaching. Theravada Buddhism emerged from the factions into which Buddhism had split shortly after Siddhartha's death. The emergence of the Theravada school apparently happened around the fourth century BCE. The Theravada school became particularly prominent in Sri Lanka and several countries of Southeast Asia. Theravada schools pride themselves in being the most accurate followers of the original teachings of the Buddha. The ultimate goal of the Theravada teachings is to end the cycle of rebirth (*Samsara*) and enter liberation (*Nirvana*). The path to attain Nirvana is to become an *Arahant* (Pali) or *Arhat* (Sanskrit), a saint who will never be reborn.[6] Within the Theravada tradition, awakening is therefore only possible for *bhikkhus* (ordained male Buddhist monastics). The Dalai Lama explains that the Early Buddhist traditions are also referred to as the "Individual Vehicle."[7]

The Theravada school is rather rigorous in its monastic traditions, even though laypeople may participate in the beliefs, support the monks, and engage in the basic ethical principles of this tradition. Theravada Buddhism is today the predominant form of Buddhist practice in South Asian countries, such as Sri Lanka, Cambodia, Laos, Burma, and Thailand.[8] This "senior" vehicle of Buddhism holds some of the earliest teachings of the Buddha, which are captured in Pali language. Meditation is considered the main approach toward transformed consciousness.[9]

Within the Theravada teachings the main message of the Buddha is a plain and simple one: abstaining from evil in any way, gathering all that is good, and purifying the mind. The way this triangular goal can be achieved is through three trainings: developing ethical conduct, meditating, and gaining insight wisdom.[10]

The Theravada philosophy teaches us that all earthly things are: 1) temporary and fleeting, 2) imperfect, and 3) not our own. Most of the tangible things around us have both a material and a nonmaterial element. The nonmaterial part can be further distinguished into sensations, perception, mental formatives, and consciousness.[11]

Upon understanding the above, which the Buddha referred to as "the true nature of things," we find that nothing in the world is substantial. Once we realize that, we also see the uselessness of either excessive indulgence in sensual pleasures, and self-mortification. Such understanding, then, may mentally pave the way to the Noble Eightfold Path, which will be further discussed in chapter 7. A person who attains the level of awareness that all our worldly suffering is based on craving and aversion, and who subsequently decides to thread the Noble Eightfold Path can reach *Nirvana* and become an *Arahant*, or "perfected one."[12]

Mahayana

Mahayana Buddhism, also known as "The Great Vehicle," aims to serve a larger group of people. This form of Buddhism is more prominent in North Asia. As with Theravada, Mahayana Buddhism also emerged from factions in the tradition, but at a somewhat later stage: around the first century ce. Mahayana Buddhists perceive their tradition as more authentic to the Buddha's teachings. While the canonical texts of Theravada are accepted, there is a large body of additional material to which Mahayana adheres.[13]

Within the Mahayana concept, everybody can become a *Bodhisattva* (enlightened being). The basic premise in this school of Buddhism is that "all sentient beings possess the Buddha nature and hence are capable of being enlightened."[14] Main focus points in the Mahayana tradition are: 1) the emptiness of all things, 2) the importance of compassion, and 3) the acknowledgment that everyone can become a Buddha, because we all have Buddha nature. Because the Mahayana described the ideal state of being as the "Bodhisattva state," this school is sometimes called, "The Bodhisattva Path."[15]

The most important teaching within the Mahayana school is that compassion is a critical component of enlightenment. Compassion is therefore always manifested in *Bodhisattvas*, who deliberately postpone *Nirvana* (final enlightenment) in order to help and guide other living beings who still suffer in *Samsara* (the cycle of rebirth).

The Mahayana is often seen as an overarching body for a variety of Buddhist streams, including the Tantra school of Tibet and Nepal; the Pure Land sect in China, Korea, and Japan; and Zen Buddhism in China and Japan.[16] Mahayana also includes a sub-school, known as Vajrayana, which is mainly practiced in Bhutan, Mongolia, Siberia, and foremost in Tibet (where five schools still exist). Tibetan Buddhism invests great effort in the practice of *Bodhicitta* (becoming aspired to obtain an awakened mind, and seeing everyone as our mother from a previous life) and the attainment of the *Bodhisattva* state.

The Mahayana vehicle, being broader and more general in approach, is believed to consist of some modifications from the original teachings of the Buddha. Multiple sources agree that this vehicle stems from a Buddhist sect called the *Mahasanghikas*, who were very enthusiastic about their purpose and became very popular. They made some changes to the interpretations of various Buddhist discourses and texts, and rejected some portions of the initial standards that were set after the Buddha's passing.[17]

The Bodhisattva

Mahayana Buddhism teaches us that our mind has two domains, the cognitive and the affective, which complement one another. Within our cognitive belief, we develop an inflated sense of a separate self. We feel, "I am," and thereby think, "I am a separate entity from others." As soon as we do so, our affective or emotional state becomes one of being primarily concerned with ourselves and less caring about the wellbeing of others. In other words, we become self-centered and develop negative emotions about our connection with others.

In order to become a *Bodhisattva* we must become aware of the delusions that give rise to this false sense of self and this misplaced self-centered behavior. A *Bodhisattva* works on simultaneous development of wisdom and compassion. The *Boddhisattva* aims to overcome emotional misconceptions by developing loving-kindness and compassion, and to overcome cognitive misconceptions by developing wisdom that sees the inherent selflessness and emptiness-of-all phenomena.[18]

Bodhisattvas are the "Buddhas-to-be" who pledge to better themselves in order to help better others. Everything they do, whether at work, home, or in other social settings, is focused on helping others. In order to do that, they work on purifying and transforming their minds. The vow to improve oneself to improve others is called "arousing the thought of awakening," or *Bodhicitta*. So, this is the commencement of Mahayana practice: the motivation to benefit all beings (human and nonhuman) in a responsible way. All actions are a result of this root intention. In Mahayana teaching, the incitement of *Bodhicitta* is considered more precious than the proverbial wish-fulfilling jewel.[19]

Accords and Discords Between Theravada and Mahayana

While the most important aspects of the teaching are still common between these two main schools of Buddhism, there are various areas in which they differ. In this section we will review a selection of the main differences.

One of the most important differences between the Theravada and Mahayana teachings is that the Theravada school holds true to the notion that only *bhikkhus* (inaugurated hermits) will ever awaken, while the Mahayana school teaches that Buddhas are all around, and that awakening can thus be obtained by each one of us. The Buddhas we find among us are referred to as *Bodhisattvas*.

Another critical difference between the two schools is the perspective on the Buddha: the Theravada school considers Siddhartha Gautama to be the only Buddha, while the Mahayana school proclaims that there is "Buddha-nature," a universal phenomenon aside from the historical Buddha, Siddhartha Gautama.

The schools also differ in their training focus: while Theravada trains its followers to become *Arahants*, Mahayana trains its followers to become Buddhas.[20]

Main Vehicles of Buddhism **69**

Perceptions on the purpose of *Bodhicitta* differ also between the two schools. *Bodhicitta* is the common term used for "enlightened mind," or the mind that strives for awakening and compassion to help all living beings. In Theravada, the liberation through *Bodhicitta* is aimed at awakening and improving the individual, while in Mahayana, the awakening is not merely aimed toward one individual, but also to help others.[21]

The Theravada school has a modest number of rituals, while the Mahayana school has many.[22]

The Theravada school has remained more authentic over the centuries due to its relative protection of the teachings, while the Mahayana tradition has opened itself to other influences such as Confucianism and Taoism in China, as well as influences from other parts of the world.[23]

Yet, both schools acknowledge that Gautama Buddha is the primary teacher. They also commonly take refuge in the Three Gems (also called Jewels, Treasures, or Refuges), which are; 1) the Buddha, 2) the *Dhamma* (Pali) or *Dharma* (Sanskrit, his teaching), and 3) the *Sangha* (the community).

Both Theravada and Mahayana Buddhists focus on: a) ceasing all unwholesome conduct, b) doing only what is good, and c) purifying the mind. They consider this triangular mission a foundation to end suffering and ensure good fortune, regardless of the effects of the times we live in and the influences thereof.[24]

> The intention of a) ceasing unwholesome conduct, is to refrain from doing anything that can cause harm, pain, or suffering, to ourselves or others. The non-harming theme is very essential in Buddhism and is generally acknowledged by the term "ahimsa" (non-harming). The concept of non-harming is a very broad one, as it relates to a large scope of actions, personal and interpersonal. At the personal level there is a range of conducts to consider, such as ensuring that our speech and thoughts remain positive, that our digestive habits—what we eat and drink—don't harm us, and that we don't engage in any type of action that could be considered unwholesome. At the interpersonal level the range of attention points is even larger, entailing our discontinuation of doing or saying hurtful things to others, stealing, and harming the environment.
>
> The intention of b) doing only what is good, is to help ourselves and others to suffer less, thus engaging in deliberate actions to stay healthy, happy, compassionate and kind, and release any negative habits or energy. We should try to do this for ourselves, but also for others.
>
> The intention of c) purifying the mind, pertains to abstaining from a self-centered focus, and respecting others in their ways. Even if they hold different beliefs than we do, we should be mindful and respect them. Hatred and discrimination have no place in this practice, as they only enforce suffering and disparity.[25]

Main Vehicles of Buddhism

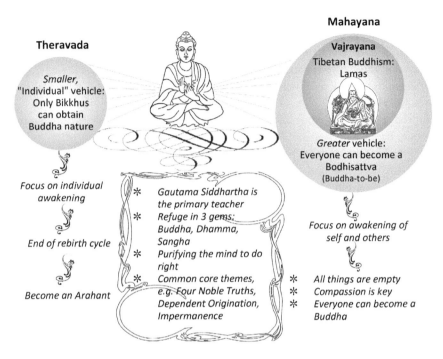

FIGURE 6.1 Main Buddhist vehicles and their focus

Both Theravada and Mahayana Buddhism, agree on core themes such as:

- Suffering (due to our craving and attachment)
- Impermanence (because everything ultimately passes)
- No-self (because nothing and no one lasts and clinging to anyone ultimately leads to suffering)
- Karma (the cycle of cause and effect)
- Nirvana (serenity through liberation)
- Dependent Origination (everything arises in dependence upon multiple causes and conditions)
- Mindfulness (awareness, as in not being distracted)
- The Four Noble Truths and the Noble Eightfold Path, which we will further discuss in chapter 7.

Figure 6.1 depicts the most essential elements of the Theravada and Mahayana schools.

Buddhism in the United States: A Brief Overview

Since we provided an overview of business from its early days on, and provided one of the life of Gautama Siddhartha (the Buddha) as well, it is fair to also provide some information about the way Buddhism evolved in the United States. In the next section, we will present this brief overview.

Establishment

The first significant Buddhist presence in the United States was noted around 1850 during the Gold Rush era, with the arrival of Japanese and Chinese immigrants. Whereas the initial Chinese Buddhist arrival took place in 1849 in California,[26] early Japanese Buddhists settled in Hawaii around 1868, after which some arrived in California in 1869.[27] The early Buddhist settlers were confronted with a Christian-dominated environment and little tolerance for other religious practices.[28] There was quite a lot of pressure on these Chinese and Japanese Buddhist settlers from the existing U.S. population to adopt the American lifestyle and incorporate Protestant or Catholic religious traditions into theirs.

There were, however, two particular events that had a positive influence on Buddhism's presence in the United States. One was the instatement of the Theosophical Society in the 1870s, supported by white American Buddhists and advocating greater religious, philosophical, and scientific tolerance, and the other was the World Parliament of Religions in 1893, which greatly promoted and popularized the Buddhist philosophy in the United States.[29]

Another important reason for Buddhism's emergence in the United States in the late nineteenth century was the emergence of an intellectual crisis in American Protestantism, fed by contemporary pressures such as increasing scientific skepticism and immense population shifts caused by the Industrial Revolution.[30] There is an epic poem, published in 1879 by Sir Edwin Arnold, titled *The Light of Asia*, that illustrates commonalities in the lives of Gautama Buddha and Jesus Christ, and became a great success, thus sparking the interest of many discontented American intellectuals of those days, and presenting them with a more tolerant and open-minded religious alternative to Christianity.[31] It has been proven throughout history that receptiveness to alternatives increases when crises hit. In the United States, Buddhism benefited from a crisis in Christian circles in the late nineteenth and early twentieth centuries.

Growth

Various sources[32] affirm that the manifestation of Buddhism in the first part of the twentieth century was predominantly maintained by the Japanese, and was mainly focused on Zen Buddhism. The attraction that Zen Buddhism held for white Americans could be found in the fact that it provided an alternative to those who had become uncomfortable with the traditional Christian traditions, or who wanted to use Buddhism for nonreligious (intellectual and behavioral) purposes.[33] Near the end of the first half of the twentieth century, interest in Asian traditions in general was spurred by the U.S. occupation of Japan right after World War II, as many Americans traveled to Japan and learned about the local culture.

72 Main Vehicles of Buddhism

When we consider the entrance of Tibetan Buddhism in the United States, names such as Tarthang Tulku and Kalu Rinpoche surface. Tulku was an incarnate lama, who escaped the Chinese invasion of Tibet in 1959, along with other prominent Tibetans such as the Dalai Lama. Rinpoche was a Tibetan yogi who made many trips to the West, starting in 1971, at the request of the Dalai Lama.[34] Tulku established the Nyingma Meditation Center in Berkeley, California, and Rinpoche established his main North American center in Vancouver, Canada. Yet, it is the name Chogyam Trungpa, also referred to as Trungpa Rinpoche, which is most recognizable when discussing the popularization of Tibetan Buddhism in the United States. Trungpa was also a Tibetan refugee, identified as the 11th Trungpa Tulku when he was 13 months old. Passing away in 1987 at the age of 49, he remains a controversial but highly intelligent figure, who studied in India and England, and gave up his monastic vows after a paralyzing car accident earlier in his life.[35] He had not been keeping those vows anyway, and decided to continue his teachings as a layperson. Trungpa was known for his unconventional ways of behaving, including drinking heavily, smoking, and having sex with his students. He founded the Naropa Institute and had a way about him that attracted a large group of white American followers. The Naropa Institute now offers bachelor's and master's degrees in Buddhist studies, while several of Trungpa's Buddhist centers in the United States also engage in Shambhala training, a secularized path to spiritual awakening, which is still in debate as to whether it was Trungpa's own invention or an existing secret Tibetan tradition.

As times progressed, American Buddhism developed along two main lines: the ethnic Buddhists, consisting of "immigrants and their descendants,"[36] and the white American Buddhists or "occidentals."[37] These two groups are described by some as "ethnic Asian-American Buddhist groups" and "mostly members of European-derived ancestry,"[38] while others refer to them as "ethnic" versus "convert."[39] The two groups often held opposing views about what Buddhism in the United States should reflect, based on their specific preferences.[40] The scholarly attention toward Buddhism, ignited in the 1970s, was primarily focused on the converts, which were predominantly white Americans.[41]

Beginning in the 1990s, controversy grew between the two groups, starting with the white group claiming responsibility for all the progress made for Buddhism in the United States, and rebutted by representatives of the Asian Buddhists through a declaration that they had contributed significantly as well by weathering harsh initial opposition in order to achieve the current level of acceptance of their religion or philosophy.[42] This controversy led to the introduction of the term "two Buddhisms"[43] in The United States, which has led to some divergence of opinion among the scholars who study American Buddhism. Some scholars acknowledge and elaborate on the division, while others feel that the division is relatively insignificant, as it is subsumed by much an overall Buddhist unity.

Those who acknowledge the division have introduced other typologies such as a sub-division of the ethnic-Asian category into "old-line" and "recently arrived"

Buddhists. Others have divided Buddhists in the United States into the categories "baggage Buddhists" and "converts," pointing out that the first of these two categories consists of those who were born into the religion culturally, and the latter of predominantly white Americans. Yet others have created three categories: elite, ethnic, and evangelical;[44] and some even listed four categories: traditional, ethnic, convert, and Americanized.[45] Then there are those who feel that the division should not be ethnic-based, but rather focused on the approaches toward Buddhism, which leads to a division of "traditionalists" versus "modernists",[46] with members of both Asian and white American groups represented in each category.

Those who oppose the perspectives of multiple Buddhisms in the United States prefer to speak of diversity under the banner of one Buddhism, and stress that there are plenty of occasions where there is positive interaction between White, Asian, and other Buddhists in the United States. These scholars feel that the classification of multiple Buddhisms in the United States worsens tensions and implies a segregation that is not as pronounced as it sounds.[47]

Current Standing

As the popularity and diversification of American Buddhism grows, scholars continue to debate the classifications. One Buddhist scholar reviews all of the above classifications as an ongoing trend common in all religions, emphasizing similar diversifications in Christianity, Hinduism, Sikhism, and Islam.[48] Another one compares the modest Zen Buddhist environment with the colorful Tibetan halls in the United States, and emphasizes the division that still exists among American Buddhists in class, culture, and ethnicity, with the white American "elite" group in the financial and intellectual lead.[49] To add to this confusion, yet another scholar emphasizes that, due to the fact that most current Chinese immigrants enter the United States for work or study purposes, they also represent a rather privileged group, free from financial hardship, and with relatively high levels of education.[50] This, of course, is in opposition to Chinese immigrants in previous centuries.

Perspectives between members of the various groups differ to this day, often stimulated by cultural and ethnic convictions. One scholar[51] points out that there are some interesting perceptional differences among American Buddhists. There is, for instance, the discrepancy in views between a Chinese Buddhist woman who describes her shame upon insight into prior selfishness, and White American Buddhist women who praise their newly gained sense of self-realization. Another interesting discrepancy is the enthusiasm gap between "baggage" Buddhists (those born into the religion), and converts.[52] Many white American, or "elite," Buddhists have no interest in becoming nuns or monks, but see their devotion to Buddhism rather as a way to enhance the quality of their lives as laypeople. These elitists don't seem to be bothered by ethical codes or the lack thereof. The main interest of this elite group is "individualism, freedom of choice, and personal fulfillment."[53] This interest is very much based on the dominant cultural mindset in the United States.

74 Main Vehicles of Buddhism

A possible factor supporting the growing popularity of Buddhism in the United States is the increased visibility of the Dalai Lama, who frequently visits the United States and has gained support from a growing number of white American elites and several high-profile celebrities such as Steven Segal, Richard Gere, and Harrison Ford. It is the Dalai Lama's unique blend of political leadership, peace activism, and personal charisma that has elevated his popularity worldwide.

There are currently multiple levels of diversity in American Buddhism. In line with the general trend in the United States, American Buddhist *sanghas* (communities) are now also trying to enhance understanding and acceptance of racial diversity within.[54] Another type of diversity that is increasingly entering the picture of Buddhism in the United States is the diversity in the teaching itself. Several prominent Buddhist teachers, such as Jack Kornfield, have started to incorporate Western psychology into their teachings, developing unique diversifications that one may or may not want to identify as Buddhism. A growing number of Western Buddhist teachers obtain training in more than one Eastern tradition, and subsequently combine insights from several Buddhist, Sufi, Taoist, Hindu, and Western traditions, creating a blend of content and a multifaceted teaching style.[55]

Critical Review of American Buddhism

It is interesting to take notice of all of the past and current issues of American Buddhism. Throughout the development of this psychology (also referred to as religion or philosophy) in the United States, it seems that the unfortunate history of racism, financial and intellectual discrimination and segregation, and a strong sense of individualism, have trickled into many instances of organized Buddhism. Author Rick Fields capitalizes on the racist foundations of the United States and stresses the white, also labeled as the "elite" or "convert" group, is defining Buddhism in this country, and unsurprisingly, doing so "in their own image."[56] Fields, who describes himself as a White middle-class American, criticizes white American Buddhists, more or less referring to them as segregationists in regards to their approach to ethnic Buddhists in the United States. He also labels them as arrogant, naïve, and engaging in "a lay practice based on monastic models."[57]

Another interesting note pertains to the recent attempts to restore relational respect in American Buddhist circles. In the 1970s and 1980s several American Buddhist centers experienced crises resulting from the loose sexual relationships between leaders and students, causing recurring turmoil and disruption among members and Buddhist adherents in general.[58]

In more recent years, American Buddhist organizations have undertaken efforts to streamline their codes of conduct, and refocus on Buddhist precepts. It may be the Vietnamese monk Thich Nhat Hanh who deserves most credit for spearheading this positive turnaround in organized American Buddhism.[59] To ensure clarity and end the chaotic situation that had emerged in earlier decades, Thich specifically detailed the issues of sexual misconduct and the use of intoxicants as taboos in the practice of Buddhism. In several meetings with Western Buddhist teachers throughout the 1990s, the Dalai Lama also spoke out against casual sexual relationships between teachers and students, referring to them as sexual misconduct.

One remarkable deviation from Eastern Buddhism is the role of women. While men are still in the majority when it comes to leadership positions, an increasing number of women are rising to prominence in the American Buddhist community, and men and women practice Buddhism as equals.[60] It seems that the United States is currently experiencing the birth of a new Buddhism, which may emerge over the next few decades and which may not look and sound like, or even be named, Buddhism once fully developed. Buddhism has seen many ups and downs over the past 2,500 years, and has typified itself by diversity and change.[61] The new Buddhism in the West is marked by fundamental sociological differences from the Eastern traditions of this religion,[62] which is therefore even more in line with Buddha's initial idea: the new American Buddhism is based on looking at the nature of things from the American individual's experience, and that happens to be an entirely different one than the experiences of Buddhist practitioners in the East.

The emerging American Buddhism has been described as practice-oriented, lay-oriented, influenced by feminism, Western psychology, societal concern, and democratic principles, authority-, competency-, and ethics-based.[63] Because of the major transformations that American Buddhism is still undergoing at this time, it is somewhat understandable that Asian Buddhists and others are puzzled by Western Buddhism, and wonder if this tradition should be called Buddhism at all. Yet, if we consider that the Dalai Lama repeatedly stresses that the beauty and strength of Buddhism is the fact that it reinvents itself under different circumstances, and that this may be the reason why this religion or philosophy has withstood the hands of time, and if we consider the many faces and streams of Buddhism that currently coexist in Asia alone, this Americanization of Buddhism may, after a few decades, become another fully established type, listed along the lines of Theravada and Mahayana, as Buddhism "Americana."

The Dalai Lama and Tibetan Buddhism

Since we mentioned him above, this may be the proper location to take a deeper look into the most well-known Buddhist leaders of our times, Tenzin Gyatso, the Fourteenth Dalai Lama. He is the Tibetan religious and political leader who was exiled to Dharamsala, India, when the Chinese invaded Tibet in 1959. Tibetans practice a form of Buddhism that consists of Theravada, Mahayana, and Vajrayana. The latter is sometimes described as a sub-school of Mahayana, and sometimes as a third school or vehicle of Buddhism, also known as "the Diamond Vehicle."[64]

The reason why Vajrayana is sometimes referred to as a sub-school of Mahayana is because it emerged out of that vehicle. Vajrayana spread quickly out of India, and became the dominant Buddhist tradition in Tibet. This may be why Vajrayana is

76 Main Vehicles of Buddhism

sometimes also referred to as "Tibetan Buddhism." It is also known as "Tantric Buddhism," and has a complex philosophical and ritual system. This form of Buddhism claims to be a swifter and more effective path to enlightenment. Congruent with the Mahayana tradition, Tibetan (Vajrayana) Buddhism focuses on becoming a *Bodhisattva*. In Vajrayana, religious teachers, or lamas, fulfill an important role. The lamas are considered to master the philosophical and ritual traditions. Tibet, being the primary Vajrayana community, holds a long lineage of lamas who serve as religious and political leaders. The Dalai Lama is the most well-known among them.[65]

Tibetans define their culture by an experience of real Buddhas dwelling among them. They feel that the Buddha is all around: he is not a dead hero who awaits resurrection. Tibetans find proof of their stance in the presence of many people who they consider living Buddhas.[66]

The problems of Tibet are of great concern to the global community. The country has been occupied by the People's Republic of China since 1950, causing the then young leader of the Tibetans, the Fourteenth Dalai Lama, and members of his government, to flee over the Himalayas to Dharamsala, India. This is where the Tibetan government-in-exile still resides. Over the decades, several hundreds of thousands of Tibetans have been killed by the Chinese occupants, and about 6,000 monasteries destroyed. It is generally claimed that human rights are being violated to this day in the area, leading to atrocities and unrest.

Perspectives about the Tibetan plight vary widely. Some Buddhist scholars, such as Robert Thurman, the first American Buddhist monk of the Tibetan Buddhist tradition, who studied together with the Dalai Lama in the 1960s and became a close friend of the Tibetan leader, claim that Tibet has been crushed in the past six decades, and is still suffering tremendously under the oppression of the Chinese occupants. Others, such as Alan Wallace, also a prominent American Buddhist scholar and translator of works for many Tibetan Lamas, present a more upbeat view and look at the Tibetan Diaspora as a way of spreading Tibetan Buddhism to many Western countries, thus gaining popularity for this form of Buddhism and for the Dalai Lama. The Chinese invasion could therefore, according to these thinkers, be considered a blessing in disguise. Wallace emphasizes that his exile from Tibet freed the Dalai Lama from his isolated lifestyle, and drove him into more intimate contact with his people. It also expanded the Dalai Lama's horizons in ways that were unthinkable before.

The Dalai Lama is currently, indeed, one of the most popular religious and political leaders in the world and Tibetan Buddhism has gained tremendous popularity in the West. The Dalai Lama has shared on several forums that he now realizes how his extensive travels serve as a powerful marketing instrument for Tibetan Buddhism.

Two of the Dalai Lama's recurring concepts in his books, interviews, and teachings, are the critical Buddhist concepts of *altruism* and *compassion*. He calls for more individual responsibility toward the direction in which the world is evolving, and warns that we should not merely put all the blame on politicians and others

Main Vehicles of Buddhism **77**

who seem to be directly responsible for bad situations. In his speeches, the Dalai Lama stresses that compassion and altruism are not fixed notions: they can be elevated: we can change our mind through training, and then improve our attitudes, thoughts, and outlook, so that we reduce negative mindsets.[67]

Within the Tibetan tradition, there are two main actions to become fully awakened in order to help others: 1) purify negativities, and 2) accumulate positive qualities.[68] For this to happen, we must first awaken and cultivate our relative and ultimate *Bodhicitta*. Relative *Bodhicitta* is the unselfish desire to attain awakening for the benefit of others. Ultimate *Bodhicitta* is the awareness that all things are void of inherent self-existence.[69] The stimulation of *Bodhicitta* and subsequent engagement in *Bodhisattva* actions and thoughts represent the essence of the Mahayana/ Vajrayana path, as taught by the Tibetan Buddhist tradition.[70]

Summary

In this chapter we presented:

- Some initial views on foundational principles of Buddhism, as a way of living righteously by keeping our minds awake, and remaining healthy and serene. Buddhism presents a particular worldview and way of living that enhances our personal understanding, happiness, and wholesome development. It primarily focuses on an understanding of the interrelation between causes, conditions, and effects. The Buddha is not worshipped as a god but revered as an awakened teacher.
- Two main schools of Buddhism: Theravada and Mahayana. These two schools should be seen as different expressions of the Buddha's teaching. In spite of their differences, they adhere to the same foundational concepts, and there is no hostility between followers of the two vehicles.
- Theravada Buddhism, also referred to as "The Teachings of the Elders," which is the more conventional of the two schools. It is more individualistic-based in its teaching. Its ultimate goal is to end the cycle of rebirths (*Samsara*) and enter liberation (*Nirvana*). Within the Theravada tradition, awakening is only possible for ordained male Buddhist monastics. The main Theravada message is abstaining from evil in any way, gathering all that is good, and purifying the mind. The Theravada philosophy teaches us that all earthly things are, 1) temporary and fleeting, 2) substandard, and 3) not our own.
- Mahayana Buddhism, also known as "The Great Vehicle," aims to serve a larger group of people. While accepting the canonical texts of Theravada, Mahayana also adheres to a large additional body of additional material. Within the Mahayana concept, everybody can become a *Bodhisattva* (enlightened being). The basic premise in this school of Buddhism is that all sentient beings possess Buddha nature and, hence, are capable of being enlightened. The main focus points in the Mahayana tradition are: 1) the emptiness of all things,

78 Main Vehicles of Buddhism

2) the importance of compassion, and 3) the acknowledgment that everyone can become a Buddha. The most important teaching within the Mahayana school is compassion as a critical component of enlightenment.

- The *Bodhisattva*, which is the state of being Mahayana Buddhists aim to achieve. In order to become a *Bodhisattva* we must become aware of the delusions that give rise to our false sense of self and misplaced self-centered behavior. A *Bodhisattva* aims to overcome emotional misconceptions by developing loving-kindness and compassion, and to overcome cognitive misconceptions by developing wisdom that sees the inherent selflessness and emptiness of all phenomena.
- Accords and discords between Theravada and Mahayana.

The main differences between the two schools are:

  - Theravada maintains that only *bhikkhus* (inaugurated hermits) will ever awaken, while Mahayana teaches that Buddhas are all around, and that awakening can be obtained by each one of us.
  - Theravada considers Siddhartha Gautama to be the only Buddha, while Mahayana proclaims that there is "Buddha-nature," a universal phenomenon aside from the historical Buddha.
  - Theravada trains its followers to become *Arahants*, Mahayana trains its followers to become Buddhas.
  - In Theravada, liberation is aimed at awakening and improving the self, while in Mahayana, awakening is not merely aimed toward the self, but also to help others.
  - Theravada has a modest number of rituals, while Mahayana has many.
  - Theravada has remained more authentic over the centuries due to its protection of the teachings, while Mahayana has opened itself for other influences in several parts of the world.

The main commonalities between the two schools are:

  - Both acknowledge that Gautama Buddha is the primary teacher.
  - Both take refuge in the Three Gems (also called Jewels, Treasures, or Refuges), which are: 1) the Buddha, 2) the *Dhamma* or *Dharma* (his teaching), and 3) the *Sangha* (the community).
  - Both Theravada and Mahayana Buddhists focus on: a) ceasing all unwholesome conduct, b) doing only what is good, and c) purifying the mind.
  - Both Theravada and Mahayana Buddhism agree on core themes such as suffering, impermanence, no-self, karma, *Nirvana*, dependent origination, mindfulness, and the Four Noble Truths and the Noble Eightfold Path.

- A brief overview of Buddhism in the United States:

  - Influxes of Japanese and Chinese immigrants in the mid-nineteenth century brought Buddhism into the United States with early settlements in California and Hawaii.
  - A movement toward greater religious freedom, and an increased sense of dissatisfaction among Protestants created a fertile climate for the growth of a Buddhist following.

Main Vehicles of Buddhism **79**

- The manifestation of Buddhism in the first part of the twentieth century was predominantly maintained by the Japanese, and was mainly focused on Zen Buddhism.
- One of the most well-known Tibetan Buddhist promoters in the United States was Chogyam Trungpa, or Trungpa Rinpoche, a Tibetan refugee, who founded the Naropa Institute and gathered a large group of white American followers.
- Over time, American Buddhism developed along two main lines: the ethnic Buddhists, consisting of "immigrants and their descendants," and the white American Buddhists or "occidentals."
- During the 1990s, controversy grew between the two groups, with the white group claiming responsibility for all the progress made for Buddhism in the United States, and rebutted by representatives of the Asian Buddhists that they had contributed significantly as well by weathering harsh initial opposition in order to achieve the current level of acceptance of their religion or philosophy. There are proponents and opponents of this divergence today.
- Buddhism is increasing in popularity in the United States, even though scholars are still displaying divergent views on its development in this country. There are, however, some interesting perceptional differences within American Buddhists, where, for instance, Asian Buddhists see selflessness as the ultimate goal, and a large group of American followers see finding the self as their main purpose.
- In more recent years, American Buddhist organizations have undertaken efforts to streamline their codes of conduct, and refocus on Buddhist precepts. It may be the Vietnamese monk Thich Nhat Hanh deserves most of the credit for spearheading this positive turnaround in organized American Buddhism.
- One remarkable deviation from Eastern Buddhism in the United States is the role of women. While men are still in the majority when it comes to leadership positions, an increasing number of women are rising to prominence in the American Buddhist community, and men and women practice Buddhism as equals.
- Because of the major transformations that American Buddhism is still undergoing, it is somewhat understandable that Asian Buddhists and others are puzzled by Western Buddhism, and wonder if this tradition should be called Buddhism at all. Yet, the Dalai Lama stresses that the strength of Buddhism is its self-reinvention, so the Americanization of Buddhism may become another fully established type, listed along the lines of Theravada and Mahayana as Buddhism "Americana."
- The Dalai Lama as the leader and main propagator of Tibetan Buddhism. Tibetans practice a form of Buddhism that consists of Theravada, Mahayana, and Vajrayana, which is sometimes described as a sub-school of Mahayana,

80 Main Vehicles of Buddhism

and sometimes as a third school or vehicle of Buddhism, also known as "the Diamond Vehicle." It is also known as "Tantric Buddhism," and claims to be a swifter and more effective path to enlightenment. Congruent with the Mahayana tradition, it focuses on practitioners becoming a *Bodhisattva*. Lamas fulfill an important role. They are considered to master the philosophical and ritual traditions. Within the Tibetan tradition, there are two main actions to become fully awakened in order to help others: 1) purify negativities, and 2) accumulate positive qualities.

Questions

1. Buddhist scholars consider Buddhism more a psychology or a way of living than a religion, because it aims to consider practical matters, such as how to lead a righteous life, how to keep our minds awake, and how to remain healthy and serene. Explain in about 300 words how you feel that this chapter has underscored this notion.
2. Theravada Buddhism claims that one has to first become an ordained monastic in order to become enlightened, while Mahayana claims that all persons can become a Buddha. Consider these notions and try to formulate your stance about them in about 200 words.
3. *Bodhisattvas* are explained as enlightened beings who deliberately stay around to assist others in releasing their suffering and attaining enlightenment. Can you think of a person that you would consider a *Bodhisattva*? Explain your reasons for selecting this person.
4. Review the differences between Theravada and Mahayana Buddhism. Select two and critique them.
5. Tibetan Buddhism, most prominently represented by the Dalai Lama, is also known as Vajrayana or Tantric Buddhism. Lamas are considered important teachers within this tradition. Engage in some online research on the tradition of lamas and present your findings in about 200–300 words. Be prepared to share in groups.

Notes

1 Yeshe, Lama (1998). *Becoming Your Own Therapist* (trans. S. Carlier, Trans.). Lama Yeshe Wisdom Archive, Weston, MA.
2 Johansen, B.-C. & Gopalakrishna, D. (2006). A Buddhist View of Adult Learning in the Workplace. *Advances in Developing Human Resources, 8*(3), 337–345.
3 Lyu, S. (2012). Development and Mission of Theravada and Mahayana Buddhism in an Era of Globalization. *Religion East & West,* (11), 45–51.
4 Ch'en, K.K.S. (1968). *Buddhism: The Light of Asia.* Barron's Educational Series, Inc., Hauppauge, NY.
5 The Buddhist Schools: Theravada and Mahayana (2008). Retrieved on November 9, 2013 from www.buddhanet.net/e-learning/buddhistworld/schools1.htm

Main Vehicles of Buddhism **81**

6 Patheos (2008–2013). *Religion Library: Theravada Buddhism*. Retrieved on November 10, 2013 from www.patheos.com/Library/Theravada-Buddhism.html

7 His Holiness The Dalai Lama (1995). *The World of Tibetan Buddhism*. Wisdom Publications, Boston, MA.

8 The Buddhist Schools: Theravada and Mahayana (2008). Retrieved on November 9, 2013 from www.buddhanet.net/e-learning/buddhistworld/schools1.htm

9 Ibid.

10 Ibid.

11 Ibid.

12 Ibid.

13 Patheos (2008–2013). *Religion Library: Mahayana Buddhism*. Retrieved on November 10, 2013 from www.patheos.com/Library/Mahayana-Buddhism.html

14 Ch'en, K.K.S. (1968). *Buddhism: The Light of Asia*. Barron's Educational Series, Inc., Hauppauge, NY, pp. 62–63.

15 Bercholz, S. & Kohn, S. C. (1993). *An Introduction to the Buddha and his Teachings*. Barnes & Noble, Inc., New York.

16 The Buddhist Schools: Theravada and Mahayana (2008). Retrieved on November 2013 9, 2013 from www.buddhanet.net/e-learning/buddhistworld/schools1.htm

17 Ibid.

18 Kyabgon, T. (2001). *The Essence of Buddhism: An Introduction to its Philosophy and Practice*. Shambhala, Boston, MA.

19 Khyentse, D. (2006). *Enlightened Courage: An Explanation of the Seven Point Mind Training*. (trans. Padmakara, Trans.) Snow Lion, New York.

20 Differences Between Theravada and Mahayana Buddhism (1996–2013). Retrieved on November 9, 2013 from www.buddhanet.net/e-learning/snapshot02.htm

21 Ibid.

22 Ibid.

23 Ibid.

24 Lyu, S. (2012). Development and Mission of Theravada and Mahayana Buddhism in an Era of Globalization. *Religion East & West*, (11), 45–51.

25 Ibid.

26 Chandler, S. (1998). Chinese Buddhism in America: Identity and Practice. In C.S. Prebish & K. K. Tanaka (Eds.), *The Faces of Buddhism in America*. University of California Press, Ltd., Berkeley and Los Angeles, 13–30; Dugan, K. & Bogert, H. (2006). Racial Diversity in Buddhism in the U.S. *Harvard University*. Retrieved on May 1, 2014 from www.fas.harvard.edu/~pluralism/98wrb/indexa.htm

27 Bloom, A. (1998). *Shin Buddhism in America: A Social Perspective*. In C. S. Prebish & K. K. Tanaka (Eds.), *The Faces of Buddhism in America*. University of California Press, Ltd., Berkeley and Los Angeles, 31–47.

28 Prebish, C. S. (1999). *Luminous Passage*. University of California Press, Berkeley and Los Angeles.

29 Ibid.

30 Coleman, J. W. (2002). *The New Buddhism: The Western Transformation of an Ancient Tradition*. Oxford University Press, New York.

31 Ibid.

32 Coleman, J. W. (2002). *The New Buddhism: The Western Transformation of an Ancient Tradition*. Oxford University Press, New York; Numrich, P. D. (2003). Two Buddhisms Further Considered. *Contemporary Buddhism*, 4(1), 55–78; Prebish, C. S. (1999). *Luminous Passage*. University of California Press, Berkeley and Los Angeles.

33 Numrich, P. D. (2003). Two Buddhisms Further Considered. *Contemporary Buddhism*, 4(1), 55–78.

34 Coleman, J. W. (2002). *The New Buddhism: The Western Transformation of an Ancient Tradition*. Oxford University Press, New York.

82 Main Vehicles of Buddhism

35 Ibid.
36 Numrich, P. D. (2003). Two Buddhisms Further Considered. *Contemporary Buddhism, 4*(1), 57.
37 Ibid.
38 Baumann, M. (2002). *Protective Amulets and Awareness Techniques, or How to Make Sense of Buddhism in the West.* In C. S. Prebish & M. Baumann (Eds.), *West-ward Dharma: Buddhism beyond Asia.* University of California Press, Los Angeles and San Francisco, p. 53.
39 Masatsugu, M. K. (2008). "Beyond This World of Transiency and Impermanence": Japanese Americans, Dharma Bums, and the Making of American Buddhism During the Early Cold War Years. *Pacific Historical Review, 77*(3), 425.
40 Ibid., 425–451.
41 Numrich, P. D. (2003). Two Buddhisms Further Considered. *Contemporary Buddhism, 4*(1), 55–78.
42 Ibid.
43 Numrich, P. D. (2003). Two Buddhisms Further Considered. *Contemporary Buddhism, 4*(1), 59.
44 Nattier, J. (1997). Buddhism Comes to Main Street. *The Wilson Quarterly, 21*(2), 72–80.
45 Numrich, P. D. (2003). Two Buddhisms Further Considered. *Contemporary Buddhism, 4*(1), 55–78.
46 Ibid., 67.
47 Ibid., 55–78.
48 Ibid.
49 Nattier, J. (1997). Buddhism Comes to Main Street. *The Wilson Quarterly, 21*(2), 72–80.
50 Chandler, S. (1998). Chinese Buddhism in America: Identity and Practice. In C. S. Prebish & K. K. Tanaka (Eds.), *The Faces of Buddhism in America.* University of California Press, Ltd., Berkeley and Los Angeles, 13–30.
51 Nattier, J. (1997). Buddhism Comes to Main Street. *The Wilson Quarterly, 21*(2), 72–80.
52 Ibid.
53 Ibid., 76.
54 Dugan, K., & Bogert, H. (2006). Racial Diversity in Buddhism in the U.S. *Harvard University.* Retrieved on May 1, 2014 from www.fas.harvard.edu/~pluralism/98wrb/indexa.htm
55 Coleman, J. W. (2002). *The New Buddhism: The Western Transformation of an Ancient Tradition.* Oxford University Press, New York.
56 Fields, R. (1998). Divided Dharma: White Buddhists, Ethnic Buddhists, and Racism. In C. S. Prebish & K. K. Tanaka (Eds.), *The Faces of Buddhism in America* (pp. 196–206). University of California Press, Berkeley and Los Angeles, p. 200.
57 Ibid., 205.
58 Coleman, J. W. (2002). *The New Buddhism: The Western Transformation of an Ancient Tradition.* Oxford University Press, New York.
59 Ibid.
60 Coleman, J. W. (1999). The New Buddhism: Some Empirical Findings. In D. R. Williams & C. S. Queen (Eds.), *American Buddhism: Methods and Findings in Recent Scholarship* (pp. 91–99). Curzon Press, Richmond, Surrey.
61 Ibid.
62 Ibid.
63 Prebish, C. S. (1999). *Luminous Passage.* University of California Press, Berkeley and Los Angeles, pp. 253–254.
64 Patheos (2008–2013). Religion Library: Vajrayana Buddhism. Retrieved on November 10, 2013 from www.patheos.com/Library/Vajrayana-Buddhism.html
65 Ibid.

Main Vehicles of Buddhism   **83**

66 Thurman, R. A. F. (1995). *Essential Tibetan Buddhism*. HarperCollins, New York.
67 His Holiness The Dalai Lama. (1995). *The World of Tibetan Buddhism*. Wisdom Publications, Boston, MA.
68 Gyeltsen, T. (1997). *Compassion The Key to Great Awakening: Thought Training and the Bodhisattva Practices*. Wisdom Publications, Boston, MA.
69 Ibid.
70 Ibid.

7

THE PLACE OF SUFFERING AND HARMING IN OUR LIVES

There is no permanency but change. From the most minute atom to the highest heaven everything is becoming. It comes into being, stays for a time and passes away, like the volume of water in the flowing stream.

Anagarika Dharmapala[1]

Buddhism: Some Basic Concepts

In the times that Siddhartha Gautama was struggling toward enlightenment, he became aware of a number of critical facts of life, which were later included in his teachings. He wandered for 45 years through many cities and villages in the Ganges valley area, and constantly taught his *Dhamma*[2] to those who were interested. He did not write any books or scriptures. His close followers did not do so either. Yet, shortly after his passing, some of his oldest followers held a council, which was to be followed by several others afterwards. During that first council, hundreds of *Arahants* (enlightened individuals), led by the Buddha's longest living disciple, Ananda, gathered to formulate a cluster of community rules, as they remembered it from the Buddha's teachings. During the subsequent councils, the teachings were expanded, and summaries, reflections, and important points of teachings were noted and grouped.

The Four Noble Truths

The Four Noble Truths, as the Buddha defined them, became foundational in the Buddha's post-enlightenment lectures. The Four Noble Truths are, in fact, a sequence of insights:

The Place of Suffering **85**

1. The truth of suffering[3] (suffering exists)
2. The truth of the origin of suffering (suffering has a cause)
3. The truth of the cessation of suffering (suffering can be ended)
4. The truth of the path, the way to liberation from suffering (the path to end suffering)

The Four Noble Truths and the Noble Eightfold Path, which is embedded in them, represent the essence of the Buddha's teaching.[4] The first three Noble Truths are intended to be points of understanding, and the fourth, which entails the Noble Eightfold Path, as a practice to be implemented if one wants to address the issue of suffering. A good way of looking at it is that the First Truth has to be understood, the Second Truth has to be abandoned, the Third Truth has to be realized, and the Fourth Truth has to be developed.[5]

The Noble Eightfold Path entails the following practices:

- Right View
- Right Intention
- Right Speech
- Right Action
- Right Livelihood
- Right Effort
- Right Mindfulness
- Right Concentration

There is no specific sequence in this set of insights, because they are interrelated. However, it might be prudent to start the review of this path with right view. Right view does not only help the practitioner understand the first three Noble Truths better, but it also helps understanding the need for this interconnected set of behaviors. In other words, it links the awareness of the initial three Noble Truths to the contents of the Fourth. Yet, that is just one way of perceiving "right view." In fact, the entire scope of the Four Noble Truths and the Noble Eightfold Path can be reduced to two essentials: 1) Suffering, and 2) The end of suffering.[6]

The First Noble Truth

The First Noble Truth, the starting point of this essential teaching, claims that suffering exists. When stating this, we should not think of being in pain or suffering from a debilitating disease. In the context used here, life can bring us many forms of suffering: birth, aging, illness, death, unpleasant experiences, inability to hold on to something desirable, inability to get what we want, or all-pervasive suffering; these are eight general ways in which we suffer. To briefly explain these eight ways:

1. Birth is considered suffering, even though we don't remember our own birth. But considering the notion of an unborn child, safe and satisfied in the

86 The Place of Suffering

mother's womb, and then suddenly purged or pulled out of the comfort zone, this is suffering, which explains the crying of newborns: they land in an unfamiliar, unsafe, noisy world that they have to get used to.[7]

2. Aging is another way of suffering. The easiest interpretation of this is old age, when we lose our mobility and our senses, and find that it becomes harder to do the things we could easily do before. However, aging as a form of suffering should be seen within a wider scope: it is also the process of changing. With this continuous change process, we gradually lose our zest for new things. We don't get as excited anymore as we were at a younger age. So, aging should be considered as a physical as well as a psychological process.[8]

3. Illness is a form of suffering we can experience at any age or stage of our life. Illness also varies in intensity. We can speak about being ill when we have a simple cold, but also when something much more seriously is going on. When we are ill, we become dependent on the care of others: loved ones, physicians, perhaps even the hospital. Illness can bring tremendous discomfort and can force us to give up the things we enjoy doing for a shorter or a longer time, and sometimes for the rest of our lives.[9]

4. Death may be considered the biggest suffering in the sequence of birth, aging, and illness. Death entails a total loss of everything: friends, loved ones, the things we cherished, and even our own body. Death is a radical experience that very few of us feel to be ready for. Even if we all know that we will die, we prefer to think that it will take a long time before it will happen to us. Getting close to death is serious suffering for most of us.[10]

5. While the first four types of suffering were more physical in nature, unpleasant experiences are more psychological. Unpleasant experiences overcome us, whether we like them or not. Many of the unpleasant experiences we encounter are unexpected, and can therefore be very traumatic. We can lose dear ones, get into an accident, lose our job, or get entangled in a bad situation at work or home; the variations of unpleasant experiences are plentiful.[11]

6. The inability to hold on to something desirable is a form of suffering we all encounter, whether it pertains to material or immaterial things, or even people. We may cherish people, pets, and things, but there is no guarantee that they will still be with us tomorrow. Losing something or someone dear is suffering.[12]

7. Inability to get what we want. We all have dreams and desires. We achieve some, and we have to forego others. Sometimes we really put our senses on something: a job, a position, a person, a car, a house, but then someone else gets it instead of us, leaving us with a sense of dissatisfaction, or maybe even despair. This inability to get what we want is also suffering.[13]

8. All-pervasive suffering. This type of suffering is the hardest to explain and understand, because it is very subtle. It is that sense of gnawing discomfort we feel all the time, even when things are going well. We question ourselves, and have an eternal chat going on in our mind that can be very troubling and

destructive to our internal serenity. While we head for new experiences we still try to digest past ones, and we often wonder where we may have gone wrong, how we could have made things better, why this had to happen, and why that did not happen. All of this internal turmoil elicits a very private, very innate sense of suffering that no one else knows about, feels, or can take away from us.[14]

It needs to be emphasized that it was not the Buddha's intention to make life seem as a sequence of miseries, but rather, to make us aware of the basics of existence, because we all have to deal with suffering and we do so at many stages in our lives.[15] If we contemplate deeply on life, we will conclude that there is almost always some imperfection, as if the ends don't quite meet. Things always end up appearing somewhat (or a whole lot) different from what we had envisioned them to be.[16] This is not to say that everything is always one gray mass, because we do find joy and pleasure at many stages of our lives. It is just that there is always an underlying factor of insufficiency or imperfection in things, which prevent life from being a smooth and rosy experience.[17] That being said, it also needs to be underscored that the Buddha did acknowledge happiness. He often referred to the happiness that we can experience at many stages and in many setting of our lives: as a family, as a recluse, physical, mental, or emotional happiness, happiness of passion, and happiness of dispassion. Yet, we should remain aware that enjoyment in life is always subject to a cycle: 1) there is attraction and enjoyment, 2) there is disappointment or frustration, and 3) there is freedom or liberation.[18] We may desire something or someone very much, and dream of this thing or person all the time. However, we may have this thing or person with us for a while and then lose it or him/her again, whether that is due to a change in our feelings, their feelings, or just the cycles of life that take them away from us. In the end, this great desire did not stay, and we had to deal with its impermanence. The Buddha explains that everything that is impermanent causes suffering. And since our entire life is impermanent, we cannot even hold on to that, so in the greater scheme, it brings suffering as well.[19]

It is this understanding that the Buddha conveys in the First Noble Truth: nothing lasts, and if we can understand that, our happiness levels will increase, because we will not be trapped into expectations that things will never end. It is mostly our denial that our happiness is a temporary experience that makes us suffer.[20]

The Second Noble Truth

The Second Noble Truth, suffering has a cause, is easily explained once we understand the First. There is an ongoing sense of disenchantment in our lives: we gain things, and then lose them again. So, what is the underlying factor to the suffering we experience when we lose something? It is our sense of possessiveness, to be explained in many shades of manifestation: thirst, desire, craving, greed, in short, our drive to gain and gather, have and hold. This nature, which we all carry to

88 The Place of Suffering

some extent, causes us to suffer.[21] We have a tendency to cling to people, places, experiences, wishes, ideas, or mindsets, and this causes suffering.[22]

This sense of desiring or wanting usually starts at a very small level. It is conceived just as a baby, almost undetectably small. We may, for instance, mentally place ourselves in a situation that we consider pleasant. This seed of imagination then starts to grow if we nurture it. And by doing so, this flicker of an idea becomes a flame, and we start filling in more details in the picture in our mind. The flame may eventually escalate into an entire blaze, turning into an all-consuming obsession. We start thinking about it all the time. Our obsession can even start controlling our behavior, and cloud our sense of fairness, honesty, and decency. We all have a tendency to "want" things, even though the degree to which we allow this sense of desire to flourish may differ, depending on how well we have trained our mind to deal with it. Yet, whether we fulfill our desires or not, the cause of suffering was created, and we endure it. Craving for things that we currently don't have also means that we crave for a state in which we currently don't reside. We want to become something else than we are at the moment.[23]

As long as we carry desires with us, we will experience births, decay, death, and rebirth. This does not have to be interpreted as absolute birth and death of our physical body as a whole, but rather, birth of our mental and emotional state of being: we desire things, attain them, get over them or lose them, and move on to new desires. That, too, is a firm of birth, decay, death, and rebirth, and it can become very tiring. Within this lifetime, we experience millions of these rebirths, so we change all the time.

The Third Noble Truth

The Third Noble Truth, suffering can be ended, is a very hopeful one and important to realize: it is possible to become free from suffering. In order to do this, we need to discontinue the cause of our suffering, which, as we explained in the Second Noble Truth, is our sense of desiring or craving. Once we have released our desires completely, our suffering has ended, and we have reached *Nirvana*.[24] *Nirvana* is not easy to explain, which is why many authors explain it in negative wording, not to be negative, but to clarify its intentions with the limited language we have at our disposal. They may, for instance, explain *Nirvana* as "extinction of thirst,"[25] or "absence of desire,"[26] or "destruction of craving."[27]

Because of the negative referrals to *Nirvana*, many people think that it entails the extinction of the self, but such is not the case, because the "self" is an illusion. It is a sense that we developed over time, and have allowed to emerge as the driver of our physical and mental states. This illusion becomes clear to those who reach *Nirvana*, and because of that, they let go of the illusion.[28]

The fact that we move from one desire to another is often the result of ignorance, in this case, the ignorance of understanding that nothing is permanent, and therefore hollow. Once *Nirvana* is reached, and the false sense of "self" has been released, we are no longer ignorant, but have obtained awareness of how things really are.

The Noble Eightfold Path (The Fourth Noble Truth)

The Eightfold Path is considered the core of the Buddha's teaching. Buddhist scholars agree that it is the insight of this path that elevated the Buddha from a great teacher to a timeless and globally renowned authority. Ever since he presented the Noble Eightfold Path for the first time, his followers have credited him as a wizard, who aroused, produced, and declared a path that had never been brought forth before.[29] They did so while he was still alive, and they are still doing so today.

The strength of the path lies in various aspects. First and foremost in the challenge it offers to those who want to practice it. Buddhas can only teach the path, but practitioners hold the responsibility to implement it. Therefore, only they can get themselves released from unwholesome thoughts and acts, and only they can lead themselves to liberation of suffering.[30]

Another strength of the path emerges in its understanding. It is based on practice rather than intellectual knowledge. While the eight treads of the path are not intended to be followed in any particular sequence, "right view" may be a good way to start for multiple reasons, one of which is the perspective on the purpose of engaging in this practice in the first place. When considering the path, the practitioner soon realizes that each part is integrated and can serve as a good preparation to the next. For instance, right mindfulness, which can be attained through meditation, leads to right concentration.[31]

In the following section, we will engage in a brief contemplation of each tread of the path.

Right View

As indicated before, "right view" may be considered a good starting point of the path, even though there is no specific requirement to do so. However, when engaging in right view, one can begin with acquiring a deeper understanding of the Four Noble Truths: the fact that we suffer; the reasons why we suffer; and the reality that we can choose to end our suffering.

Thich Nhat Hanh, one of the most well-known and revered Buddhist monks of our time, explains that right view can help us nurture the good intentions we have and keep the bad intentions dormant. He alerts us that we all have both in us, but that we have the choice to decide which mindset we will allow to prevail.[32] There is a beautiful story on the internet that explains this well: a grandfather once taught his grandson that there are two wolves in us, which fight each other all the time. One wolf represents jealousy, meanness, spite, anger, negativity, and hate, while the other represents generosity, tolerance, understanding, peace,

90 The Place of Suffering

and harmony. Upon the grandson's question which wolf wins, the grandfather responded, "The one you feed."

Right view entails our ability to detect which internal seeds are positive and constructive and nourish those. It also influences our perception: the way we consider things that happen with us and around us. We can choose to maintain a negative view and see everything as an attack to our dignity and quality of life, or we can decide to look at things from a positive angle and try to detect the positive lessons in each experience. Right view therefore influences our attitude.

Right view can help us contemplate on many aspects of our lives, such as our notion of happiness. Do we think that happiness is tied to certain achievements and material assets, or do we believe that it can be attained right here and now, if we just release all the conditions we have mindlessly erected and maintained over time? Those of us who have been around for a while have found out that happiness is a moving target if we keep attaching it to achievements. If we say, "I will be happy when I have bought this new car, earned this degree, got married to that person, or acquired this job," we find that within a few months after fulfilling our desire, our mind has formulated a new definition of happiness, which we now have to attain.

Right view adjusts limiting perspectives, and may even lead us to understand that actually, all perspectives are limiting. This is why we speak of a "point of view": it is still only one point.[33] Hence, in the end, right view would be the release of any view.

Right Intention

Right intention is often also described as "right thinking": it boils down to the same thing: mental focus. Maintaining the right intention sounds easier than it is. Therefore Thich[34] suggests four simple activities that can help us refocus whenever we get distracted from our right intention:

1. Questioning ourselves if we are sure of what we see, hear, or read. There are often multiple ways of interpreting something, and our first inclination may not be the right one. Taking some time to contemplate everything could help us refocus and engage in right intentions.
2. Asking ourselves what we are doing can also help us refocus, as we often tend to perform on "auto pilot" and engage in behaviors and actions that we have simply adopted from others or from what we have learned in the past.
3. Critically reviewing our habits is another way to keep our intentions on track. We all have good and bad habits, and it is very easy to fall into them. Our bad habits, especially, have a tendency to emerge when we least need them. Remaining alert, and regularly evaluating our behaviors, responses, and actions, could help us refrain from falling back into habitual patterns.
4. Maintaining *Bodhicitta*, which is the aspiration to obtain an awakened mind for the benefit of others. When we engage in *Bodhicitta*, we become filled with

the intention to do well unto others, and help them become happier, more fulfilled beings.

Right Speech

In these times of massive communications in many diverse ways, the importance of right speech should be fully understood. Words have the power to heal or wound. They can be constructive or destructive. Engaging in right speech means that we deliberately refrain from saying things that have negative effects on others. It also means that we remain cautious with spreading news of which we are unsure, or of which the contents can be devastating to some.

Engaging in right speech means that we attempt to resolve division and disharmony, and try to promote or restore unison and harmony. Right speech entails telling the truth to our best of abilities, not creating divisiveness by telling different people different things, refraining from cruelty in our speech, and withholding ourselves from exaggerating facts, only to make them (or us) seem more interesting.[35]

When we listen well, we can better engage in right speech, because we have absorbed the other party's words and intentions well, and can digest them thoroughly before responding. It may now be clear how right view and right intention, as well as the other treads of the Noble Eightfold Path, can assist us in performing right speech.

Right Action

Right action starts, interestingly enough, with the discontinuation of an action: the action of harming ourselves and others.[36] The context of right action is a very broad one, as it entails careful guarding of our practices, helping to protect life, and the wellbeing of all living beings, in the broadest sense possible. This also means no killing, no stealing, and not engaging in any type of misconduct.

Because temptation is all around us, it is not as easy as it may seem to engage in right action. Killing, for instance, is a very broad topic. It also entails, for instance, refraining from killing for pleasure (hunting). We are in need of right action in in our time, where wrong actions have led to global warming, and the loss and destruction of many innocent lives as well as the environment, due to inconsiderate, selfish behavior.

While the human community has progressed in many ways, its progress has happened at the expense of many other beings: the imbalance in income is greater than ever, which means that some pay for the prosperity of others. Human beings and animals in many parts of the world are victimized on a daily basis by those who allow themselves to be driven by mindless greed, leading to selfish actions. The unbridled destruction of natural resources in our few global rainforests without proper replenishment, for instance, has demanded its toll, and since we are not living on an island, we will all ultimately feel the negative effects of these mindless actions.

92 The Place of Suffering

Right Livelihood

Right livelihood pertains to the way in which we earn our living. Are we engaging in constructive activity when we perform our job?

Are we refraining from producing, dealing in, or promoting weapons of any kind that are being used to kill and destroy?[37]

Are we refraining from engaging in slave trade, where people are not paid or heavily underpaid for the work we let them do, so that we can take ruthless advantage of that?[38]

Are we refraining from producing, trading, or promoting destructive goods, such as alcohol and drugs, intended to intoxicate others and expose them to danger and life-threatening situations?[39]

Are we refraining from engaging in dishonest practices such as preying on people's naiveté, and making prophecies or telling fortunes?[40]

Each of the above is an example of wrong livelihood, indented to destroy others, diminish happiness and quality of life, and prey on those who have no means to stand up against the powerful ones. Wrong livelihood may not seem problematic right away, and many people who work in the weapons industry, for cigarette or alcohol manufacturing companies, or in other entities where people and other living beings are abused, will try to justify why their actions are useful. Yet, as their life progresses and they mature, they may eventually awaken and realize their contribution to the misery and suffering in the world.

Right Effort

Right effort is sometimes also listed as "right diligence." Effort is a commendable practice, but we can direct it to constructive or destructive activities, as the previous section indicated. People who work in the weapon or drug industry undeniably invest effort in their job, but, unfortunately, this is not right effort, due to the suffering this effort causes.

As is the case with right view (and all other treads of the path), right effort requires that we carefully distinguish our actions, thoughts, and intentions, so that our effort remains constructive.[41]

Right effort is a very personal task, just like all other elements of the path: it also pertains to the act of contemplating about the roots of our suffering, and then engaging in the effort to release those roots.

Right Mindfulness

When we are mindful, we engage in right view, right intention, right speech, right action, right livelihood, right effort, and right concentration. In Sanskrit, the word *smriti* is used for mindfulness, and it means, literally, "to remember." Remembering here, means returning to the present moment when we realize that our mind starts wandering. When we are mindful, we see things that we usually take for granted:

The Place of Suffering **93**

the grass, the trees, our partner, our colleagues, our pet, and we realize fully that they are here now. Thanks to our mindfulness, we may be able to truly appreciate what we see, and where there is responding life involved (a person or pet), we may indicate our gratitude for their presence, so that they, too, may become mindful of the moment. The appreciation that is part of such mindfulness can alleviate the suffering of mindlessness, and encourage us to go a step further, so that we concentrate on the other, understand him or her better, and transform our own suffering and theirs into joy.[42]

Mindfulness can be incited in several ways. A frequently practiced way is meditation. One of the most well-known forms of meditation is Vipassana, or insight meditation, which is the meditation practice in which Siddhartha Gautama engaged when he gained enlightenment. In its origins associated with Theravada Buddhism, Vipassana is now used in various denominations of Buddhism to bring about attention, awareness, and mindfulness. Vipassana has emerged as a global movement, and is even more westernized than, for instance, Zen, because it does not require traditional techniques.[43] There are Vipassana meditation centers in all parts of the world. Because it can be practiced in a non-sectarian way, it is attractive to Buddhists and non-Buddhists alike.

Vipassana literally means "special seeing" or insight. Being a system of mindfulness techniques, Vipassana draws attention to the breath and to every object of consciousness.[44] Business people, academicians, and also prison inmates, seem to experience significant transformations when engaging in this meditation practice. In the past decade, popular U.S. sources such as *Publishers Weekly* and the *Philadelphia Inquirer*[45] have written about the usefulness of Vipassana for prison inmates, stating that it has helped them break their cycles of anger and revenge. Vipassana is a useful instrument in attaining expanded and purified consciousness, and it appeals to people from all religions, cultures, and backgrounds, because it only requires concentration of the mind by observing one's natural, normal respiration, without adding any sectarian verbalization, visualization, or imagination. There is little to object to purifying the mind at the deepest level, by observing the interaction of mind and matter within oneself, at the level of body sensations, because that, too, is universal.[46]

Engaging in Vipassana meditation starts with finding a suitable place where you can sit comfortably without interruptions. It is also recommended that you wear comfortable clothes, so that you don't get distracted by tightness or pain.

- Most people meditate in sitting position. This is particularly useful for beginners. You will develop your most favorite seating position over time. This can be full or half lotus, tailor cross-legged position, one leg in front, kneeling on a soft bench or cushion, or sitting in a chair.[47]

94 The Place of Suffering

- Sit straight, yet relaxed, and close your eyes.
- Focus on your breathing. You can do so by concentrating on the airflow in and out of your nose, and sensing how it enters and exits or you can focus on your abdomen, right above the navel. You will then start experiencing the sense of rising and falling of the breath: as you inhale, it rises, as you exhale, it falls.[48] This is an awe-inspiring activity, which our body does all the time, even when we sleep, yet we pay so little attention to it. Now is the time to focus on the miracle of your breath, and release thoughts of past or future. Just focus on your breathing at this very moment.
- Your mind may start wandering as you continue breathing. Don't get upset or disheartened. It takes time to take control of the ever-chattering, moving mind. Once you become aware of the wandering, just bring your mind gently back to the moment, and re-concentrate on your breathing. Don't worry about the nature or contents of your thoughts. Just see them as "thoughts," neither good nor bad. Perceive them as an outsider, and redirect your attention back to your breath. To increase your focus, you may think of the movement your breathing makes, and speak out the words in your mind: "rising, falling, rising, falling,"[49] or "breathing in, breathing out, breathing in, breathing out." While doing so, make sure you don't force your breathing in any particular pattern or speed. Let it happen naturally, as it always does.
- During your meditation, you will notice the sense of itching, tingling, or tickling. It's something we deal with all the time, but normally don't pay much attention to. During meditation, however, these physical sensations become obvious and may even be experienced as annoying. Don't get upset. Observe your physical sensations with a calm outsider's perspective, and you will find that they will subside. Just like your breathing rises and falls, you will find your physical sensations arising and passing. In fact, observing the arising and passing of your bodily (e.g., itching) and mental (thoughts) sensations is very helpful in realizing that everything in life arises and passes the same way: difficult situations and people, but also good ones: they arise and pass. The awareness of arising and passing is critical for understanding the uselessness of many of the things we frustrate ourselves with.

Right Concentration

Right concentration pertains to being focused on what is important. Sometimes it is important to focus selectively, which is a focus on one particular thing, such as our breathing when we engage in Vipassana meditation. Sometimes it is important to concentrate actively, which encapsulates the wholeness of activities. An example is driving: when we drive, we focus on our driving as well as the lights,

FIGURE 7.1 The Four Noble Truths

other cars, people crossing the streets, our speed, the condition of the road, possibly the weather, and so on.

Concentration is required to be present, and when we do so, we enjoy each moment to the fullest. By enjoying each moment to the fullest instead of worrying about past and future, we detect beautiful details that used to escape us when we were not concentrating. Right concentration therefore holds the ability to lead us to greater happiness, as we are more focused on what matters now. If we engage deep enough in right concentration, we will ultimately start realizing the impermanent nature of many of our cravings, and learn to release them.[50] Figure 7.1 presents the Four Noble Truths, with inclusion of the Noble Eightfold Path.

The eight threads of the Noble Eightfold Path are interrelated. Right intentions emerge from right views, and incite right efforts and right actions. A point of caution here: just as the right interpretation of all elements of the path are interrelated and supportive of one another, just so are malicious implementations and interpretations interrelated and mutually supportive.[51]

Buddhism and Consciousness

Studies of consciousness have a long and well-considered history in Eastern traditions such as Buddhism. In her article "In Search of the Real You," in which she questions the meaning and validity of authenticity, Wright[52] annotates, "Eastern spiritual traditions have long furnished ways to glimpse the messiness of the self, and to view with detachment the vicissitudes of mind and emotion that roil human consciousness." Focusing in on Buddhist practice, Wright points out that Buddhism takes the self in all its inconsistency as the main subject of reflection; self-study is considered to be of great importance. If we consider the above analysis of perceptions on "the new Buddhism" as it develops in the United States (see chapter 6), highly tailored to the American individualistic mindset, and focusing on personal wellbeing *first* and *then* on wellbeing of others, Wright seems to be making a point in favor of this type of American Buddhism.

Yet, Wright is by far not the only one in America who has been contemplating on the role of Buddhism in individual consciousness. Alan Wallace, one of the best known writers and translators of Tibetan Buddhism in the West, has also written extensively about this topic. In his review of the Buddhist perspective on consciousness, Wallace explains that consciousness is not *produced* but rather *conditioned* by the brain. Wallace[53] first notes that, in Buddhism, consciousness is preserved with reflection to Buddha's experiences and numerous Buddhist contemplatives after them. He then points out that, in Buddhist theory, consciousness arises from consciousness. The Buddhist premise is that an individual's consciousness does not arise from the consciousness of his or her parents, because each individual has his or her own range of consciousness. Explaining where human consciousness comes from, according to Buddhist teaching, Wallace declares, "Individual consciousness exists prior to conception, arising from a preceding, unique continuum and will carry on after this life."[54]

The Buddha's Perspective on Consciousness Through Current Interpretations

Consciousness, or *viññāna* (Pali), is a widely discussed topic in Buddhist teachings. According to Buddhist philosophy, there is no permanent, unchanging spirit which can be considered "Self," or "Soul," or "Ego, as opposed to matter.[55] Consciousness (*viññāna*) should therefore not be seen as spirit in opposition to matter.[56] The Buddha's perspective on consciousness has been described as follows:

> Consciousness is named according to whatever condition through which it arises: on account of the eye and visible forms arises a consciousness, and it is called visual consciousness [1]; on account of the ear and sounds arises a consciousness, and it is called auditory consciousness [2]; on account of the nose and odors arises a consciousness, and it is called olfactory consciousness

[3]; on account of the tongue and tastes arises a consciousness, and it is called gustatory consciousness [4]; on account of the body and tangible objects arises a consciousness, and it is called tactile consciousness [5]; on account of the mind and mind-objects (ideas and thoughts) arises a consciousness, and it is called mental consciousness [6].[57]

From the above it can be concluded that the Buddha considered consciousness as something that depends on matter, sensation, perception, and mental formations and that it cannot exist independently of them.[58]

The Buddhist perspective on consciousness can also be explained from a more holistic standpoint, as Thich Nhat Hanh says: "Our consciousness is composed of all the seeds sown by our past actions and the past actions of our family and society. Everyday our thoughts, words, and actions flow into the sea of our consciousness and create our body, mind, and world."[59] We can nurture our consciousness by practicing the Four Immeasurable Minds of *love, compassion, joy*, and *equanimity*, or we can nourish our consciousness with greed, hatred, ignorance, suspicion, and pride.[60] We should, above all, be aware that our consciousness is consuming all the time, day and night, and whatever it absorbs becomes the foundation and texture of our life. This is why we should be mindful about the mental nutrients we ingest.[61]

Thich Nhat Hanh shares an interesting story from Buddha about the way we treat our consciousness. The story is about a vicious murderer who was arrested and led before the king, who sentenced him to death by stabbing. The verdict was harsh: the man would have to be stabbed with 300 sharp knives. After a few hours, a guard approached the king and told him that the man was still alive. The king ordered to stab him an additional 300 times. Yet, as night fell, the guard reported to the king that the man was still alive. The king then ordered to find the 300 sharpest knives in the entire kingdom and plunge them into the man. The Buddha explained to his followers that we treat our consciousness just like this man was treated. It is like stabbing ourselves with 300 knives, and as we get more miserable, we spread the misery to those around us.[62]

In one of the most revered books on Buddhism, the *Abhidhammattha Sangaha—a Comprehensive Manual of Abhidhamma,*[63] great attention is devoted to *citta*, which is the Pali word for consciousness or mind. In an earlier translation of this manual[64] *citta* is explained as deriving from "*cit,*" which means "to think." Both books emphasize the importance of paying attention to *citta*, because the focus of Buddhist analysis is experience, and "consciousness is the principal element in experience, that which constitutes the knowing or awareness of an object."[65]

Citta is defined in three different ways:

1. As agent, where *citta* is that which cognizes an object.[66]
2. As instrument, where *citta* is the path through which our mental factors understand the object.[67]
3. As activity, where *citta* is the process of understanding the object.[68]

98 The Place of Suffering

The third definition is considered to be the most sufficient perception of the three, because *citta* is not really an agent or instrument but rather "an activity or process of cognizing or knowing an object."[69] The first two definitions of *citta*, as agent and instrument, are merely included to disarm the erroneous notions of those who think that they have a permanent self or ego, which is the agent and instrument of their understanding.[70] So, Buddhist thinkers hope that with these definitions it becomes clear that it is not a *self* but *citta* or *consciousness* that performs any act of cognition or understanding.

There are different ways of classifying consciousness. Some authors distinguish between moral and immoral types of consciousness, stating some types of consciousness are immoral, because they spring from attachment, aversion or ill-will, and ignorance. In contrast, there are the moral types of consciousness, which are rooted in nonattachment or generosity, goodwill, and wisdom. The immoral types of consciousness produce undesirable effects, which makes them unwholesome. The moral types result in desirable effects, so they are wholesome.[71]

It should be noted that, while some Buddhist authors perceive consciousness as the entire drive behind our performance, they also share the notion that consciousness is an experience related to our own experiences rather than others'.

The Dalai Lama's Perspective on Consciousness

The Dalai Lama considers consciousness to be an important aspect to spiritual growth. He affirms, "On the spiritual path, it is also on basis of this continuity of consciousness that we are able to make mental improvements and experience high realizations of the path."[72] This Buddhist leader explains that the continuity of consciousness, which we could call our "Buddha nature," is responsible for our ultimate state of awareness. The Dalai Lama stresses that consciousness has no end and no beginning. "Any instance of consciousness requires a substantial cause in the form of another preceding moment of consciousness. Because of this, we maintain that consciousness is infinite and beginningless."[73]

In his book, *The Universe in a Single Atom*, The Dalai Lama stresses that the experience of consciousness is an entirely subjective one.[74] He comments that, in spite of the reality of our subjectivity, and several millennia of philosophical study, there is still very little consensus on what consciousness is. The Dalai Lama also refers to the six-fold typology of the mind, earlier explained in the section about the Buddha's perspective of consciousness, entailing experiences of sight, hearing, smell, taste, touch, and the mental states. He presents the definition, which Tibetan thinkers formulated for consciousness, based in earlier Indian sources: "The definition of the mental is that which is luminous and knowing."[75] These two features—luminosity, or clarity, and knowing, or cognizance—have come to characterize "the mental" in Indo-Tibetan Buddhist thought.[76]

According to the Dalai Lama, *clarity*, in this regard, pertains to the ability to reflect, while *knowing* pertains to the ability to observe and understand what

The Place of Suffering **99**

happens. He then underscores the difference between Buddhist and Western perspectives on consciousness by stating that Western philosophy and science have generally attempted to understand consciousness solely in terms of the functions of the brain.[77]

Addressing the importance of cause and effect within the Buddhist perspective of consciousness, the Dalai Lama affirms that the theory of causation is critical in understanding the Buddhist concept of consciousness, and its rejection of the reducibility of mind to matter.[78] This theory has always been an important focus of Buddhism.

Buddhism, states the Dalai Lama, proposes two principal categories of cause: 1) the substantial cause, and 2) the contributory or contemplatory cause. He illustrates this by reflecting on a clay pot. In the case of the clay pot, the *substantial cause* is everything that turns into the clay that becomes the pot. Everything else, such as the skill of the potter, the potter himself, and the furnace that heats the clay, are *contributory or contemplatory causes*. The Dalai Lama stresses that this distinction between the substantial and the contributory cause of a given event or object is of the utmost significance for understanding the Buddhist theory of consciousness.

A Western Perspective on Consciousness

Consciousness is a growing topic of interest from non-Buddhist sides these days as well. In his book *Power vs. Force*, David Hawkins agrees with the Buddhist perspective that causality should be seen beyond a linear sequence, and that the things we don't see (unobservable phenomena) should also be considered.[79] Hawkins identifies various levels of human consciousness. In the book, he presents a chart with rising levels of human consciousness, starting with shame (20) at the lowest level, and gradually increasing with guilt (30), apathy (50), grief (75), fear (100), desire (125), anger (150), pride (175), courage (200), neutrality (250), willingness (310), acceptance (350), reason (400), love (500), joy (540), peace (600), and enlightenment (between 700 and 1,000). "The numbers represent the logarithm (to the base 10) of the power of the respective fields."[80] The main point that Hawkins makes in this and other books he wrote on the topic of consciousness is that anything below the energy level of 200 represents a non-constructive foundational motivation for the individual as well as for his or her surroundings. On the other hand, asserts Hawkins, energy levels over 200 are generally positive, uplifting, and constructive to the wellbeing of humanity.

Hawkins' distinction of consciousness drivers corresponds with some of the Buddhist-based perspectives presented earlier, that some types of consciousness spring from attachment, aversion, or ignorance, while others are rooted in generosity, goodwill, and wisdom. The only difference is that Hawkins has converted the various drivers into levels.

In order to illustrate his theory, Hawkins evaluates well-known world leaders, such as Mahatma Gandhi. According to Hawkins' calibrations, Gandhi scored

100 The Place of Suffering

around 700, which he considers close to the top of normal human consciousness. In his review of the levels 700–1,000, Hawkins affirms that, "at this level, there is no longer the experience of an individual personal self [lowercase "s"] separate from others; rather, there is an identification of Self [capital "S"] transcending beyond the personal level with Consciousness and Divinity. The Unmanifest is experienced as Self beyond mind."[81]

Hawkins elaborates, "There's no longer any identification with the physical body as 'me,' and therefore, its fate is of no concern. The body is seen as merely a tool of consciousness through the intervention of mind, its prime value that of communication. The self merges back into the Self. This is the level of non-duality, or complete Oneness. There is no localization of consciousness; awareness is equally present everywhere."[82]

Explaining the possibility of and the path toward attaining enlightenment as the highest humanly attainable level of consciousness, Hawkins affirms that the quickest way we can attain enlightenment is by engaging in deep self-reflection, meditation, and contemplation about our ego and its workings, so that we can understand consciousness.[83]

Hawkins shares the interesting finding that 85% of the human race calibrates below the critical level of 200, but fortunately, the general average level of humanity's consciousness has risen to about 207.[84] He attributes the consciousness levels to cultural conditions, and points out that we will mostly find energy levels below 200 in very primitive living conditions; energy levels in the low 200s among unskilled labor; levels in the mid-200s among semiskilled labor; high 200s among skilled labor, blue-collar workers, tradesmen, retail commerce, and industries; levels around 300 among technicians, skilled and advanced craftsmen, routine managers, and a more sophisticated business structure; levels around the mid-300s in upper management, artisans, and educators; levels of around 400 in those who have tapped into their intellect, such as those in higher education, the professional class, executives, and scientists. Hawkins claims that 500 is the point at which awareness makes a major leap, and excellence becomes the common trend in every field of performance.[85]

Hawkins' consciousness analysis may make good sense, but could be disputed at the point where he asserts that lower income- and educational levels generally calibrate lower in consciousness. Hawkins' opinion may come across as prejudiced, even though there may very well be some solid foundation to his findings. It is not hard to understand that extremely poor people have survival on the mind, and will do whatever it takes to attain that. Yet, Hawkins' perspectives also have quite some common areas with Buddhism. Conform to the Buddhist perspective; Hawkins claims that the problem with low consciousness or low energy levels can be attributed to ego.

In his book, *The Eye of the I*, he clarifies that we usually see letting go of the ego or mind as a major sacrifice, because we consider it something unique and personal, and the reason why we consider it unique and personal is because we

The Place of Suffering **101**

believe in a singular "me" or "my."[86] Hawkins encourages us to come to the realization that the ego is impersonal and not unique at all. He points out that everybody's ego operates about the same as that of everybody else. He goes on to explain that the ego or "self" displays the same traits of self-service, egotism, vanity, deception, and focus on gain of position, possession, status, wealth, renown, praise, and control. This can only change, writes Hawkins, when the ego is modified by spiritual evolution. If we don't undertake any effort toward spiritual evolution, the ego will consistently result in energy levels that rank below 200, such as "guilt, shame, greed, pride, anger, rage, envy, jealousy, hatred, and so forth.[87] In one of his other books, *Transcending the Levels of Consciousness*, Hawkins explains that we cannot overcome our ego by seeing it as an enemy. It is our biological inheritance, and without it, nobody would be alive to lament its limitations.[88] He cautiously adds that we should understand the origin and intrinsic importance of the ego to survival, and when perceived in that light, it could be considered beneficial, yet at the same time inclined to becoming disruptive, and causing problems of emotional, psychological, and spiritual nature if we are unable to transcend it.[89]

Another important analysis Hawkins makes in *Power vs. Force* is the comparison of various religions, and how their collective level of consciousness evolved through history. Christianity, for instance, is based on the teachings of Jesus Christ, who calibrates at 1,000 (fully enlightened) according to Hawkins. However, the religion itself, he says, has gradually decreased through various misinterpretations and mistranslations, causing some contemporary fundamentalist Christian groups to calibrate as low as 125.[90] In the same vein, Hawkins calibrates Lord Krishna at 1,000 (fully enlightened), but the religion that exists on basis of his teachings, Hinduism, at 850. He calibrates Abraham at 985, but the religion that exists on basis of his teachings, Judaism, between 499 and 730. He calibrates Mohammed at 740, but the fundamental level of his currently implemented teachings at 130. As for Buddhism, Hawkins calibrates Buddha at 1,000 (fully enlightened), and the "religion" that exists on basis of his teachings, Buddhism, as the highest form all religions of our times. He states, "Hinayana Buddhism [the smaller or lesser vehicle, preferably referred to as Theravada Buddhism, since "Hinayana" contains a derogatory connotation to some Eastern nations] still calibrates at 890; Mahayana Buddhism (the greater vehicle) calibrates at 960; Zen Buddhism is 890."[91]

Aside from the classification of "higher" and "lower," Hawkins' Western perspectives on consciousness demonstrate great overall concurrence with the Buddhist perspectives on consciousness, particularly in areas such as causality as a phenomenon that should be perceived in a broader scope than merely linear; ego as a major hurdle toward general human wellbeing, and consequently self as a hurdle toward realizing Self as an interconnected part of all that is; meditation and contemplation as sources to elevate consciousness; and the authenticity of Buddhism compared to other major religions.

102 The Place of Suffering

Summary

In this chapter we presented:

- The Four Noble Truths, as the Buddha defined them. The Four Noble Truths are:
  1. The truth of suffering (suffering exists)
  2. The truth of the origin of suffering (suffering has a cause)
  3. The truth of the cessation of suffering (suffering can be ended)
  4. The truth of the path, the way to liberation from suffering (the path to end suffering)
- The Noble Eightfold Path, which is the Fourth Noble Truth, and entails the following, non-sequential practices:
  1. Right View
  2. Right Intention
  3. Right Speech
  4. Right Action
  5. Right Livelihood
  6. Right Effort
  7. Right Mindfulness
  8. Right Concentration
- A more detailed view of the First Noble Truth, which entails the understanding that suffering exists. We generally suffer in eight ways. The first four are physical forms of suffering, and the last four psychological:
  1. Birth, because we get purged or pulled out of the comfort zone that is our mother's womb.
  2. Aging, because we lose our mobility and our senses, cannot do the things we did before, and have to deal with changes that we may not enjoy.
  3. Illness, because we may suffer tremendous discomfort and be forced to give up the things we enjoy doing.
  4. Death, because it entails a total loss of everything: friends, loved ones, the things we cherished, and even our own body.
  5. Unpleasant experiences, which are often unexpected, and therefore traumatic.
  6. Inability to hold on to something desirable, because losing someone or something dear is suffering.
  7. Inability to get what we want, because we are devastated when we finally learn that we will not get what we hoped for.
  8. All-pervasive suffering, which is the everlasting sense of discomfort we feel, even when things are going well.
- A more detailed view of the Second Noble Truth, which entails that suffering has a cause. It stems from the ongoing trend of gaining and losing things in our lives. We have a tendency to cling to people, places, experiences, wishes, ideas, or mindsets, and this causes suffering.

The Place of Suffering **103**

- A more detailed view of the Third Noble Truth, which entails that suffering can be ended. In order to do this, we need to discontinue the cause of our suffering, which is our sense of desiring or craving.
- A more detailed view of the Noble Eightfold Path (the Fourth Noble Truth), which is considered the core of the Buddha's teaching, and consists of:
  1. Right View, which can help us understand the Four Noble Truths, and help us nurture the good intentions we have and keep the bad intentions dormant. Right view positively influences our attitude, and can help us contemplate many aspects of our lives, such as our notion of happiness.
  2. Right Intention, which is also described as "right thinking." Maintaining the right intention requires regular wake-up calls to ourselves, such as: 1) questioning ourselves if we are sure of what we see, hear, or read, 2) asking ourselves what we are doing so that we can refocus, 3) critically reviewing our habits to keep track of our intentions, and 4) maintaining *Bodhicitta*, which is the aspiration to obtain an awakened mind for the benefit of others.
  3. Right Speech, which is highly important in these times of massive communications. Engaging in right speech means that we deliberately refrain from saying things that have negative effects on others.
  4. Right Action, which entails carefully guarding our practices, helping to protect life, and the wellbeing of all living beings, in the broadest sense possible.
  5. Right Livelihood, which pertains to the way in which we earn our living. Are we engaging in constructive activity when we perform our job?
  6. Right Effort, which is sometimes listed as "right diligence." Right effort requires that we carefully distinguish our actions, thoughts, and intentions, so that our efforts remains constructive.
  7. Right Mindfulness, which can help us truly appreciate what we see, and where there is responding life involved (a person or pet), we may indicate our gratitude for their presence, so that they, too, may become mindful of the moment. Mindfulness can be incited in several ways. A frequently practiced way is meditation. One of the most well-known forms of meditation is Vipassana, or insight meditation, which is the meditation practice in which Siddhartha Gautama engaged when he gained enlightenment. Vipassana literally means "special seeing" or insight.
  8. Right Concentration, which pertains to being focused on what is important. Sometimes it is important to focus selectively, which is a focus on one particular thing, and sometimes it is important to concentrate actively, which encapsulates the wholeness of activities.
- Buddhism and Consciousness, reviewing Eastern and Western considerations of this ever-fascinating topic.
  - Some Western authors, such as Wright, focus on deep and frequent self-reflection as an effective way to attain expanded consciousness. Others,

104 The Place of Suffering

such as Wallace, concur with the Buddhist theory that consciousness arises from consciousness.

- The Buddha's perspective on consciousness through current interpretations teaches us that there is no permanent, unchanging spirit which can be considered "Self," or "Soul," or "Ego," as opposed to matter. Consciousness should therefore not be seen as spirit in opposition to matter. Six conditions of consciousness are presented: 1) visual consciousness; 2) auditory consciousness; 3) olfactory consciousness; 4) gustatory consciousness; 5) tactile consciousness; and 6) mental consciousness.
- Thich Nhat Hanh suggests a holistic standpoint, stating that our consciousness is composed of all the seeds sown by our past actions and the past actions of our family and society. We should, above all, be aware that our consciousness is consuming all the time, whether day or night, and whatever it absorbs becomes the foundation and texture of our life.
- The *Abhidhammattha Sangaha* devotes great attention to *citta*, the Pali word for *consciousness* or *mind*. *Citta* is defined in three different ways:
  1. As agent, where *citta* is that which cognizes an object.
  2. As instrument, where *citta* is the path through which our mental factors understand the object.
  3. As activity, where *citta* is the process of understanding the object.
- The Dalai Lama considers consciousness to be an important aspect to spiritual growth, and explains that the continuity of consciousness, which we could call our "Buddha nature," is responsible for our ultimate state of awareness. He also stresses that the experience of consciousness is an entirely subjective one. Addressing the importance of cause and effect within the Buddhist perspective of consciousness, the Dalai Lama affirms that the theory of causation is critical in understanding the Buddhist concept of consciousness, and its rejection of the reducibility of mind to matter. This theory has always been an important focus of Buddhism.
- David Hawkins, a popular author who holds a Western perspective on consciousness, agrees with the Buddhist perspective that causality should be seen beyond a linear sequence, and that the things we don't see (unobservable phenomena) should also be considered.
  - Hawkins identifies various levels of human consciousness, such as shame (20), guilt (30), apathy (50), grief (75), fear (100), desire (125), anger (150), pride (175), courage (200), neutrality (250), willingness (310), acceptance (350), reason (400), love (500), joy (540), peace (600), and enlightenment (between 700 and 1,000).
  - Hawkins compares various religions, and the evolution of their collective level of consciousness through history. He calibrates Christ at 1,000 (fully enlightened), but Christianity, due to various misinterpretations and mistranslations, as low as 125; Lord Krishna at 1,000 (fully enlightened), but Hinduism, at 850; Abraham at 985,

The Place of Suffering **105**

but Judaism between 499 and 730; Mohammed at 740, but the most fundamental levels of Islam at 130; Buddha at 1,000 (fully enlightened), Hinayana Buddhism at 890, Mahayana Buddhism at 960; and Zen Buddhism at 890.

Questions

1. Review the eight general ways in which we suffer (see First Noble Truth): select two of these ways that you consider the most critical forms of suffering, and reflect on these.
2. The Second Noble Truth explains that our suffering comes from our attachment to people, places, experiences, ideas, and so on. Do you agree that attachment causes suffering? Please explain your response.
3. The Third Noble Truth explains that we can end suffering by getting rid of our desires. Do you think this is attainable? Please explain your answer?
4. Please select two of the threads in the Noble Eightfold Path, and explain how you could possibly engage in them.
5. Please engage in some research online about Vipassana meditation, and formulate in about 300 words a description of this meditation form.

Notes

1 Dharmapala, A. (2011). *Great Sayings of Anagarika Dharmapala*. Collected by Bhikshu Sangharakshita. With a Life Sketch by Buddhadāsa P. Retrieved on April 23, 2014 from Kirthisinghe www.bps.lk/olib/bl/bl022.pdf
2 The Pali word *Dhamma* can mean many things. It is, for instance used as part of the "Triple-Gem," which entails: 1) the Buddha, 2) the *Sangha* (community of Buddhist hermits), and 3) the *Dhamma* (where Buddhists take refuge). In this context, it is more appropriate as the principles uncovered by the Buddha, which we should verify for ourselves before internalizing them fully.
3 Suffering is, in this context, actually an insufficient term, because the Buddha intended to encompass much more with the word that he used, which was *Dukkha*. *Dukkha* pertains to more than suffering, pain, or misery. It suggests the foundational unsatisfactory sense we get from existing. It refers to the lack of perfection and the constant struggle and strive that is associated with life. Bodhi, B. (n.d.). The Four Noble Truths. Retrieved on November 17, 2013 from www.beyondthenet.net/dhamma/fourNoble.htm
4 Bodhi, B. (1994, 2000). *The Noble Eightfold Path: Way to the End of Suffering*. BPS Pariyatti First U.S. Edition, Onalaska, WA.
5 Bodhi, B. (n.d.). The Fourth Noble Truth—The path leading to the cessation of Dukkha—The Noble Eightfold Path. Retrieved on November 17, 2013 from www.beyondthenet.net/dhamma/fourthNoble.htm
6 Gethin, R. (1998). *The Foundations of Buddhism*. Oxford University Press, Oxford.
7 Trungpa, Y. (2009). *The Truth of Suffering and the Path of Liberation*. (ed. J. Lief, J. Ed.). Shambhala Publications, Boston, MA.
8 Ibid.
9 Ibid.
10 Ibid.
11 Ibid.

106 The Place of Suffering

12 Ibid.
13 Ibid.
14 Ibid.
15 Gethin, R. (1998). *The Foundations of Buddhism*. Oxford University Press, Oxford.
16 Nanamoli, B. (1992). *The Life of The Buddha: According to the Pali Canon*. BPS Pariyatti Editions, Seattle, WA.
17 Rahula, W. (1974). *The Heritage of the Bhikkhu: The Buddhist Tradition of Service*. Grove Press, New York.
18 Ibid.
19 Ibid.
20 Carrithers, M. (1988). *The Buddha*. Oxford University Press, Oxford.
21 Rahula, W. (1974). *The Heritage of the Bhikkhu: The Buddhist Tradition of Service*. Grove Press, New York.
22 Nyanatiloka, T. (1970). *Buddhist Dictionary: Manual of Buddhist Terms and Doctrines* (3rd Revised ed.). (ed., Nyanaponika). Buddhist Publication Society, Kandy, Sri Lanka.
23 Carrithers, M. (1988). *The Buddha*. Oxford University Press, Oxford.
24 Rahula, W. (1974). *The Heritage of the Bhikkhu: The Buddhist Tradition of Service*. Grove Press, New York.
25 Rahula, W. (1959). *What The Buddha Taught*. Grove Press, New York.
26 Ibid.
27 Ibid.
28 Ibid.
29 Bodhi, B. (1994). *The Noble Eightfold Path: Way to the End of Suffering*. BPS Pariyatti First U.S. Edition, Onalaska, WA.
30 Ibid.
31 Gombrich, R. F. (1988). *Theravada Buddhism: A Social History from ancient Benares to modern Colombo*. Routledge & Kegan Paul, London.
32 Thich, N. H. (1998). *The Heart of the Buddha's Teaching: Transforming Suffering into Peace, Joy, and Liberation*. Broadway Books, New York.
33 Ibid.
34 Ibid.
35 Ibid.
36 Ibid.
37 Ibid.
38 Ibid.
39 Ibid.
40 Ibid.
41 Ibid.
42 Ibid.
43 Coleman, J. W. (2001/2002). *The New Buddhism: The Western Transformation of an Ancient Tradition*. Oxford University Press, New York.
44 Wrye, H. K. (2006). Sitting With Eros and Psyche on a Buddhist Psychoanalyst's Cushion. *Psychoanalytic Dialogues, 16*(6), 725–746.
45 Rickey, C. (March 5, 2009). Teaching Meditation to Prisoners: Transformative Silence? *The Philadelphia Inquirer*. Retrieved on November 22, 2013 from www.correctionsone.com/treatment/articles/1843777-Teaching-meditation-to-prisoners-Transformative-silence/; Martinez, J. (September 22, 2008). New Age Pragmatism: Crystals and Tarots Give Way to More Practical and Mainstream Subject Matter. *Publishers Weekly, 255*(38). Retrieved on July 8, 2010 from www.publishersweekly.com/pw/print/20080922/10447-new-age-pragmatism-.html
46 Goenka, S. N. (2006). *Peace Within Oneself for Peace in the World*. Vipassana Research Institute, Dhammagiri, Igatpuri; Goenka, S. N. (2008). Goenka, S. N. (2007). *The Discourse Summaries: talks from a ten-day course in Vipassana Meditation*. Vipassana Research Institute, Dhamma Giri, Maharashtra, India.

47 Thatcher, C. (2012). How to Meditate. *Vipassana Dhura Meditation Society*. Retrieved on March 8, 2014 from www.vipassanadhura.com/howto.htm

48 Ibid.

49 Ibid.

50 Thich, N. H. (1998). *The Heart of the Buddha's Teaching: Transforming Suffering into Peace, Joy, and Liberation*. Broadway Books, New York.

51 Bodhi, B. (1994). *The Noble Eightfold Path: Way to the End of Suffering*. BPS Pariyatti First U.S. Edition, Onalaska, WA.

52 Wright, K. (2008). In Search of the Real You. *Psychology Today, 41*(3), 70.

53 Wallace, B. A. (2001). *Buddhism with an Attitude: The Tibetan Seven-Point Mind Training*. Snow Lion Publications, Ithaca, NY.

54 Ibid., 47.

55 Rahula, W. (1959). *What The Buddha Taught*. Grove Press, New York,: p. 23.

56 Ibid.

57 Rahula, W. (1959). *What The Buddha Taught*. Grove Press, New York, p. 24.

58 Ibid., 25.

59 Thich, N. H. (1998). *The Heart of the Buddha's Teaching: Transforming Suffering into Peace, Joy, and Liberation*. Broadway Books, New York, p. 36.

60 Thich, N. H. (1998). *The Heart of the Buddha's Teaching: Transforming Suffering into Peace, Joy, and Liberation*. Broadway Books, New York.

61 Ibid.

62 Ibid.

63 Bodhi, B. (1993). *Abhidhammattha Sangaha: A Comprehensive Manual of Abhidhamma— The Philosophical Psychology of Buddhism* (trans. M. Narada). BPS Pariyatti Editions, Onalaska, WA.

64 Narada, M. T. (1959). *A Manual of Abhidhamma*. The Buddhist Missionary Society, Kuala Lumpur, Malaysia.

65 Bodhi, B. (1993). *Abhidhammattha Sangaha: A Comprehensive Manual of Abhidhamma— The Philosophical Psychology of Buddhism* (trans. M. Narada). BPS Pariyatti Editions, Onalaska, WA, p. 27.

66 Ibid.

67 Ibid.

68 Ibid.

69 Ibid.

70 Ibid.

71 Narada, M. T. (1959). *A Manual of Abhidhamma*. The Buddhist Missionary Society, Kuala Lumpur, Malaysia.

72 His Holiness The Dalai Lama. (1995). *The World of Tibetan Buddhism*. Wisdom Publications, Boston, MA, p. 29.

73 Ibid., 49.

74 His Holiness The Dalai Lama. (2005). *The Universe in a Single Atom: The Convergence of Science and Spirituality*. Broadway Books, New York.

75 Ibid., 124.

76 Ibid.

77 Ibid.

78 Ibid.

79 Hawkins, D. R. (1995). *Power vs. Force: The Hidden Determinants of Human Behavior*. Hayhouse, Inc., Carslbad, CA.

80 Ibid., 52.

81 Ibid., 93–94.

82 Ibid., 94.

83 Hawkins, D. R. (2003). *I: Reality and Subjectivity*. Veritas Publishing, West Sedona, AZ: 291.

108 The Place of Suffering

84 Hawkins, D. R. (1995). *Power vs. Force: The Hidden Determinants of Human Behavior.* Hayhouse, Inc., Carlsbad, CA.
85 Ibid., 97–99.
86 Hawkins, D. R. (2001). *The Eye of the I: From Which Nothing is Hidden.* Veritas Publishing, West Sedona, AZ: 109.
87 Ibid.
88 Hawkins, D. R. (2006). *Transcending the Levels of Consciousness.* Veritas Publishing, West Sedona, AZ.
89 Ibid.
90 Hawkins, D. R. (1995). *Power vs. Force: The Hidden Determinants of Human Behavior.* Hayhouse, Inc., Carlsbad, CA.
91 Ibid., 273.

8

BUDDHISM AND BUSINESS

Friends or Foes?

There simply is nothing to which we can attach ourselves, no matter how hard we try. In time, things will change and the conditions that produced our current desires will be gone. Why then cling to them now?

Hsing Yun

A Fertile Climate for Change

The contemporary world of work is undergoing some fascinating changes. First, the entire fabric of the workforce is changing. There is much more diversity than ever before, thanks to a greater influx of women and minority members. This trend has its origins in the changed structures of society. For instance, women no longer feel that they should be the default homemakers, especially since large groups of women are obtaining college educations nowadays, so we find more women in the workplace, gradually moving into increasingly higher managerial positions. Then there is the increased financial pressure of contemporary life, which often requires both partners in a household to earn an income. Furthermore, we experience increased degrees of urbanization and migration thanks to an unstoppable globalization trend, introducing different groups of people from different regions and continents into the workforce. Westerners get increasingly exposed to Eastern traditions vice versa. Also, the nature of work has changed, and with that, the requirements to be in the physical work environment all the time. This change has also enabled groups of potential workers, such as young mothers, or individuals with elderly parents at home, to work from the comfort of their home.

110 Buddhism and Business

In the midst of all these developments are the human emotions, experiencing a growing sense of discontentment, and not exactly sure why that is.

- It may partly be due to the growing insecurity, because the formation and pace of work and life has tremendously increased thanks to the massive availability of the internet. This has caused a lot of jobs to be outsourced from industrialized nations with relatively high wages to countries where labor is cheaper.
- It may partly be due to the increased pace of change: even before the dust on a previous change has settled, it is time for a new series of transitions. People are, by nature, creatures of habit, so change, no matter how functional, does not come natural to us. We dread letting go of our comfort zones, especially if we have to do so time and again.
- The fact that the nature of our work, especially in industrialized nations, requires higher levels of education, may also be a critical factor in the growing overall discontentment. Educated workforce members are more aware of inequalities, and see, hear, and read more about the greed and dishonesty of their leaders. Upon comparing their salary to their CEO's, which is sometimes more than 500 times theirs, they may feel used.
- The growing discontentment could also be due to the changed nature of the work we are doing today: less predictable and steady, more surprising and inconsistent. Many of us may secretly feel ill-prepared for this ambiguous work climate, and question our education, our intelligence, or even our suitability for the job.
- Another major foundational reason for the growing discontentment in professional circles today may be the mismatch between the nature of our work and the way we are rewarded: while most of us clearly perform in tasks that represent the knowledge revolution, our rewards and punishment are still attuned to the Industrial Revolution. People with self-managing tasks still have to clock in, still find that they are micro-managed, and still receive only extrinsic rewards, such as larger offices, bigger desks, and raises, while they actually crave intrinsic rewards, such as freedom to perform, appreciation, and recognition.
- And then, we should not forget another mismatch: the one between what people want to do, and what they actually do. Many people are merely following trends, and either choose a profession that has been traditionally held over multiple generations in their family, or they follow their peers and popular developments. They do all these things without taking a deep and intense look at themselves in order to find out what they would really enjoy. In other words, they don't engage in self-reflection. When they finally wake up and realize their discontentment with their profession, they are already so deeply embedded into the profession that they don't dare to make a bold career change.

Buddhism and Business **111**

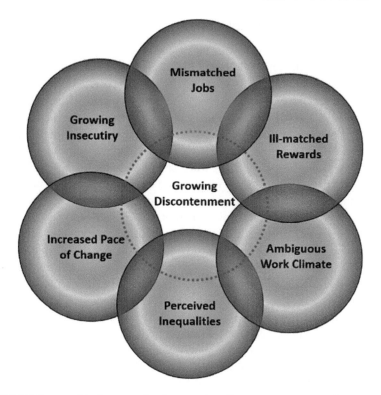

FIGURE 8.1 Some critical reasons for the growing discontentment at work

There are definitely more reasons why people are discontent with their work today and it may be that all of the above (and other) reasons contribute their share to this trend. Figure 8.1 depicts the previously mentioned reasons for work-related discontentment.

The aspects enumerated above don't just cause discontentment. They also trigger growing awareness. Workforce members are starting to realize things that they did not consider before. They get exposed to the religions, traditions, and cultures of their colleagues, and realize that there is more than one way to happiness. In other words, they realize that the way they always did things is not the only right way. So, they start questioning their sense of reality, and gradually become aware that they were trapped in ill-suited mental models that were instilled into them by their parents, peers, education, culture, religion, and other local factors.

As we can conclude from the reasoning above, there are two major work related trends taking place at the same time: 1) a growing discontentment[1] and, consequently, 2) a growing call for more meaning.[2] Because workplaces are so diverse in many ways today, people learn new insights, and break through traditional boundaries.

112 Buddhism and Business

Buddha Enters the Workplace

In reviewing the Western workplace, we mainly focus on the American workplace in this book, even though a number of the developments may ring true for other Western work societies as well. With the growing diversity levels in the American workplace, along with all the other reasons for discontentment and desire for more meaning, there seems to be an increased gravitation toward Buddhism.[3] This is not to say that there were no U.S.-based Buddhist practitioners prior to recent decades. In fact, there was a massive rise of Buddhist temples in the United States in the Gold Rush era (1850s) when large groups of Japanese and Chinese immigrants entered the country.[4] Yet, due to the change-driven climate of recent decades, the general interest in Buddhism has grown, and we have seen prominent academicians and entertainers converting to it.[5]

Buddhism may have been able to make such critical progress in professional American circles because it seems to provide a useful template to the movement of workplace spirituality in general. This movement, while growing, struggles with divergence in viewpoints: some proponents of Spirituality at Work[6] feel that it is closely related to religion, while others feel that workplace spirituality does not necessarily have to be tied to religion.[7] Due to the fact that Buddhism is not only presented as a religion, but increasingly as a psychology or an ethical system, it appeals to both of the above-mentioned spirituality-at-work advocacy groups. The main concepts of Buddhism make perfect sense from a secular standpoint, and can therefore be adopted by members from different religious traditions without them feeling that they would have to surrender their original beliefs. The Buddhist focus on mindfulness and awareness in all our actions and thoughts is not threatening to any religion, and can therefore find easy acceptance in large communities. The authenticity of Buddhism, throughout the centuries and the creation of multiple schools of Buddhism, has managed to sustain the main message of its founder, which is human consciousness. When consciousness is practiced, we gradually rise above our ignorance, and move toward wisdom.[8]

Issues of Appropriateness

Does Buddhism fit into capitalistic American society?[9] This is a very legitimate question when we consider that the United States is a highly individualistic country, where people develop a sense of self at very early stages in their lives, resulting in a mentality of individualism, and often, greed, and envy. In stark contrast to that, Buddhism teaches the importance of *selflessness* in our actions, leading to social behavior, moderation, and transcending greed and envy. So, how should we look at this apparently incompatible set of ideologies? There may not really be an answer to this last question yet, but history has already provided an unequivocal fact: Buddhism has found its way into capitalistic American society. While the Western Buddhist community predominantly consists of more affluent and highly educated members who seem to have little problem investing decent sums of money in Buddhist books and materials, it should be emphasized that adhering to this ethical system does not require any financial investment. The Dalai Lama, who was made aware of the fact that Buddhism is becoming so popular among elite groups, stressed that, while it is nice if people want to invest the money they have in gimmicks, the basic activity should still be geared toward developing compassion and freedom from greed and anger, even in the United States.[10] Many American Buddhists feel that they don't need to attend a congregation of any sort to adhere to their beliefs. Similarly, they feel that they can still make money while doing the right thing.[11]

Several prominent Buddhists have deliberated on the question whether Buddhism has a proper place in the capitalistic American world of work. In an article titled "Dharma and Greed: Popular Buddhism Meets the American Dream," David Templeton poses the question as to whether one can be truly Buddhist while being truly American.[12] He does so after observing the obvious contradictions between the Buddhist ideals of social behavior, moderation, and transcending greed and envy, and the American way of living that is based on the opposite: individualism, affluence, greed, and envy. Templeton reviews a meeting held in June 2000, in which 220 prominent Buddhist leaders in America, as well as the Dalai Lama, participated. Templeton reports that the Dalai Lama was informed about the fact that, in the United States, Buddhism mainly appealed to more intellectual and affluent Americans who could afford expensive retreats and pricey Buddhist paraphernalia: the "spiritual" materialists. As a consequence, the Dalai Lama stressed that Buddhist practitioners in the United States should still focus on compassion and freedom from anger and greed, even in such a money-mad nation.

Templeton also analyzes various American Buddhist businesspeople, among them Peter Bermudes, director of a successful Boston-based nonprofit Buddhist book publishing company, and draws the conclusion that most American Buddhists are independent. They read books and don't feel compelled to be part of a congregation of any sort. Templeton further analyses other American Buddhist ventures, such as Greyston Bakery in New York, and finds that the combination of being commercial while still adhering to spiritual values is possible, even though it requires thorough and regular self-examination. Templeton leaves the question as to whether this is being truly Buddhist while being truly American unanswered. Templeton's comments are also included in Holender's book Zentrepreneurism,[13] in which he introduces a number of new terms such as zentrepreneurism, zenployees, and zenvesting, in an attempt to combine Buddhist virtues and American commercialism.

The increased popularity of Buddhism in the United States may very well be attributed to the fact that it fits in well with the contemporary trends of greater awareness, environmental sustainability, and increased social responsibility. Buddhism fits well to the call for spirituality at work, which is fueled by a number of factors such as increased diversity in U.S. workplaces, greater insight into the motives of greed of American corporate leaders, and a desire toward greater satisfaction at work. Bookstores, online sources, and management speakers are capitalizing on this trend, and gearing their product offerings accordingly.

As the Dalai Lama, the most prominent Buddhist in the world, travels and speaks worldwide, writes one book after the other, and gains popularity among American celebrities, knowledge and understanding of Buddhism continues to expand. It is difficult, at this point in time, to distinguish whether the current growth in affection for Buddhism in the United States will merely be a fad that will subside as soon as a new one emerges, or whether this trend should be viewed within the greater scope of increased human, thus also American, awareness of the developments of the twenty-first century: greater access to information, more international human interaction, and socially conscious decision making.

The first part of the twenty-first century brought upsetting events and changes to the United States that caused Americans to reconsider their society's conventional way of careless spending, adhering to external appearances, and mindlessly following trends. Among these events were the September 11, 2001 terrorist attacks on U.S. soil; the fall of several prominent U.S. businesses due to unethical activities and the major losses that many Americans consequently suffered; the massive outsourcing of manufacturing, engineering, and service operations of large corporations to emerging economies such as China and India; and most recently, the tremendous economic recession of 2008 in which large numbers of U.S. citizens lost their homes, jobs, and savings. All these occurrences may have contributed to the creation of a change in mentality in the United States, to which Buddhism may provide useful inspiration. So, while the Americanization of Buddhism is a fact, it may also be that Americans are deviating from their traditional ways (de-Americanizing) and redefining themselves (re-Americanizing). This may mean that the ultimate look and practice of "Americanized Buddhism" is still in process of development.

Useful Buddhist Practices at Work

In a qualitative study, conducted with six highly acclaimed Buddhist scholars (American and Tibetan), and four Buddhist business leaders, an interesting overview emerged of what these individuals commonly considered to be prerequisites for a workplace that nurtures Buddhist practices. Table 8.1 reflects these

Buddhism and Business **115**

TABLE 8.1 What should be present in a workplace that nurtures Buddhist practices.

Internally	Externally
Principles of compassion, ethics, altruism; the seeking of genuine happiness; and a positive paradigm. Yet, no one in the company would be forced toward participation in any of these tendencies.	
A spirit of service and a tendency toward charitable support.	
Respect and support for diverse religious and/or nonreligious practices from workers.	
An atmosphere of support, collaboration, team spirit, mutual appreciation, and good communication.	
Positive attempts to guide coworkers, and patience.	
Remembering cause and effect.	
Hard work, and awareness of the larger purpose of this organization to the wellbeing of all sentient beings. In that, there will be no harmful production.	
Positive mindsets, speech, and actions.	

TABLE 8.2 What should be absent in a workplace that nurtures Buddhist practices.

Internal	External
Unethical behavior, including self-centeredness and harming others, from management as well as employees' sides.	
The thought of things coming independently and randomly.	
Anger and other afflictive emotions.	
Bias or partiality: measuring with multiple scales in treatment of people.	
Production of goods and services that are harmful to others.	
★ Nothing: these workplaces would just try to deal with human cruelty and insensitivity in a compassionate way.	

prerequisites with the understanding that the elements flush left only pertain to internal aspects of the organization, while the centered sections pertain to both internal and external aspects.

When asked what should be absent in a workplace that nurtures Buddhist practices, the interviewed Buddhist scholars and business leaders provided several common responses, shown in Table 8.2.

The last point in Table 8.2 demonstrates the sober view of the interviewed individuals, as they were all very aware that every work environment brings challenges due to the variety of participants, their backgrounds, and mindsets.

116 Buddhism and Business

Before we focus on some specific Buddhist practices that are useful in work environments, it may be good to underscore that implementing these practices is always a personal choice. It is no use to attempt any indoctrination toward others, as this will only draw out aversion within them. The best way to convince other people of the use of anything is to practice it. If it appeals to them, they will start inquiring or simply follow suit.

The many changes our workplaces are experiencing today, as well as the many reasons that trigger these changes, have led to increased interest in Buddhist practices, because they are generally perceived as positive paradigm shifters. The fact that several Eastern nations, led by China and India, are demanding an increasingly prominent position in the global business scheme is not insignificantly contributing to this growing interest in Eastern traditions, not only in workplaces, but also in educational institutions.[14]

The main message of Eastern traditions, and specifically Buddhist psychology, is to gravitate toward a more people-centered approach in the workplace, where employees get breaks to renew their energy and regain their serenity, and where they receive more positive reinforcement instead of the negative reinforcement that has been so embedded in many work environments. What this means is that managers will not only refrain from dwelling on the mistakes their employees make (negative reinforcement), but also give them positive feedback and recognition when they do well (positive reinforcement). If implemented cautiously, a Buddhist-based approach can therefore help transform the work environment, whether for-profit or nonprofit, in a positive way. In the following sections, we will review five qualities that this psychological approach upholds, which can be of value in contemporary work environments. For the reader's convenience, we project the main points in Figure 8.2.

Buddhism is Pro-Science

The Dalai Lama is undoubtedly the most celebrated Buddhist in the world. He travels around the globe, and participates in a wide variety of dialogues. Stemming from a Mahayana-based school of Buddhism; the Dalai Lama has a strong belief that everyone can develop Buddha nature. He also believes that science is important in human development. His reasons for supporting science among his followers and in general is due not only to his personal fascination with science, but also to his awareness that the underlying cause for Tibet's current predicament lies in its past refusal to open itself up. It is this closed-mindedness that instigated Tibet's political tragedy.[15]

Today, the Dalai Lama writes and talks about the need for us to educate ourselves, and support science and technology. He astutely reviews the concepts of science and spirituality, and underscores that these two concepts don't have to be mutually exclusive. In fact, it should be quite the contrary, because both science and spirituality are seeking the truth, even though they do so from a different

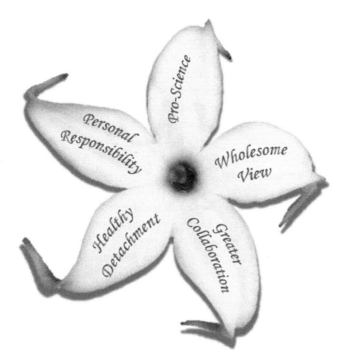

FIGURE 8.2 Buddhist values in the workplace

starting point. The Dalai Lama therefore warns that those who claim to be spiritual but ignore the discoveries of science, place themselves at risk of becoming fundamentalists.[16]

In Dharamsala, where the Dalai Lama resides along with almost 90,000 Tibetan refugees, all society members, especially those who want to become monks, are encouraged to engage in the highest education possible. The enthusiastic approach of the Dalai Lama and his followers toward science makes Buddhism a very appealing psychology to consider for Westerners. While other ideologies are still struggling with science and how to include it in their perspectives, Buddhism has been leading the way in receptiveness to new scientific developments.

Considering the fact that today's work environment is increasingly science and technology based, there seems to be a great foundation to embrace Buddhist thinking as the inter-human guide in professional circles.

Buddhism Supports Personal Responsibility

Buddhist psychology focuses heavily on the principle of cause and effect. It holds that our current experiences are based on our past actions and choices, and that our future circumstances will similarly be determined by our current actions and choices.[17] Karma, as this concept of cause and effect is widely known, is important

118 Buddhism and Business

for us to consider, because it can help us stay on the right path with our actions and choices, so that the quality of our life remains sound.[18]

A Buddhist business leader interviewed for this study stressed that his belief in karma helps him make decisions focused on the broadest wellbeing for all stakeholders. He stated that he engages in meditation daily, because he has found that it calmed his mind, and helped him make more rational decisions. Because of the calmer mind, he also found that he was better able to face challenging situations at work, and consider issues that arose in a less defensive and more positive light.

Belief in the cause and effect cycle of karma is useful in the workplace, because it will prevent the worker who is a practitioner of Buddhist psychology to readily blame others for problems that emerge. This person will develop the will to first take responsibility for his or her actions, and reflect on everything that occurs within a larger view. True to the karmic principle, he or she will consider the past as the foundation of what happens at the moment. When workforce members engage in such a mental mode, they will be less defensive, less upset, and less prone to engage in mean-spirited actions toward coworkers.

One of the numerous personal responsibility–based teachings of Buddha pertains to releasing: not just the bad feelings, thoughts, and habits we encountered or developed along the way, but also the good ones. And although this may seem senseless at first it can be explained quite easily.

Every feeling, thought, or habit you develop at one time was initially created for a certain purpose. Purposes evolve, and so do you. After some time, your feeling, thought, or habit, directed toward that predetermined purpose, becomes obsolete.

Fortunately, "obsolete" is not a strange word anymore in modern day society. On the contrary. We have grown very accustomed to this word in today's ever-changing world. We hear it all the time when we talk about computers, transportation devices, communication methods, and even job processes.

So, if we should "release" feelings, thoughts, or habits to prevent obsolescence, what is it, then, that really works? The answer is simple, and probably already obvious: continuous renewal.

In fact, this advice for continuous renewal should not be limited to such intangible phenomena as feelings, thoughts, and habits; it should also be perceived in regards to the tools we work with, the patterns we develop to solve our problems, and the vehicles we build to get us from one place to another, whether physically, mentally, or emotionally.

This brings to mind a story the Buddha once told about a man who encountered a river that he would have to cross in order to move on, while there were no boats or ferries available. After the initial despair of being stuck, the man built a raft from branches and sticks, and crossed the river. So, what happened when he reached the other side? Well, here is where Buddha warns for the logical tendency to take the raft under one's arm in order to have it ready for use in future encounters with large waters.

The general counsel here is, that carrying all the "rafts" we build along our way through life is not just a tiresome and decelerating process, but also one that prevents us from nurturing a creative spirit. We will become like the man, in another parable, who has a hammer and treats every problem that he encounters as if it were a nail. Or, in the above example, like the man who carries a raft and treats every challenge as if it were a river.

What we should understand is that, once having built a raft, we have now gained insight, experience, and confidence to build others with different, more applicable components in the future, so we can safely leave the old one behind.

Getting rid of our old "rafts," whether they are thoughts, feelings, habits, work devices, vehicles, organizational strategies, or mind patterns, is a must. We will not be able to stay active in the increasingly competitive game of life if we refuse to do this. Worse, we will rob ourselves of our most precious quality if all we do is cling to old solutions. We will lose our sense of creativity and ingenuity, and our touch with the child inside of us. And, believe it or not, it is exactly the sense of creativity and ingenuity, together with the naïve curiosity within us, that gives us a competitive and comparative advantage these days, in business as well as in other social settings. Those who don't fear to release old feelings, thoughts, habits, devices, strategies, and methods, and dare to come up with new ideas, inventions, and insights are the ones who thrive.

Isn't it interesting that this advice given more than 2,500 years ago has now become more practical than it ever was? Makes you wonder how much has really, fundamentally changed . . .

Buddhism Promotes Healthy Detachment

Healthy detachment is a state of mind in which a person chooses to be alert, and refrain from harboring preconceived notions or judging others.[19] Because Buddhism assumes "no self" for all of us, an attentive practitioner of this psychology will not take anything personal, because there is "no self" to do so. Observing healthy detachment also makes it easier to deal with setbacks, because you don't take them personally.[20] Thanks to this mentality, suffering becomes less, at home, at work, or in any setting.[21] A person that observes healthy detachment is aware that everything is temporary: our jobs, our positions, our colleagues, and even us. It is therefore senseless to get too attached to any of these fleeting things.

When we decide to practice healthy detachment in the workplace, we find that our stress levels diminish, because the struggle and strive are no longer a problem

120 Buddhism and Business

to us. We become aware of and compassionate about the stress that our still-attached coworkers deal with, especially if they define themselves by their position, their office, or other status symbols.

When the no-self mindset has become part of how we see the world, we will feel less affected by the daily ups and downs, have less need to engage in gossip or complaints, feel less fearful or angry, grieved or proud, and are less pressured when changes happen in our work environment. Developing and nurturing the mentality of healthy detachment is therefore beneficial to us, and may also be helpful for our coworkers and our work environment as a whole.

A Buddhist business leader who was interviewed for this study explained that daily engagement in the workplace can be challenging, because we see people who are attached all around us, and become involved in their struggle and strife. If we don't remain mindful and regularly reflect on healthy detachment, we may lose it and start suffering again. This is why we should turn inward regularly, through meditation, reflection, or anything that we consider helpful, to nurture our awareness. The business leader also underscored how good it is for our health and wellbeing when we practice healthy detachment: we are largely free of anxiety, approach problems with an open heart, have no fear for retaliation, and are free from regret, because we make more deliberate, less selfish, decisions.

Although it is not easy to refrain yourself from all desire while wandering on the face of the earth, and even to detach the from your "self," you can grow toward a more mature state of spiritual being. This state will limit, if not eradicate, desolation and exultation, resentment and lust, excessive fear and extreme ruthlessness, as well as every other disproportionate state of mind that only causes inner disturbance and disparity. This state will enhance, if not entirely establish, inner-balance and acceptance of life as it presents itself.

Once you manage to obtain a state that is free from wrath, disproportionate expectations, greed, or envy, you can start enjoying your current circumstances more, and live more fully, and with increased gratitude, in the here and now.

Obtaining such a state takes time and effort, and you will encounter multiple conditions along the way, even after obtaining the aimed-for state, that will seemingly justify a relapse into old patterns and behaviors. After all, living in a civilization that is built on influence, possessions, a need for security, and a pressing prerequisite to engage in manipulative maneuvers, almost seems to be an undeviating inconsistency with the attainment of this liberated state.

How can you achieve liberation of the self and still live in a subjugated world? How can you achieve spiritual boundlessness and still perform up to daily expectations? How can you discover, and hopefully find a lasting way

Buddhism and Business **121**

to dwell on the inner nirvana while remaining part of a controlled system, entangled in, oftentimes, ridiculous and rigid rules and regulations?

The answer cannot be given as a pre-formulated, all-fitting set of directions, as this in and of itself would once again be a manifestation of the boundary establishment, which we tend to struggle with in our modern culture of excessive organization and control. The answer can actually only be found within yourself after thorough inward turning, concentrating on your circumstances and character, formulating your personal perception of freedom, and determining your capacity to persevere in reaching the discovered personal definition of spiritual liberation.

Acceptance may be a key concept here. And gratitude for all that you are and could not have been without carrying yourself with dignity and sincerity. And respect for all that lives and grows around you: family, colleagues, strangers, flora, and fauna. And awareness of matters, without giving in to the tendency of falling into the trap of mass-hypnosis, thoughtlessness, and justification of wrongdoing due to partisanship.

Enlightenment starts with encouraging yourself to be awake. And being awake starts with distancing yourself from mass thinking and elevating yourself toward thinking for yourself in order to develop your own views. It also entails recognizing that your personal view starts with detaching yourself from mindless adoption of group perspectives, while being alert enough to retain social graces and manners. Detaching yourself from group perspectives starts with obtaining respect for your own perceptions. Obtaining respect for your own perceptions starts with valuing yourself. Valuing yourself starts with accepting yourself. Accepting yourself starts with loving yourself. Loving yourself starts with knowing yourself. Knowing yourself starts with realizing the difference between you and self. Realizing the difference between you and self will provide insight in what matters to you without necessarily incorporating self. Having insight in what matters to you without necessarily incorporating self will provide awareness into what is beneficial to all. Awareness into what is beneficial to all will lead to doing things right without fearing consequences, because you are now detached from politics and insincerity, and freed from excessive desires.

Such is the reward of being awake: tranquility, peace, and serenity. It may not always be present at the level you would prefer, because you are still part of the world, part of a family, and part of teams; and you still have feelings and emotions; but it can be maintained and enhanced if you recognize when you regress into previous states of mind and recommit your awareness. All you need to do is train yourself to stay in touch with the inner source, and detect alienation from this source as soon as it occurs, and growth will be assured.

122 Buddhism and Business

Buddhism Provokes Greater Collaboration

In today's work environment, team performance is critical. Team performance comes natural to those who practice a Buddhist mindset. Because you have the best intentions at heart for your workplace and your coworkers, you will share your insights and contribute optimally with no selfish agenda.[22] Since Buddhist psychology promotes a giving mentality, practitioners are encouraged to share their knowledge and skills as well as they can, to not shy away from difficult chores, refrain from complaining, admit their mistakes, ask for help when needed, help others when possible, and be loyal to those in trouble.[23] It is similar to what we learn in the golden rule: "do unto others as you would want them to do unto you."

Because people who follow the Buddhist psychology are aware of the importance of generosity, respect, collaboration, and compassion in their behavior, they will be great team players, and hold no selfish agenda, other than the thought that they need to do right in order to establish good karma for the future.

Many of the Buddha's insights are as applicable today as they were during his lifetime. He stated, for instance, "All that we are is the result of what we have thought. The mind is everything. What we think we become." This powerful statement reminds us that the world, as we see it, is a reflection of our thoughts. When we consider others enemies, we establish an impression in our mind that only we can alter. We can therefore make our life miserable or cheerful, simply by the perspective we choose to maintain. This is important in work settings.

A friend of mine approached me a few weeks ago with this very problem: one of her supervisors seemed to utterly dislike her, no matter how hard she tried to do well. I explained to her that the problem was not hers, and that she should not make it hers either. She could try compassion based on the understanding that there might be issues with this person, which she is not aware of. It is important to understand that you will not be able to please everybody, and that there will be people who will dislike you for the very fact that you breathe. Yet, that does not have to become your problem.

In a more specific citation, the Buddha clarified:

> "All that we are is the result of what we have thought. If a man speaks or acts with an evil thought, pain follows him. If a man speaks or acts with a pure thought, happiness follows him, like a shadow that never leaves him."

How many of us cannot come up with examples on both sides of this statement? I have worked with a person who always resented any initiative that would enhance the team spirit in our department. His bitterness

> followed him as a dark cloud wherever he went. With his unpleasant demeanor he alienated many colleagues who would have liked to get to know him better. Similarly, I have a coworker who always responds with the phrase "Life is good!" when anyone asks him how he is. I have no doubts that he has his share of challenges, but his positive approach works wonders for the general atmosphere at work, and colleagues are always ready to do him a favor, knowing that he would be happy to help them out as well.[24]

Buddhism Incites a Wholesome View

When we practice Buddhist psychology, we keep our eyes on the bigger picture of what we do. We consider our work, and make sure it is a constructive activity, and that the output of our labor, directly or indirectly, does not harm anyone.

In chapter 7 we discussed the Noble Eightfold Path, and its various threads. When we look deeper into the qualities Buddhist psychology brings to us, we can see all these reflected: right view, right intention, right speech, right action, right livelihood, right effort, right mindfulness, and right concentration.

We practice *right view* by focusing on the larger scope, and not on details that could upset us. Within this larger scope, we realize that work is a blessing that fulfills multiple functions in our lives, such as: a) providing us a chance to develop and display our talents, b) helping us to overcome our ego-centeredness through collaboration with other people in a joint purpose, and c) allowing us to help deliver products and services that contribute to the overall quality of life.[25] With this wholesome perspective in mind, we focus on progress for the organization we work for, and don't allow petty issues to get the better of us.

We practice *right intention* (or thinking) by carefully screening the reasons why we make our decisions. Because we operate from a no-self mindset, we don't harbor a selfish agenda and therefore make no self-centered decisions that can be harmful to others. Yet, working with a compassionate and constructive mind does not mean that we may not enjoy the fruits of our labor. If we work hard and honestly, there is no sin in earning a decent living, and appreciating the comfort that may bring,[26] as long as we don't become obsessed with it, and remain vigilant that the desire for comfort and luxury does not become our priority.

We practice *right speech* by speaking the truth, sharing our insights to the best of our abilities, and avoiding backstabbing or hurtful expressions. Practicing right speech requires right view, intention, effort, mindfulness, and concentration, because it is so easy to go along with the flow and find ourselves caught in a web of gossip or badmouthing when something does not go as planned.

We practice *right action* by taking on challenging tasks, and not leaving them to others. We help our colleagues where we can, and perform in teams at our level

124 Buddhism and Business

best. We don't engage in any activities in which we are aware that they are harmful to anyone, so we stay away from practices that involve killing, stealing, sexual misconduct, greed, lying, and drug abuse.[27] In other words, we ensure that neither we nor others are harmed by our actions.

We practice *right livelihood* by examining the nature of our work, and not working for a company that engages in practices or productions that can lead to harm. There are millions of people who work in the weapons industry, and help produce weapons, whether directly or indirectly, or work in human trafficking, or help produce destructive drugs or intoxicants that get people addicted. This is wrong livelihood.[28] While our vocation is intended to nurture our understanding and compassion for others, such negative sources of livelihood only erode our inter-human senses.[29] We should always keep ourselves aware of the consequences of our personal and professional actions, not only for the present, but also for the near *and* distant future.[30] So, even if someone is an accountant, and doesn't have anything to do with the production aspect of the company, he or she remains aware that anything they do for the workplace contributes to its purpose.

We practice *right effort*, because we make sure that our mental and physical output is pure and void of malicious intentions. When performing in a business (or non-business) setting, we make sure that the organization is successful. In business settings, this means that it should make a profit. While the Buddhist practitioner will not cooperate in making a profit at any cost and through wrong livelihood, he or she will have no problem with making a profit in a morally sound way.[31] As explained under *right intention*, there is nothing wrong with earning a decent income for our earnest efforts. We should keep in mind that our income does not only provide a more comfortable living for us and those that directly depend on our income, but it can enable us to do more for others as well.

We practice *right mindfulness* by remaining alert about our work, our actions, our speech, and all other segments of our behavior. One area that we should be particularly mindful about is our attitude toward our work. Workaholism is easily acquired when our jobs are very enticing and challenging. Habits quickly grow, even from practices that are not healthy or positive.[32] If we become workaholics, we will start clinging to our work, and undo the healthy detachment we carefully nurtured. As a result, we will become stressed, consumed, and victimized again by the daily struggle and strife in our workplace.

We practice *right concentration* by not allowing ourselves to get distracted by things that can derail us from our noble path. A simple yet wise set of questions we should regularly ask ourselves are: 1) Who am I? 2) What am I doing here? 3) How can I fulfill my life's potential?[33] By formulating the answers to these questions, we make sure we are still focusing on the right thing, and prevent ourselves from falling into the trap of hopeless tedium that gives rise to anger, frustration, and boredom.

The Buddha warned:

"Holding on to anger is like grasping a hot coal with the intent of throwing it at someone else; you are the one who gets burned."

In 2,500 years nothing has changed about that: angry people get absorbed by their anger still today. The party we are angry with may not even be aware of our feelings. Sometimes people have no idea how hurtful their comments can be. They move on with their day, unaware of any emotional damage they may have caused. But even if they deliberately caused the damage, should we allow them the pleasure of our suffering? Those of us who have decided to choose for our own wellbeing to release our anger and continue our strides toward personal mastery are aware of the gratification this decision brings. So why risk hypertension if we know that releasing anger contributes to our own wellness?

In my conversations with workforce members I have found that they are often concerned about the volatility of the job market. They constantly fear that they might lose their job to outsourcing, and fall into the trap of chronic distress. The Buddha understood the importance of living in the moment and the distraction of focusing too much on past or future:

"Do not dwell in the past, do not dream of the future, concentrate the mind on the present moment."

One of my past MBA students who was living on financial aid constantly feared that she would not be able to find a job after earning her degree. I kept encouraging her to live more in the moment and enjoy her study time instead of looking too far ahead. This was not a matter of sweet-talking on my end, but rather a reflection of having been there and done that. Upon her graduation, she received a job offer, and realized that I was right. Whether she will take the lesson she learned to heart or not: living in the moment is a gift that too many of us take for granted.[34]

Summary

In this chapter we presented:

- A number of reasons why today's world of work is subject to such tremendous change. Some of these reasons are increased diversity, increased financial pressure, increased degrees of urbanization and migration, and increased exposure to other traditions than the one(s) we grew up with.
- A number of reasons why so many people feel discontented at work. Some of these reasons are growing insecurity, increased pace of change, higher educated employees with more critical views, the changed nature of the work we are doing today, the mismatch between the nature of our work and the way

126 Buddhism and Business

we are rewarded, and the mismatch between what we do, and what we *want* to do. From the discontentment that emerges through all these (and more) factors, a growing awareness arises for more meaning.

- The growing interest in Eastern traditions in the Western (specifically the American) workplace. Buddhism has become by far the most popular Eastern psychology in U.S. professional and academic circles because it seems to provide a useful template for the general movement of workplace spirituality, and because Buddhism make perfect sense from a secular standpoint, which makes it acceptable to people from all walks of life.
- A closer review on the appropriateness of Buddhism in American society. The United States is a highly individualistic country, where people develop a sense of "self" from very early stages in their lives, while Buddhism teaches the importance of "selflessness" in our actions. Yet, Buddhism has thus far successfully found its way in the capitalistic American society.
- Useful Buddhist Practices at Work, which are to be considered on a very personal basis by anyone who is interested:
  - Buddhism is Pro-Science: Buddhists agree that science is important in human development. The Dalai Lama, the world's foremost Buddhist leader, writes and talks about the need for us to educate ourselves, and support science and technology. The pro-science approach is very much in line with trends in today's world of work.
  - Buddhism Supports Personal Responsibility: because Buddhists believe in karma (cause and effect) they make decisions focused on the broadest wellbeing for all stakeholders. Rather than blaming others for problems that emerge, they will first take responsibility for their actions, and reflect on everything that occurs within a larger view.
  - Buddhism Promotes Healthy Detachment: because Buddhism assumes "no self," an attentive practitioner will not take anything personally, and not get too attached to anything, because it is all temporary. Thanks to the notion of healthy detachment, stress levels diminish, because the struggle and strive are no longer a problem.
  - Buddhism Provokes Greater Collaboration: team performance comes natural to those who practice a Buddhist mindset. They have the best intentions at heart for their workplace and coworkers, and will share their insights, and contribute optimally, with no selfish agenda.
  - Buddhism Incites a Wholesome View: when we practice Buddhist psychology, we keep our eyes on the bigger picture of what we do. We consider our work, and make sure it is a constructive activity, and that the output of our labor, directly or indirectly, does not harm anyone. Within the wholesome view, we can see all the threads of the Noble Eightfold Path reflected: right view, right intention, right speech, right action, right livelihood, right effort, right mindfulness, and right concentration.

Questions

1. In the first part of this chapter, a number of reasons are mentioned for the changes we experience in the world of work. Which of these changes seems most challenging to you, and why?
2. This chapter also presents a number of reasons why workforce members may be so discontented in our times. Which of these reasons do you consider to be the most compelling, and why?
3. Why do you think that Buddhism may have such great appeal to U.S. workforce members, in spite of the major ideological differences between U.S. culture and Buddhist foundations?
4. The term "workplace spirituality" is mentioned in this chapter as one that may have facilitated the receptiveness of Buddhist practices in the U.S. workplace. Please engage in some research about this trend, and share a definition and brief explanation about your findings (400–500 words).
5. Five useful Buddhist practices for the workplace are discussed in this chapter. Please review them critically, and try to formulate a well-considered point of caution you consider necessary in the application of each of these practices at work?

Notes

1 Mohamed, F., Taylor, G. S., & Hassan, A. (2006). Affective Commitment and Intent to Quit: The Impact of Work and Non-Work Related Issues. *Journal of Managerial Issues, 18*(4), 512–530; Stewart, S. M. (2007). An Integrative Framework of Workplace Stress and Aggression. *The Business Review, Cambridge, 8*(1), 223–233.
2 Cash, K. C., Gray, G. R., & Rood, S. A. (2000). A Framework for Accommodating Religion and Spirituality in the Workplace/Executive Commentary. *The Academy of Management Perspectives, 14*(3), 124–134; Morgan, J. F. (2004). How Should Business Respond to a More Religious Workplace? *S.A.M. Advanced Management Journal, 69*(4), 11–19.
3 Netland, H. (2008). Into the Jaws of Yama, Lord of Death: Buddhism, Bioethics, and Death. *Ethics and Medicine, 24*(2), 124–125; Gockel, A. (2004). The Trend Toward Spirituality in the Workplace: Overview and Implications for Career Counseling. *Journal of Employment Counseling, 41*(4), 156–167.
4 Dugan, K. & Bogert, H. (2006). *Racial Diversity in Buddhism in the US*. Retrieved on November 28, 2013 from http://pluralism.org/research/reports/dugan/diversity_buddhism.pdf; Masatsugu, M. K. (2008). Beyond This World of Transiency and Impermanence: Japanese Americans, Dharma Bums, and the Making of American Buddhism During the Early Cold WAR years. *Pacific Historical Review, 77*(3), 425–451.
5 Netland, H. (2008). Into the Jaws of Yama, Lord of Death: Buddhism, Bioethics, and Death. *Ethics and Medicine, 24*(2), 124–125.
6 Kakabadse, N., Collins, P., & Kakabadse, A. (2007). The Need for Spirituality in the Public Sphere. In Ramsden, J., Shuhei, A., & Kakabadse, A. (Eds.), *Spiritual Motivation: New Thinking for Business and Management*. Palgrave MacMillan, Hampshire, 161–184.; Korac-Kakabadse, N., Kouzmin, A., & Kakabadse, A. (2002). Spirituality and Leadership Praxis. *Journal of Managerial Psychology, 17*(3), 165–182.

128 Buddhism and Business

7 Fernando, M. & Jackson, B. (2006). The Influence of Religion-Based Workplace Spirituality on Business Leaders' Decision-Making: An Inter-Faith Study. *Journal of Management and Organization, 12*(1), 23–39; Giacalone, R. A. & Jurkiewicz, C. L. (Eds.) (2003). Toward a Science of Workplace Spirituality. In Giacalone, R. A. & Jurkiewicz, C. L. (Eds.). *Handbook of Workplace Spirituality and Organizational Performance*, M.E. Sharpe, New York: pp. 3–28; Marques, J. (2005). Yearning for a More Spiritual Workplace. *Journal of American Academy of Business, 7*(1), 149–153; Paloutzian, R. & Park, C. (Eds.) (2005). *Handbook of the Psychology of Religion and Spirituality*. Guilford Press, New York; Zinnebauer, B. J. & Paragament, K. L. (2005). Religiousness and Spirituality. In Paloutzian, R. & Park, C. (Eds.), *Handbook of the Psychology of Religion and Spirituality*. Guilford Press, New York: pp. 21–42.
8 Thich Nhat Hanh (1998). *The Heart of the Buddha's Teaching: Transforming Suffering into Peace, Joy, and Liberation*. Broadway Books, New York.
9 Templeton, D. (2000). *Dharma & Greed: Popular Buddhism Meets the American Dream*. Metro Publishing Inc., Northern California Bohemian, CA. Retrieved on November 28, 2013 from www.metroactive.com/papers/sonoma/10.12.00/buddhism-0041.html
10 Ibid.
11 Ibid.
12 Ibid.
13 Holender, A. (2008). *Zentrepreneurism: A Twenty-First Century Guide to the New World of Business*. Book Tree, New York.
14 Johansen, B. C. & Gopalakrishna, D. (2006). A Buddhist View of Adult Learning in the Workplace. *Advances in Developing Human Resources, 8*(3), 337–345.
15 His Holiness The Dalai Lama (2005). *The Universe in a Single Atom: The Convergence of Science and Spirituality*. Broadway Books, New York.
16 Ibid.
17 Bercholz, S. & Kohn, S. C. (1993). *An Introduction to the Buddha and His Teachings*. Barnes & Noble, Inc., New York.
18 Thondup, T. (1995). *Enlightened Journey: Buddhist Practice as Daily Life*. Shambhala Publications, Inc. Boston, MA.
19 Morvay, Z. (1999). Horney, Zen, and the Real Self: Theoretical and Historical Connections. *American Journal of Psychoanalysis, 59*(1), 25–35.
20 Ibid.
21 Metcalf, F. & Hately, B. G. (2001). *What Would Buddha Do at Work?* Seastone and Berrett-Koehler Publishers, Inc., San Francisco, CA.
22 Ibid.
23 Ibid.
24 Marques, J. (2012). The Resurgence of Human Values in Today's Organizations: Pointers From the Buddha. *Development and Learning in Organizations, 26*(1), 5–7.
25 Valliere, D. (2008). Exploring Buddhist Influence on the Entrepreneurial Decision. *International Journal of Entrepreneurial Behaviour & Research, 14*(3), 172–191.
26 Yeshe, Lama (2004). *The Peaceful Stillness of the Silent Mind: Buddhism, Mind and Meditation*. Lama Yeshe Wisdom Archive, Weston, MA.
27 Quatro, S. A. (2004). New Age or Age Old: Classical Management Theory and Traditional Organized Religion as Underpinnings of the Contemporary Organizational Spirituality Movement. *Human Resource Development Review, 3*(3), 229–249.
28 Thich Nhat Hanh (1998). *The Heart of the Buddha's Teaching: Transforming Suffering into Peace, Joy, and Liberation*. Broadway Books, New York.
29 Ibid.
30 Ibid.

31 Geshe Michael Roach (2000). *The Diamond Cutter: The Buddha on Managing Your Business and Your Life.* Doubleday, New York.
32 Thich Nhat Hanh (1998). *The Heart of the Buddha's Teaching: Transforming Suffering into Into Peace, Joy, and Liberation.* Broadway Books, New York.
33 Richmond, L. (1999). *Work as a Spiritual Practice: A Practical Buddhist Approach to Inner Growth and Satisfaction on the Job.* Broadway Books, New York.
34 Marques, J. (2012). The Resurgence of Human Values in Today's Organizations: Pointers From the Buddha. *Development and Learning in Organizations, 26*(1), 5–7.

9

A CLOSER LOOK AT THE POINTS OF CAUTION

> Two people have been living in you all your life. One is the ego, garrulous, demanding, hysterical, calculating; the other is the hidden spiritual being, whose still voice of wisdom you have only rarely heard or attended to.
>
> Sogyal Rinpoche

A Middle Path for Everything

In chapter 8 we reviewed five strengths of Buddhist psychology in work environments. While there are definitely more strengths to be distinguished, these five strengths were based on a broad view of Buddhist practice and its consequences. Most other strengths could very likely be placed in the clusters of these five strengths.

One preliminary note to be made is that almost every strength can turn into weakness, and almost every weakness into strength, depending on the intensity or moderation in which we apply it. For example, we generally see perseverance as a strong quality in attaining results. There are many wise quotes and adages that teach us the power of persevering and not giving up too quickly, such as this one from Victor Hugo: "Perseverance, secret of all triumphs."[1] Yet, extreme perseverance can turn into stubbornness, leading to relentless persistence, and a serious waste of time, energy, money, and peace of mind, long after rational behavior has ended. This is why Mark Twain once wisely alludes, "Perseverance is a principle that should be commendable in those who have judgment to govern it."[2]

On the other hand, we generally see risk-taking as a dangerous trait, and that is indeed the case when it is done in an irresponsible way. However, there is also calculated risk-taking, where we consider trends, review the factors at stake, talk to mentors, and rely on our insights. In fact, every decision we make, whether professionally or privately, is a risk to a certain degree, because we rarely have a complete overview of the circumstances and their consequences. The choices we make on a daily basis, whether simple or complex, always include a degree of risk that they may not work out as we envisioned. In the business world, quick decisions are needed, and many of those decisions are made with incomplete data, but based on experience, trend analyses, and considerations of what is at stake.

Considering the above examples of strengths that can become weaknesses and weaknesses that can become strengths, we will now take another look at four of the five strengths mentioned in chapter 8, and present some points of caution to them. Subsequently, we will consider five critical principles in Buddhist psychology that should be carefully examined, as they can become potential pitfalls in business performance. We will, however, also consider the other side of these perceived "weaknesses" and contemplate how they could become strengths.

The Cautionary Side of the Strengths

The first strength that was mentioned in chapter 8 was that *Buddhism is pro-science.* This is a broad and general advantage that has no impact on personal performance. Problems at the personal level are therefore not easy to discuss regarding the first strength. However, the picture changes significantly with the four other strengths, due to their behavioral nature:

- *Buddhism Supports Personal Responsibility*
  This strength discussed the understanding of cause and effect that followers of Buddhist psychology hold. Based on this understanding, Buddhist practitioners will have a high consideration of karmic consequences in everything they do. That means that a person adhering to Buddhist psychology will always try to do right, and prefer to take ownership of problems that arise, rather than blame others.

An interesting point that the Buddha commented on is the frequently manifested problem of victimized thinking. This is an unfortunate habit, possibly nurtured by our entire societal status quo to keep large groups of workers from becoming more proactive. When someone displays a high internal locus of control, meaning that he or she takes responsibility for his or her actions, we oftentimes perceive this person as an entrepreneur. And indeed, it is usually a great thing to see yourself as an entrepreneur, regardless if you really are one. Whether things look up or down in your life, there are always consequences of decisions you once made. The best thing to do when you get derailed is to correct your error and move on without wasting time looking for scapegoats.[3]

132 A Closer Look at the Points of Caution

A point of caution here is that coworkers may soon realize this mentality within the Buddhist practitioner, and try to pin their mistakes onto that person. It can also be that, based on the attitude of wanting to always do right, the Buddhist practitioner will be banned to the "out-group" and therefore be shirked in critical decision making for fear that he may create problems when the decisions might not be morally sound.

- *Buddhism Promotes Healthy Detachment*
  Based on the awareness of "no self," a practitioner of Buddhist psychology will not cling to material things, and not take setbacks personally. The points of caution are multiple here: coworkers may decide to take advantage of this mindset, and demand the best opportunities and spaces for themselves, claiming that it doesn't matter to the Buddhist practitioner anyway. Fortunately, the Buddhist practitioner will, indeed, not be disturbed by this behavior for long. Another point of caution is the detachment to setbacks, which can be interpreted by others as if the Buddhist practitioner does not care for the organization's progress. Such is not the case, because Buddhist psychology also entails performance to the best of abilities at all times. Nonetheless, the perception may lead to unfavorable actions against the Buddhist worker.
- *Buddhism Provokes Greater Collaboration*
  People who follow the Buddhist psychology are aware of the importance of generosity, respect, collaboration, and compassion in their behavior. Therefore, they will be great team players and hold no selfish agenda, other than the thought that they need to do right in order to establish good karma for the future.

> The Buddha stated, "Thousands of candles can be lit from a single candle, and the life of the candle will not be shortened. Happiness never decreases by being shared." This is, indeed, relevant for twenty-first century corporate workers, as they should reach out and try their best to enhance the quality of life for themselves and others. Doing so will not affect their own gratification. It is actually quite the contrary. When you know that you have done something right for someone else, you feel so much better about yourself.[4]

Yet, this heightened collaborative mentality should also be considered with caution, as less scrupulous coworkers may take advantage of the Buddhist practitioner by preying on his generosity and compassion, and letting him do all the work, even though they will demand a share in the credits.

- *Buddhism Incites a Wholesome View*
  In discussing this element of strength, we considered the eight threads of the Noble Eightfold Path. Of particular interest is the quality of focusing on the bigger picture in everything. This could become somewhat frustrating to

those who need to work with minute details, as happens so often in workplaces, especially those in academia. While filled with good intentions, the Buddhist practitioner may not be overly enthused about excessive stressing on minute details. A real point of caution, however, is the consideration of right livelihood, as this will entail that followers of Buddhist psychology will not become employed at work environments that engage in any practice or service that can cause harm to others.

Some Important Points of Caution

While there are some major advantages to following Buddhist psychology in the workplace, it would be deceptive to paint a picture that was void of areas for concern. Considering the fast-paced, competitive, money-driven, oftentimes controversial and sly climate in business, it comes as no surprise that a psychology focused solely on welfare of all living beings will encounter some tough challenges. In the following section we will review five of these challenges, with the understanding that there are undoubtedly more, but those could most likely be incorporated in the challenges to be mentioned below. For the reader's convenience, we have depicted the five points of caution in Figure 9.1.

The Principle of Non-Harming (Ahimsa)

Buddhist psychology teaches us that we are all related to each other. Coming from the belief that human beings are born thousands of times, Buddhists believe that everyone has been everyone else's mother in a previous life. Those of us who don't believe in reincarnation may have a problem accepting this particular reasoning,

FIGURE 9.1 Five challenges in applying Buddhist practices in business

134 A Closer Look at the Points of Caution

but there are other, more scientific considerations to support our interconnectedness. One of these is Charles Darwin's proposition of one single progenitor for all life forms,[5] a theory that has been revived and further popularized in recent years by, among others, Richard Dawkins.[6]

So, whether we believe the Buddhist concept, the Darwinian concept, or biblical concepts, the connectivity aspect is somehow embedded. Based on their specific notion that everyone has been everyone else's mother once, followers of Buddhism feel that we should respect all beings, even when they seem to turn against us. Non-harming is therefore a huge conviction in Buddhism, often underscored by the Dalai Lama, who says, "Always help others, and if you cannot help, at least don't harm." Buddhists use the term *Ahimsa* to refer to non-harming. It is Sanskrit for "do not injure."

Considering *Ahimsa* in life's overall scheme, we see that it may not be applied as easily as we would hope. In a more general sense, we sometimes find ourselves in a position where we have to eradicate living creatures that form a threat to our health: mosquitos, bedbugs, and flies, for instance. Keeping one fly or bug that we find in our home alive is one thing. But dealing with swarms that can cause epidemics is a different story. While every living organism serves a purpose in life, circumstances have already been skewed to a point that it would take enormous sacrifices to correct them. For this reason, we sometimes may find that we are forced to protect ourselves against destructive organisms instead of allowing them to peacefully live alongside us.

Considering *Ahimsa* in business, we face a similar dilemma: the nature of business, as it has been developed for many decades, is competitive. For one to prosper, another one has to suffer. In business dealings the situation is similar: for one corporate representative to win a bid, for instance, others will have to lose. The win-lose mentality is deeply embedded in business practices worldwide.[7] On a positive note, we have seen a trend toward more gentleness in business performance in recent years, encouraged by a wide range of academic and popular authors, who attempt to instill a more cooperative mindset among business leaders. One of the famous efforts in this regard is one of Stephen Covey's "Seven Habits of Highly Effective People,"[8] known as "Habit 4: Think Win-Win." In his description of this habit, Covey explains that we don't have to focus on "win-lose" but can try to establish a "win-win" situation, where both parties leave the negotiations with a sense of achievement. It may not result in profits of the "win-lose" magnitude, but it ensures longitudinal, mutually rewarding relationships.

The Buddhist mindset is more focused on "win-win-win" in which there are more stakeholders than just the two at the bargaining table. In this case, the third win could be considered for the environment, and in that, all other life. This is a laudable notion, and we should continue hoping that the trend toward achieving this continues to grow. The "win-win-win" mentality may gain ground in the near future, as new business entities arise of which a significant number may adhere to the social business model, in which money is still made, but wellbeing of others is considered.

The Principle of Equanimity (No Cravings and No Aversions)

Equanimity is explained as calmness or level-headedness. In Buddhist psychology, it pertains to inner balance, which comes from the absence of cravings and aversions.

When we participate in a work environment, regardless whether it is for- or nonprofit, we deal with people: colleagues, supervisors, subordinates, clients, and other stakeholders. In our daily confrontations, we sometimes encounter situations that can be hurtful, aggravating, or disheartening. People may do things to us or to others, which are very disappointing. They may lie, cheat, or steal from us. They may decide not to follow up on their agreements, and place us in a difficult predicament. They may quit on us when we need them most. They may undermine our workplace by sharing confidential information with competitors. All these actions are part of work relationships, and can lead to major frustration, hence, a disturbance of our equanimity.

In reviewing the concept of equanimity, we approached a Buddhist business leader in Dharamsala, India. He was a highly revered monk, a *geshe* (an academically educated Tibetan Buddhist monk), but at the same time he also performed as the manager of several business facilities in the Tibetan refugee community. Even in this rather devout community, he admitted to losing his equanimity at times during work. However, he also pointed out that, thanks to his habit of meditating, he never stayed out of balance for long. The *geshe* stated that lack of equanimity causes internal afflictions, which are more destructive enemies to our wellbeing than external ones. He would therefore release the anger or disappointment, based on his awareness of the impermanence of all things, and he would carefully refrain from clinging to any negative emotion, based on his awareness of healthy detachment.

Nurturing equanimity becomes an even greater challenge when we perform in Western workplaces such as the American business environment, because we deal with much more craving and aversion. The media play a very important role in our lives, and they have developed shrewd ways to arouse our cravings. The numerous advertisings we see every day on television, in newspapers and magazines, on the internet, on billboards, and everywhere else, constantly awaken desires within us. We see our colleagues with new outfits and acquire the craving to get ourselves some as well. Then there are the standards of society and the demands of trends: we don't want to be the oddball in our groups, so we crave newer models of cellphones, notebooks, laptops, cars, shoes, or purses, even if our current ones are still in perfect condition. Another set of cravings comes forth from the nature of our work: we need to reach goals, not only for our supervisors, but also for ourselves. Our ambition drives us to work harder in order to realize our dreams. These are all cravings. They are not all bad, but they do disrupt our equanimity.

136 A Closer Look at the Points of Caution

While nurturing our equanimity is a great purpose to have, we should also realize that the craving that is our ambition drives us toward higher achievements. The Dalai Lama encourages education among his followers, and is a major proponent of science. Without ambition, scientists would not care to make strides toward further development. It is therefore the very craving for improvement of our circumstances that brings progress in the world. Craving is the cornerstone of performance. If there was nothing to be craved anymore, there would also be no interest in progress-based activities.

Similarly, aversion can lead to positive outcomes as well. If, for instance, we witness immoral performance at our workplace, we may either choose to stay detached, exit the workplace, or give in to our aversion for the unhealthy situation, and report it. By reporting it, and causing measures to be taken, we have ended a negative cycle that would otherwise continue to harm large groups of people. This example shows that there are some cases where senses of aversion in the workplace can lead to betterment for all. Craving and aversion therefore have a place in business and non-business workplaces, as long as they are used constructively and responsibly. That being said, it is still important to reduce senses of craving and aversion to a minimum for a more peaceful life.

The Principle of No Competition

Whether we like it or not, competition is an essential element in business. In any environment where more than one organization delivers a similar product or service, there will be competition. And with the internet as global connection tool, anyone from any country, region, or continent can have access to any product, which means that companies are facing known and unknown competitors all the time. Competition serves a purpose in the dynamics of business: we can see it all around. When many corporations deliver a similar product or service, they have to make sure that they stand out, and do so either through price, service, or product differentiation. The customers benefit greatly from this because the corporate participants are aware that they have to stand out in some way.

We are also aware what the problem can be when a company has no competitors. In a situation of monopoly (one corporate player), or oligopoly (few corporate players), we often see that we, the customers, have very little choice but to accept what is offered to us at the price it is offered. Customers feel victimized in situations with one or few products or service suppliers, because the quality of the product may also suffer.

In Buddhist psychology, competition is considered a source of internal imbalance. If you are in competition with another person, you are always trying to top that person's performance. If the company you work for is in competition with others, a similar pattern unfolds on a larger scale. When we place Buddhism and business alongside one another, the competition element may be the most

A Closer Look at the Points of Caution **137**

apparent dichotomy, considering that Buddhism focuses on compassion, respect, and mutual support, and not on strife, competition, and mutual elimination.

If we imagine a world with no competition, however, one of the problems we may run into is stationary development, because without competition the very act of doing business loses its attraction, and a large number of businesses will cease to exist. They will do so, because they will see their incentives dwindle, and therefore will lose their motivation to continue with innovations of existing products and services, or developments of new ones. As a result, advancement will stall.

A Buddhist business leader in Los Angeles, whom we interviewed for this study, provided his perspective on competition. He was affiliated with the financial market at the time. The company, in which he held a fairly high management position, was prominent in stocks and bonds transactions. The business leader admitted that, while he did not support the usual competitiveness among his financial advisors, he could not always prevent it from happening. When it happened, he had to make an assessment about the seriousness, and call the competing parties to order. He was, however, never able to rule the competitive mindset out completely. Competition is extremely high in the financial industry because there is so much money involved, and as a result, so much commission to be earned! Members of this work environment have an extremely hard time staying away from aggression because they are aware that this is the fuel of their job performance. An employee in this environment, who wants to adhere to noncompetitive behavior, will soon find himself sidetracked and void of any client portfolios.

It came as no surprise when, within a year after being interviewed, the Buddhist business leader exchanged his prestigious position in the finance industry for a much more cooperative work environment in spiritual books and music, where profits were still important, but not as critical as the financial world, and where the nature of his professional performance was much more in line with what is considered "right livelihood." It turned out that this business leader had been on the lookout for a new opportunity for quite some time, and felt fortunate when he could exit his hectic, high-pressure financial workplace.

Competition will never be eradicated in business, but it may become less aggressive as corporations find their niche and serve a specific customer base. Yet, just like the business leader described in this section, followers of Buddhist psychology may rather consider a nonprofit work environment, or one that does not focus on profit at any cost, performs morally and socially responsible, and delivers a product or service that is constructive to the wellbeing of others.

The Application of Bodhicitta

"The Sanskrit word Bodhi means awakening, and one who is awake is called a Buddha. Chitta [citta] means mind, heart, and spirit."[9] *Bodhicitta* could therefore be translated as a "spirit of awakening."[10]

138 A Closer Look at the Points of Caution

The Dalai Lama[11] regularly emphasizes that Buddhism holds the perspective that everyone was once our mother, father, brother, sister, or other loved one in a previous life. It is an established mindset within the Buddhist tradition that creates a sense of connection, tolerance, acceptance, gratitude, and even affection within those who accept it.[12] Why? Because when we consider that our colleague, customer, student, fellow customer in the store, neighbor, or even the stranger passing us by in the street, was once a dear one to us, we approach this individual with more kindness. Holding this consideration may enable us to develop a greater sense of compassion to all living beings.[13]

The problem this attitude may experience in contemporary work environments is that most people we encounter there don't harbor such gentle feelings toward one another. In fact, they often struggle with such low self-esteem and so little self-love that they can barely muster enough compassion of their own, let alone extend such gentleness to others. Their mental and emotional suffering is at such a level that they are constantly seeking to build up their ego with selfish behavior.[14] These people, which form a large part of our colleagues, customers, and others we encounter professionally, will compare themselves to others and compete all the time, trying to get rid of the enormous insecurities that trouble them. They are so busy doing that, that there is no space in their mental and emotional bandwidth to nourish compassion for others.[15]

Seen from the Buddhist practitioner's side, applying *Bodhicitta* may not go without unpleasant surprises either. Because people are so self-absorbed in many work environments, especially those that are highly bottom-line driven, there is little trust in a person who supports, cooperates, and embraces others selflessly. It may seem just too unreal, and since people see the world as a reflection of their own mind, others may distrust this behavior and think that the person performing *Bodhicitta* is "out to get them" or maintains a "hidden agenda." They may therefore either be on guard against this person and stay out of his way, or try to take advantage of this person,[16] because the Buddhist practitioner will most likely refrain from retaliation. Such nonresponsive behavior may be seen as demoralizing to the vigor in the workplace.

The Reality of Attaining Higher Consciousness

In life, we always have choices. When it comes to shaping our consciousness, we can also choose to either nurture it with love, compassion, joy, and equanimity, or fill it with senses of greed, hatred, ignorance, suspicion, and pride.[17] In this chapter, we refer to a consciousness based on senses of love, compassion, joy, and equanimity as a "higher consciousness." Choosing to maintain a higher level of consciousness is admirable, because it helps us see the interconnectedness and the mutual dependency of things so much clearer. It enables us to respect every effort, whether done at the executive level or the janitorial level, and it allows us to realize that one action is not more or less important than another, only because society or

A Closer Look at the Points of Caution **139**

a workplace labels it as such. However, all of this may not be very well understood in social environments, particularly those that are business related, because these environments are still very attached to and dictated by an "us versus them" mentality, which drives every decision. In these environments people are judged and ranked on basis of predetermined criteria in order to maintain a system that was set in place at the birth of our current societal performance system.

When considering this obvious dichotomy in the dominant mindsets of Buddhist psychology and conventional business performance, it is hard to imagine how a person adhering to the Buddhist mentality would care to stay in an aggression-driven business environment. The author of this book tried the higher consciousness approach in a previous workplace, and soon discovered that the resulting *Bodhicitta*, non-harming, more collaborative way of performing, resulted in mistrust from colleagues and supervisors, as they could not understand her motives, and suspected a hidden agenda. Moreover, colleagues started to expect increased coverage for their repeated absences, thus taking advantage of the mindset of selfless serving. Soon enough, the author decided to change workplaces and seek out a more entrepreneurial-based work setting with less chance of these situations to recur.

One often-overlooked effect of being seriously devoted to a "higher consciousness" is that the practitioner will focus on an all-encompassing sense of love to all living beings, and may lose focus on the immediate environment. The immediate result is loss of intimacy and togetherness with loved ones for the sake of serving a larger purpose. Using the examples of some major spirits that went before us, such as Buddha, Jesus, and in more recent times Gandhi, Mother Theresa, and Nelson Mandela: these individuals devoted themselves fully to a higher consciousness, and thereby distanced themselves from those closest to them in order to devote their efforts to a greater cause. While this is laudable for life on earth as a whole, it may weaken the intimacy at the personal level at the same time, and therefore cause suffering within the loved ones around this person.

The above-discussed principles of non-harming, equanimity, no competition, *Bodhicitta*, and higher consciousness are not to be seen as independent from one another: they are very much related and each other's cause and effect. A person who practices non-harming will not want to compete, because competition means harm to one of the competing parties. A person who practices equanimity (no cravings or aversions) will also not be prone to engage in competitive behavior, as there is nothing to strive for. A person who practices *Bodhicitta* (spirit of awakening) automatically respects non-harming, equanimity, no competition, and a higher consciousness.

While these behaviors or mindsets are presented in this chapter as "points of caution," it should be understood that this is only the case in light of business performance, but not in light of human performance overall. Business performance is just a part of the overall scheme in which we human beings operate. Within the overall scheme, the above senses are desperately needed to help us establish a better quality of life for a much larger cluster of living beings on earth.

140 A Closer Look at the Points of Caution

Some Additional Cautionary Notes on Buddhism and Work

Buddhism from a Religious Perspective

There is still a widespread tendency to perceive Buddhism as a religion, just like Christianity, Islam, Catholicism, or Hinduism. Indeed, as discussed in a previous chapter, there are people, especially from the Eastern traditions, but also many converts in the West, who consider Buddhism their religion. When considering this movement as such, the point of sensitivity emerges with flashing red lights. No one wants another person's or group's religion to be forced upon him or her. In workplaces particularly the exhibition of one religion, especially by leading individuals, can quickly create inhibitions among workers who maintain other beliefs, or counterintuitively, encourage them to openly start enforcing theirs. An aggressive manifestation of religious preferences could lead to alienation and the well-known and highly despised in- and out-group syndrome, where adherents to the leader's religion would become part of the in-group, and all others would remain in the out-group. Because of this awareness, managers should be particularly vigilant in advocating their religious preferences in the workplace. Those who adhere to Buddhism, even if they don't consider it a religion, should therefore be extremely mindful of the potential perceptions of others and the aversion this may provoke.

On the other hand, the twenty-first century has kindled a revived enthusiasm about religion in the United States. American society is known to be rather religious, with a higher emphasis in some parts of the country than in others. Overall, however, more than 90% of U.S. citizens believe in God or a higher power,[18] making this nation one of the most religious in the world.[19] When we bring the workplace into this scope, we can also detect a revival of religious prominence due to the crumbling of the tradition of keeping religion out of work environments.[20] This development can be explained as an immediate result of the increasing role of work in daily life, and the growing belief among U.S. workers that greed is the most important driver of U.S. business leaders. In addition, there is a blurred definition of what exactly religion is these days, which makes a response to the existing legal framework in the U.S. toward this growing and diversified tendency increasingly complicated.[21] Do we speak of religion when there is reverence of a god or multiple gods involved, or is it a common tendency toward wanting to do the right thing? Buddhism is not concerned with the concept or perceptions of a god, but is more concerned with living right, which makes this tradition a non-religion to those who adhere to the first consideration (presence of a god), and a religion to those who prefer the second (doing the right thing).

To make matters even more complicated, there is the growing popularity of *spirituality in the workplace*, bringing along broadly diverging perspectives from: a) entirely religious based to b) religious-induced, and even c) non-religious. The growing interest in the workplace spirituality movement has added to the confusion in perspectives on religion and its place in the U.S. workplace. With religion becoming more important at work, and work becoming an increasing part of Americans' lives, and with the overwhelming perspective of greed as a main driver of many U.S. business practices, workers are looking for a counter-balance against these developments.

Some authors believe that Buddhism might be better off and more readily accepted if it is not perceived as a religion, but more as a contemplative science.[22] These authors feel that religions, due to transfer over time and cultures, inevitably deviate from their initial purpose and often lead to violence. One only has to consider the longitudinal Israeli-Palestinian conflict, as well as a number of other religious-based clashes, to understand this point. These authors justify their pleas to cease labeling Buddhism as a religion by stating that: 1) Buddhism promotes thinking and contemplating before accepting, which is very unlike the general religious tendency to accept without thinking, and 2) Buddhism deviates from the us-versus-them mindset that lies at the foundation of many religions.[23] In addition, Buddhism, which entails a set of ethical principles and meditation, reveals valuable truths about the mind and the phenomenal world. Some of these truths are emptiness, selflessness, and impermanence. They are, however, not limited to "Buddhist" thinking.[24]

Perceived Manipulation of Buddhism

In a previous chapter, we briefly addressed the existing concern of some Buddhist scholars and followers that the Western implementation of this tradition increasingly deviates from the Eastern manifestation. We also stated at that time that the Dalai Lama took the high road in this matter by stating that flexibility is the strength that enabled Buddhism to stand the test of time, as it managed to reinvent itself in different cultures and eras. In this section, we will elaborate some more on the concerns that exist about Buddhism in the West. A number of concerned authors and followers of Buddhism[25] have stressed that Westerners have stripped Buddhism from its real purpose as a social religion, and modified it to their convenience into a solitary practice, away from traditional *sangha* settings and more leaning toward new-age mysticism. Some are worried that highly industrialized countries such as Japan and the United States are using Buddhism as a handy training tool to repress workers' dissatisfaction and distract attention from corporate malpractice.[26] They further assert that Buddhism, just like Christianity, has taught its followers to accept suffering when they should not. Particularly in Buddhism, they state, members perceive their suffering as the price they have to pay for wrongdoings from previous lives. When considered that way, the practice of Buddhism could lead to lethargic acceptance of suffering without proactive action toward improvement.[27]

There is also the concern that Buddhist psychology is too idealistic in that it only caters to a certain type of individual: the one with a higher level of intellectual

142 A Closer Look at the Points of Caution

development. This entails that the masses, with their limited levels of comprehension and resources, don't really benefit from this tradition, while those who have already reached a higher intellectual level utilize it to enhance their sense of social sensitivity.[28]

There is something to be said about the erroneous notion that suffering is something to be accepted as a karmic retaliation for wrongdoings in a previous life. A Tibetan Buddhist business leader in Dharamsala admitted that this notion exists among many people in India as well. This is unfortunate, however, since Buddhism is not intended to enhance lethargy, but rather to enforce the realization that one can improve his or her karma by engaging in actions toward advancement. The Buddhist leader stressed that it is every person's duty to improve his or her circumstances and, at the same time, those of others. "The Buddha was not [. . .] the life-denying pessimist that he is sometimes pictured to be, for he also saw the end of suffering through the cultivation of ethical behavior, meditation, and transcendent wisdom.".[29]

Summary

In this chapter we presented:

- The cautionary side of four of the strengths mentioned in chapter 8:
  - The fact that Buddhism supports personal responsibility will prevent the Buddhist practitioner from blaming others, which may invite those others to pin their mistakes onto that person, or eschew this person out of critical decision processes.
  - The fact that Buddhism promotes healthy detachment may lead to the practitioner being nonconfrontational and non-competitive, and others to demand all the opportunities.
  - The fact that Buddhism provokes greater collaboration, which may lead others to prey on the practitioner's generosity and compassion, and let him or her do all the work, while they may demand the credit.
  - The fact that Buddhism incites a wholesome view may cause the Buddhist practitioner not to be too concerned about minute issues at work, which can cause irritations among colleagues and supervisors.
- Some additional points of caution in applying Buddhist psychology in the workplace:
  - The Principle of Non-Harming (*Ahimsa*), which encourages us to see our connection to all other living beings, and therefore should not injure anyone. This would mean that we would also refrain from harming entities that can be harmful to our collective wellbeing.
    In business this would mean no competition, because in competition there is always some harm done to one or more involved parties. However, without competition, the entire spirit of business will cease to exist.

A Closer Look at the Points of Caution **143**

- The principle of equanimity (no cravings and no aversions), which provides us with inner balance. Equanimity is hard to find in work environments where it's all about striving, outperforming others, and continuously being exposed to cravings and aversions.
  In business this principle will be hard to digest because it instigates a lack of desire to be ambitious and achieve anything stellar.
- The principle of no competition, which may bring us internal peace at the personal level, but may not be received well in work environments either, especially when there is a dynamic undertone of performance at play.
  In business, no competition would equal going out of business, because the very nature of business is to compete and outperform others.
- The Application of *Bodhicitta* (spirit of awakening), which reminds us to see everyone as our mother from a previous life. In contemporary workplaces, this embracing mindset is poorly understood and even less appreciated, because people, especially in Western based workplaces, have a "me versus you" mentality.
  In business the *Bodhicitta* mindset may lead to being taken advantage of, and/or being excluded from important decision making processes.
- The reality of attaining higher consciousness, which promotes a sense of love, compassion, joy, and equanimity. Unfortunately, the world of work is more driven by greed, hatred, ignorance, suspicion, and pride.
  In business the actions driven by a higher consciousness may not be trusted, and the practitioner may find that it is better to look for work in a less competitive, or possibly nonprofit environment.
- The principles of non-harming, equanimity, no competition, *Bodhicitta*, and higher consciousness, are very much related and each other's cause and effect. For instance, a person who practices non-harming will not want to compete, because competition means harm to one of the competing parties.
- While these mindsets are presented in this chapter as "points of caution," they are laudable in human performance overall. They are needed to help us establish a better quality of life for a much larger cluster of living beings on earth.

Questions

1. In the introductory part of the chapter, the statement is made that strong qualities can become weaknesses, while weak qualities can become strengths, depending on how we use them. Examples that are given are perseverance, usually seen as a strong quality, that can degenerate into persistence that is a true strain for all parties involved, and risk-taking, which is usually seen as dangerous, but that we engage in all the time in the decisions we make. Think of one strong quality that can become a weakness, and one weak or dangerous

144 A Closer Look at the Points of Caution

quality that can become a strength. Please include your reasoning for these statements.

2. Four of the five advantages mentioned in chapter 8 are briefly reviewed in the beginning of the chapter, and some potential points of caution for these four advantages are mentioned. The advantages are: 1) personal responsibility, 2) healthy detachment, 3) greater collaboration, and 4) a wholesome view. Based on what you have read and your own reflections afterward, which of these four advantages has the greatest potential for problems in professional work environments, and why?

3. The principle of non-harming (*Ahimsa*) is discussed as an enlightened Buddhist principle, but one that can cause setbacks in business environments because it may create inhibitions in regards to the will to compete with others. Reflect on *Ahimsa* at the personal level: how could it be an impediment for you in business performance, and how could it be helpful?

4. The chapter mentioned the Buddhist concept of equanimity (no cravings and no aversions) as a potential problem in business performance. Do you agree or disagree with the stance presented in this chapter? Please share your insights in about 200 words.

5. In the final statements, the author asserts that the reviewed principles of non-harming, equanimity, no competition, *Bodhicitta*, and higher consciousness should not merely be seen as "points of caution" because they are laudable in human performance overall. Please select any two of these principles and discuss how, in your opinion, can these principles be beneficial to all life on earth?

Notes

1 Hugo, V. (n.d.). Perseverance, Secret of all Triumphs. Retrieved on November 30, 2013 from www.brainyquote.com/quotes/quotes/v/victorhugo398755.html

2 Twain, M. (n.d.). Perseverance. Retrieved on November 30, 2013 from www.twainquotes.com/Perseverance.html

3 Marques, J. (2012). The Resurgence of Human Values in Today's Organizations: Pointers From the Buddha. *Development and Learning in Organizations, 26*(1), 5–7.

4 Ibid.

5 Darwin, C. (2003). *The Origin of Species: 150th Anniversary Edition*. Signet Classics, Penguin Group, New York, NY.

6 Dawkins, R. (2005). *The Ancestor's Tale: A Pilgrimage to the Dawn of Evolution*. Mariner Books, Houghton Mifflin, New York, NY.

7 Richmond, L. (1999). *Work as a Spiritual Practice: A Practical Buddhist Approach to Inner Growth and Satisfaction on the Job*. Broadway Books, New York, NY.

8 Covey, S. (2004). *The 7 Habits of Highly Effective People: Powerful Lessons in Personal Change*. Free Press, Simon & Schuster, New York, NY.

9 Wallace, B. A. (2001). *Buddhism with an Attitude: The Tibetan Seven-Point Mind Training*. Snow Lion Publications, Ithaca NY,: p. 65.

10 Ibid.

11 His Holiness The Fourteenth Dalai Lama (1978). *Activating Bodhichitta and a Meditation on Compassion* (trans. Gonsar Rinpoche). Library of Tibetan Works and Archives, Dharamsala, India.

12 Kernochan, R. A., McCormick, D. W., & White, J. A. (2007). Spirituality and the Management Teacher: Reflections of Three Buddhists on Compassion, Mindfulness, and Selflessness in the Classroom. *Journal of Management Inquiry, 16*(1), 61–74.

13 Barad, J. (2007). The Understanding and Experience of Compassion: Aquinas and the Dalai Lama. *Buddhist-Christian Studies, 27*, 11–29.

14 Ibid.

15 Ibid.

16 Richmond, L. (1999). *Work as a Spiritual Practice: A Practical Buddhist Approach to Inner Growth and Satisfaction on the Job.* Broadway Books, New York, NY.

17 Thich Nhat Hanh (1998). *The Heart of the Buddha's Teaching: Transforming Suffering into Peace, Joy, and Liberation.* Broadway Books, New York, NY.

18 Morgan, J. F. (2005). In Defense of the Workplace Religious Freedom Act: Protecting the Unprotected Without Sanctifying the Workplace. *Labor Law Journal, 56*(1), 68–71.

19 Morgan, J. F. (2004). How Should Business Respond to a More Religious Workplace? *S.A.M. Advanced Management Journal, 69*(4), 11–19.

20 Morgan, J. F. (2005). Religion at Work: A Legal Quagmire. *Managerial Law, 47*(3/4), 247–259.

21 Ibid.

22 Harris, S. (2006). Killing the Buddha. *Shambhala Sun.* Retrieved on November 15, 2008 from www.shambhalasun.com/index.php?option=com_content&task=view&id =2903&Itemid=0; Arellano, J. T. (2006). *Why Buddhism? The Evil of Religion.* Trafford Publishing, Victoria, British Columbia.

23 Ibid.

24 Harris, S. (2006). Killing the Buddha. *Shambhala Sun.* Retrieved on November 15, 2008 from www.shambhalasun.com/index.php?option=com_content&task=view&id =2903&Itemid=0

25 Crabtree, V. (2004). Criticism of Buddhism. *Vexen Crabtree.* Retrieved on May 2, 2014 from www.vexen.co.uk/religion/buddhism_criticism.html; Fields, R. (1998). Divided Dharma: White Buddhists, Ethnic Buddhists, and Racism. In C. S. Prebish & K. K. Tanaka (Eds.), *The Faces of Buddhism in America.* University of California Press, Berkeley and Los Angeles, pp. 196–206; Nattier, J. (1997). Buddhism Comes to Main Street. *The Wilson Quarterly, 21*(2), 72–80; Numrich, P. D. (2003). Two Buddhisms Further Considered. *Contemporary Buddhism, 4*(1), 55–78.

26 Crabtree, V. (2004). Criticism of Buddhism. *Vexen Crabtree.* Retrieved on May 2, 2014 from www.vexen.co.uk/religion/buddhism_criticism.html

27 Ibid.

28 Ibid.

29 Coleman, J. W. (2002). *The New Buddhism: The Western Transformation of an Ancient Tradition.* Oxford University Press, New York: p. 5.

10

BUDDHIST BUSINESS LEADERS IN ACTION

There is no path to happiness: happiness is the path.

Buddha

Three Leaders, One Mindset

In the past decades, Buddhism has made important strides in the Western world, as was explained in earlier chapters. The very reason that this book was written is an indication that interest in Buddhism is on the rise, whether it is seen as a religion, a science, a philosophy, or a psychology. As a human community, we are exposed more than ever to different cultures and traditions, and become curious about them. The fact that the Dalai Lama and a number of other prominent Buddhist scholars-leaders, such as Thich Nhat Hanh, Bhante Henepola Gunaratana, Geshe Kelsang Gyatso, Bhikkhu Bodhi, Matthieu Ricard, and so many more, travel around the world and appear on forums and media to share their enlightened insights, has also contributed to the increased interest in Buddhism. Today, we find well-known Buddhists in many disciplines. They are authors, such as Jack Kornfield, Robert Thurman, and Alan Watts; politicians and political activists such as U Thant, the third Secretary General of the United Nations; musicians such as Leonard Cohen, k.d. Lang, Courtney Love, Herbie Hancock, and Tina Turner; actors such as Richard Gere, Jet Li, and Sharon Stone; poets such as Allen Ginsberg; and business leaders such as Steve Jobs, who practiced Zen Buddhism before he passed away in 2011.

Indeed, individuals from a wide variety of backgrounds and professional settings become enamored with the Buddhist psychology, and decide to start practicing it. Some become devout followers, and others decide to only adopt elements that they feel comfortable implementing. Regardless of what they choose, however, we can now find business leaders adhering to Buddhist practices in various environments. In this chapter, we present the findings of interviews we conducted with four Buddhist business leaders across three businesses: three American and one Tibetan in India. While these leaders' names will be withheld, their work environments will be described to provide a clear mental picture of their daily whereabouts.

The Finance Expert

In chapter 9, we briefly referred to this leader when discussing the competitive mindset that is so steadfast in the U.S. business environment, especially when large sums of money are involved. Competition occurs in multiple layers: between corporations, between departments, and between employees. At the time we interviewed this Buddhist business leader, to be referred to from here on as Craig (not his real name), he performed as President and Chief Operating Officer at a prominent financial institution in California. The fact that Craig had been with this company for over a decade may demonstrate that he was seasoned in this volatile environment.

Helpful Buddhist Practices

Craig explained that his Buddhist background had been very helpful in keeping him sober and reasonable throughout his high-stress career. Thanks to his vivid awareness of some critical Buddhist principles such as interdependence, impermanence, and karma, he could keep himself involved, yet not excessively attached. He maintained his clear perspectives through daily meditations and reading of Buddhist literature. Craig explained that the meditation and the books, as well as regular meetings and dialogues with other Buddhists, helped him to keep his priorities in order.

In the financial workplace, you have employees who handle portfolios of different sizes. There is a continuous competition going on in the workplace, and it is not always possible to keep the peace at the level that he would like it. However, we all know that such is the case in financial environments with immense capital flows. Tension occurs in every setting where people interact on a daily basis. Conflict can be both constructive and destructive. Through the years, Craig had become capable of distinguishing between constructive and destructive conflicts in his workplace, and dealt with these phenomena in different ways. He intervened in the constructive conflict cases, which led to betterment for all parties, and he ensured a swift discontinuation of destructive conflicts. And yes, sometimes he had to be direct and even radical to keep any potential damage to a minimum. This means that he sometimes had to explain matters in tough wording to employees that were trying to create and fuel toxicity among coworkers. Occasionally, he even had to fire an employee.

148 Buddhist Business Leaders in Action

While Craig admitted that such actions were hard to digest, he also explained that he only applied them when his repeated efforts to resolve the problem in less drastic ways had failed. He pointed back to his daily meditation, which helped him release negative baggage acquired through the day, and cleanse his mind for the next day. His meditations had also ignited another quality that he was grateful for: the ability to detect senses of defensiveness and other resentful emotions within, so that he could address those before they would reach proportions that would be difficult to manage. What this means is that he did get affected by the negative emotions that sometimes emerge when people work together, but that he was quick to face and disarm them.

One of the emotions Craig mentioned was fear: people always deal with this emotion to some degree, whether it is fear of losing a lucrative deal, fear of losing your job, or fear of losing a valuable customer. Yet, while fear was not an unfamiliar territory to him, he could face it thanks to his three powerful sources: his meditation, his books, and his Buddhist buddies, with whom he could deliberate in peace and comfort until the negative emotion had subsided.

Effects on Stakeholders

One of the major sources of joy for Craig was the apparent effect he had on his employees. He explained that it was more valuable to him when an employee told him that he felt more peaceful thanks to their work relationship than when he had closed a huge financial deal. While some leaders might consider the latter more important, Craig felt that rewarding relationships were so much more meaningful in the end. He emphasized, however, that he was highly cautious about giving anyone the feeling that he was trying to persuade them to follow his footsteps into Buddhist psychology. While he appreciated the positive feedback, he made it a point not to solicit more information about his balanced performance than asked.

Craig was able to make an important change in his workplace, thanks to his Buddhist background. He made his employees aware of their blessing to work in such a well-paying environment and invited them to join him in a project of giving back to the community. He had lobbied with the rest of his company's strategic managers that the company would match any donation effort from employees. The project became a big hit! As employees started giving, they increasingly became aware of how good it felt to engage in social projects, especially when supported by their employer.

Craig found his Buddhist background to be helpful in dealing with disgruntled customers. He explained that he had learned to make people aware of the suffering they were imposing upon themselves by being so upset. Whenever an angry customer landed in his office, he would invite them to sit, offered them some tea, and listened to their tirade. When it was his turn to speak, he told the customer that he understood their anger, but that he also wanted to point out that the anger made them suffer: a negative emotion that they would most likely take home with them, and project in traffic and at home, to people who did not have anything to do with it. Without using Buddhist related words, he gently made the upset customer aware of the negative effects of their anger to themselves, and gradually succeeded in calming their moods. Most of the time, the customers would leave Craig's office in a much calmer mental state, and much more aware of the importance of their behavior and thoughts to their wellbeing.

Perceived Pros and Cons

When reflecting on his management style, Craig explained that he had three focus points: 1) making his work a pleasurable experience, 2) respecting all stakeholders, and 3) keeping unpleasant surprises to a minimum.

Regarding point 1, making work a pleasurable experience, Craig focused particularly on junior employees, who still had to make their way in the unpredictable financial work environment. He tried to get to know these younger employees and empower them so that they would not get discouraged, but become zestful and convinced that they had what it took to succeed. He was very aware that engaging with employees resulted in a more pleasant work environment with employees who were smiling more often, feel more appreciated, and ultimately, performed better.

Regarding point 2, respecting all stakeholders, Craig referred to the time he set aside to personally meet with displeased customers, and ensure that they left calmer and happier than when they entered, but also the various projects he engaged in with his employees to benefit them as well as the community in which their company were located.

Regarding point 3, keeping unpleasant surprises to a minimum, Craig was mainly referring to the nature of the industry in which he worked. Such a workplace is involved with numerous financial transactions, and temptation for fraud and deception is extremely high, as well as the chance of making a mistake. Therefore, Craig considered it very important to keep communicating to his employees how important honesty was. He preferred them to admit a mistake early on, instead of hoping it wouldn't be detected and then have it snowball into a much bigger problem.

The more difficult part of Craig's work, in his opinion, was laying people off. As stated earlier, he was well aware that he sometimes had to be drastic in firing someone who had been impossible to work with, even after repeated dialogues and reprimands. While this is never a pleasant thing to do, Craig had learned to deal with it. What he considered really hard was to let good people go, due to fluctuations in the industry, which required release of part of the workforce.

> What is not easy is when you have to do what we had to do, which was laying off people due to circumstantial issues. They were doing their job; it was not because they didn't come in; it was not because they didn't ask

150 Buddhist Business Leaders in Action

> for permission; it was just because we had to cut expenses. The revenues were down and we had to cut expenses. That's not fun. I feel like the messenger of death in those situations, I don't like that, because I feel that, as senior management, we have a responsibility to look out for the employees as one looks out for children. You want to run the business responsibly: yes you want to grow, yes you want a bigger bottom line, but you need to be responsible and aware of what risk can come along that might put the house on fire and put people out on the street. [. . .] I don't like firing people. I feel it's a failure from the manager's side if you can't get people to do what they're supposed to do. But when you have a large number of people there will always be some that fall off.

Craig also explained one of the complexities of being a leader: the fact that you sometimes find yourself dealing with a toxic employee, who demoralizes the entire department, but performs so well for the company that it is irresponsible to let him or her go. He admitted that this would stretch his endurance and take a high toll on his Buddhist beliefs, because he was very well aware how much suffering it meant for other employees to keep this toxic coworker on board, only because of financial performance.

Providing a general view on contemporary work environments, Craig expressed a major concern as seen through his Buddhist lenses: the sense of entitlement that so many corporate workers seem to have today. In his many years as president and COO, he saw employees coming on board and starting to demand promotions and raises within a short time, simply because they were showing up to work, and not because of anything extraordinary in their performance.

> The thing that's wrong now is the sense of entitlement that a lot of workers have gained, and I mean entitlement in its negative sense here, where they feel they're entitled to something merely because they exist, and not because they are contributing to a team, and not because they understand and embrace the mission of the group, but simply because they're here. There was a guy once who was working here for two years in the trading department, on the track to move up. The senior traders make a lot of money here. This young man had an attitude problem. He just wasn't fitting in, but wasn't going anywhere. He just held a clerk type level job. And I remember that his manager came in saying that the young man wanted to talk to me, because he was not happy where he was. He came in and said, "I've been here two years (as if that's a long time), and I know what the people around me are making." I said, "Really? And so what is it that makes you think you deserve to make the same? Because you're sitting there?" He answered, "Yes, I've been sitting there and doing my job." I said, "Well, you haven't been doing your job well enough. Now go out and talk to your manager and ask him what it is that he wants you to do now, because if you

don't want to do that, there is not going to be a tomorrow." I wasn't happy with him. He left soon. That was no loss.

Craig felt that the attitude this employee displayed was a perfect example of the sense of entitlement that we are seeing in so many workplaces today. He felt that this is a destructive attitude that only contributes to the dissatisfaction about which so many people are complaining. He referred to this sense of entitlement as the "me" epidemic. Too many people are infected with "me," and among this crowd we find a lot of corporate managers and leaders as well. Rather than embracing a sense of spirituality and an understanding of collective progress, Craig stated, they are only concerned with their own advancement, and most of the time at the expense of others. He further stated that, when taking a hard look at himself, he had to admit that he was a much better leader today than he was 20 years ago, because he had now realized that leaders and managers largely determine the performance of their employees. Employees are reflections of how they are treated. If we treat them with compassion and understanding, they will very likely reciprocate that. If we treat them harshly and selfishly, they will also return that to us. Leaders and managers are like parents. Craig asserted that there are no bad children, only bad parents. Similarly, there are no bad employees, only bad managers and leaders.

Through this statement, Craig underscored the greater sense of responsibility in Buddhist leaders, which was mentioned in chapter 7.

The Marketing Team

The next Buddhist business performer is actually a team: husband and wife, running a small marketing and advertising company in Kansas. We shall refer to them here as Jim and Jenny (not their real names). Jim founded the company as a part-time business about 14 years ago, and ran it as a sole proprietorship. However, the business grew, and Jim left his previous job to devote all his time to his venture. He started hiring employees, and while the company remained rather small, the team started taking on larger projects. At the time of our interview, Jim's wife, Jenny, had entered the business as well, and along with a team of 20 full-time employees, they had a nice synergy going on.

Employee Ownership

Jim and Jenny attributed their good fortune with this business to several factors, first and foremost their strong team. Each employee was responsible for a set of portfolios, which provided a great sense of responsibility and ownership. This sense of responsibility seemed to provide the employees with a greater sense of dignity and job satisfaction, as they maintained direct contact with their clients, and did not feel as if they were micro-managed. Jim and Jenny were very careful to refrain from doing that, and granted all employees their space.

152 Buddhist Business Leaders in Action

Jim and Jenny also learned that the consultant-based approach encouraged employees to think more creatively, and come up with new ways to serve their clients better. Another major advantage of this hands-off approach was that employees delivered better projects at a faster rate, which increased client satisfaction.

A major part of this company's success is undoubtedly its small size: everyone knows one another, and there is a close bond at all times. Each of the employees was instrumental in formulating the mission they adhere to. Their mission is "To have a positive impact on each other, our customers, our community, and our world."

The Revival Room

Shortly after joining the company, Jenny designed a mental health room on the working premises. She named it "the Revival Room," and it enables employees to take breaks throughout the day for prayer, meditation, a brief nap, or just a quiet time of doing nothing. Jim and Jenny ensured that the room would not be associated with any religion or ideology, so that employees of any background or conviction would feel comfortable in it. And since the small team consisted of a variety of backgrounds, this was highly appreciated.

We asked Jim and Jenny whether such a room would not lead to a decline in employees' performance, because they now had a legitimate room to rest multiple times through the day. The couple responded that such was definitely not the case. In fact it was rather the opposite. Employees now had an opportunity to regenerate their energy after a stressful experience, and return to their projects after a while with much more enthusiasm than they did before. Having this "Revival Room" actually led to a revival in many projects, because employees were now even more creative than before, and made more rewarding decisions.

Morale, Performance, and General Wellbeing

Another advantage of such a small work team, according to Jim and Jenny, was the fact that there was much spontaneous interaction among team members, leading them to encourage and support each other in their projects. Similar to Craig, Jim and Jenny also proposed a charity-match project, in which the company matched up to $500 annually to each employee's preferred social project. In addition, the team votes every quarter on a common social project they will support, and then get two paid days off to volunteer for that cause.

Morale, performance, and general wellbeing have increased in Jim and Jenny's small venture, and the turnover has been extremely low. While this marketing and advertising company is still a for-profit entity, money has not been allowed to become the sole driver of all actions. Therefore, the general wellness of employees has not suffered, and harming is avoided.

The Monk-Manager

In the Indian state of Himachal Pradesh, there is a city called Dharamsala, where a Tibetan community has lived in exile since 1959. About 80,000 Tibetan refugees reside there, among whom are a number of highly esteemed Buddhist monks and the Dalai Lama. The business leader we interviewed in Dharamsala was also a highly venerated monk: a *geshe*, to whom we will refer from here on as "Lobsang" (Tibetan for "noble-minded"). This *geshe* had worked closely with the Dalai Lama for many years, and was now managing one of the premium ventures within the Tibetan community in exile. The organization was nonprofit in set-up, but still required meticulous planning, leading, organizing, and controlling, as is common in any undertaking.

Compassion and Social Involvement

In observing Lobsang's interactions, it became clear that he was well-respected and loved by his employees and members of the community, who frequently came by. He was a busy man, involved with many more business transactions than just running the nonprofit, for which he formally performed as director. Throughout his activities one thing stood out: his social awareness. Every morning, a number of young Indian men and women would arrive and ask for work, and he would assign them jobs in local building projects that he was supervising.

While he was not in a position to grant them continued employment, he kept the option open for them to come by and find out what was available as the opportunity arose. The social structure in his part of the world was very different than the one in the United States, and local poverty, especially among the Indian population, was high, while job security was slim. Lobsang's attitude was one of social involvement without judging how things became as they were, or who was at fault for it. Within his means, he did what he could, and rejoiced in that.

Availability and a Positive Mindset

Lobsang's office was on the third floor of the building, but he rarely sat in it. He practiced MBWA, management by wandering around, and frequently stopped to have a talk with coworkers, visitors, and delivery people. It seemed as if he was so balanced that he never got angry, but when asked about it he admitted otherwise: of course he was getting angry, he stated, he just didn't dwell on his anger, because he did not want it to become a negative habit. He made it a point to meditate and study daily, so that his awareness level about the impermanent nature of everything remained intact. He stated that internal, negative emotions are worse enemies than other people. Presenting the Chinese invasion of Tibet as an example, Lobsang clarified that many people see the Chinese as the enemies of the Tibetans, but in fact the negative emotions that people hold about this subject are worse

154 Buddhist Business Leaders in Action

enemies than anyone. Negative emotions are enemies, very near to us. They have an immediate effect on us, as opposed to physical enemies that are rarely around us. Our negative emotions make us bewildered, confused, silly, blind, and ignorant, so we have to get rid of them when we feel them emerging. The more we face our mental enemies, the better we become at getting rid of them, and the easier it becomes to release our anger, spite, despair, disappointment, pride, or other mental afflictions.

Lobsang reflected on the fact that there are so many people in the world, who were once beloved colleagues, close friends, or trusted family members, but who allowed negative emotions to drive a wedge between them, and stopped talking to each other for months, sometimes for years, or even for the rest of their lives. This was why he refused to hold grudges of any kind, and instead preferred to shake hands immediately after an argument.

Common Practices

There are some important common factors to be distinguished in the behaviors and statements of the Buddhist business leaders described in this chapter.

- *Relationships over the bottom line*: Based on their awareness of foundational Buddhist principles such as impermanence, interdependence, and karma, they focused more on their relationships with others than on the bottom line.
- *Collaboration*: They nurtured a sense of involvement among their workforce by engaging in collaborative projects, or regularly mingling with employees, customers, and visitors.
- *Social awareness and charity*: Craig and the couple Jim and Jenny had introduced the idea of charity projects, to be proposed by employees and matched by the company, while Lobsang involved less fortunate community members in daily projects to help them survive.
- *Stress reduction*: The leaders were aware that stress was part of the work environment, and embedded constructive strategies in resolving problem situations: Craig invited disappointed or disgruntled customers or employees in his office for constructive dialogues; Jim and Jenny built a revival room to enable coworkers to regain their enthusiasm for their work through the day, and Lobsang shook hands after confrontations, so that commotions in relationships would swiftly be addressed and restored.
- *Responsibility and ownership*: Each of the leaders nurtured their employees' sense of responsibility by leaving them ample space to perform. Craig's employees were handling financial portfolios and had a chance to make progress on the basis of their performance and service; Jim and Jenny's coworkers handled marketing project portfolios and enjoyed the sense of ownership therein; and Lobsang's coworkers could always find him if they needed anything, but were not overwhelmed by any kind of continuous micro-management.

- *Meditation and mindfulness*: Each of these leaders were aware of the advantages of meditation as a path toward practicing mindfulness.
- *Embracing others while staying true to values*: Each of these leaders shared his or her Buddhist principles at work, but refrained from applying them intrusively. Rather, they presented their values in secular ways, so that people from different cultures and traditions would feel at ease.

Figure 10.1 highlights the above-explained common practices of the interviewed Buddhist business leaders.

When considering the behaviors of the Buddhist business leaders described in this chapter, it becomes apparent that their practices are not an inhibition to the performance of their work, but rather an advantage. Indeed, ultimate wealth may come to them at a slower pace, but overall satisfaction, connectivity, and gratification are high. Besides, these business leaders did not have a problem with making money. They just tried to ensure that in the process few living beings were harmed as possible. They kept calibrating their behaviors and driving motives, because they wanted to engage in right livelihood. In fact, they wanted to ensure that they remained aware of the essence of the Buddha's teachings, the Four Noble Truths (suffering exists, has an origin, can be ended, and there is a path to do so), and as part of that, the

FIGURE 10.1 Common practices of Buddhist business leaders

156 Buddhist Business Leaders in Action

Noble Eightfold Path, entailing right view, right intention, right speech, right action, right livelihood, right effort, right mindfulness, and right concentration.

This became even more apparent when, not even a year after this interview, Craig said farewell to the hectic, die-hard financial world in order to follow the Noble Eightfold Path more closely. He immersed himself in a livelihood that was much more spiritually attuned, working as a global leader in delivering products and services in health, wellness, and spiritual practices.

This, then, may serve as a proper endnote: people who seriously engage in Buddhist psychology will reflect regularly on their actions, thoughts, motives, and other behaviors, and continuously refine their awareness. They aim to adhere to the foundational Buddhist principles as mentioned above. While it may take time, they eventually gravitate to environments that may be less lucrative, but are in harmony with their beliefs.

The Seven-Point Mind Training

In several of the earlier chapters we mentioned Vipassana meditation as a secular way of attaining peace of mind, deeper insight in life, and possibly, an enlightened view. As a final, but highly useful step, we would like to review an equally effective and reputable Tibetan-based instrument, known as the Seven-Point Mind Training, which also has high appeal among meditation practitioners.

Alan Wallace, a well-known American Buddhist practitioner and author, and Geshe Jampa Tegchok, a highly respected Tibetan monk, author, and global teacher, explain the Seven-Point Mind Training in several of their books. The tradition of the Seven-Point Mind Training can be traced back to Atīśa, an eleventh-century Buddhist teacher from the Pala Empire in Bengal, who was highly instrumental in spreading Mahayana Buddhism in Asia and promoted Buddhist thought from Tibet to Sumatra. Atīśa received the teachings of the Seven-Point Mind Training from Serlingpa, also a renowned Buddhist teacher, who lived in Sumatra in the tenth century. The Seven-Point Mind Training has therefore been confirmed to date back to at least 1,000 years ago.[1] The earliest written version of this training came from Chekawa Yeshe Dorje, in the twelfth century.[2]

The Seven-Point Mind Training has been reported as being very powerful. Even a small, partial instruction can be very effective in eliminating our selfishness. It therefore surpasses all other kinds of teachings in that regards.[3] The training entails the following seven steps:

1. Training in the preliminaries. In this stage we should reflect on four thoughts that turn the mind toward higher goals and better focused priorities:
    1. The value and preciousness of human life, in order to understand the gift of having a body and all the opportunities it provides;
    2. Death and impermanence, in order to understand the fickleness of everything including ourselves;

Buddhist Business Leaders in Action **157**

3. The unsatisfactory nature of the cycle of existence, in which the practitioner enhances his or her awareness of *samsara*, the cycle of rebirth, and all the suffering it brings; and

4. Karma, which is the Sanskrit word for "action."[4] Reflecting on karma alerts us to the long-term consequences of our actions.

2. Cultivating ultimate and relative *Bodhicitta*. While we explained *Bodhicitta* before, here is a brief reminder: *Bodhi* is a Sanskrit word that means awakening. One who is awake is called a Buddha. *Citta* means mind, heart, and spirit. *Bodhicitta* could therefore be translated as "a spirit of awakening."[5] Ultimate *Bodhicitta* pertains to the nature of reality and insight into reality. Relative *Bodhicitta* is the compassionate and altruistic dimension of practice.

Thrangu Rinpoche, a highly esteemed Tibetan Buddhist scholar, presents some useful steps in the training of ultimate and relative *Bodhicitta*.

- Toward the attainment of ultimate *Bodhicitta*, we should
  - consider all things and perceptions as dreams,
  - seek for the consciousness we had before we were born,
  - release even the remedy,
  - settle in the nature of our basic cognition,
  - between meditations, we should consider everything, even ourselves, as an illusion.
- Toward relative *Bodhicitta*, we should
  - train ourselves to give (or send) and take, and use our breath to maintain that focus. For example, breathing in could become an acceptance of the negativity and sadness of the world, and breathing out could become a sharing of your blessing to all existence.
  - observe and understand your attachments, aversions, and indifferences,
  - in all your activities, train with maxims,
  - begin the sequence of giving and taking with yourself (accept yourself as you are).[6]

3. Transforming adversity into an aid to spiritual awakening. Through this point, we learn to integrate Dharma (the Buddha's teaching) into the good and bad parts of life. Suffering is no longer avoided or rejected but used as a pathway to awakening. Self-centeredness is unmasked as the source of all evil, and the focus shifts to the kindness of others.

There are several ways in which we can transform adverse conditions into a path of awakening.

- When everything looks grim, see it as an opportunity to wake up.
- Do not blame others, but seek all faults within yourself.
- Remain grateful to everyone.
- Confusion is unreal, so there is no need to become concerned.
- Approach all things, including the unexpected, with meditation.[7]

4. A synthesis of practice for one life. Within this step lies the practice of maintaining alertness on ultimate and relative *Bodhicitta*, familiarizing the mind

158 Buddhist Business Leaders in Action

with possible tragedy, remaining devoted to spiritual practice, rejection of self-grasping and self-centeredness, and staying true to spiritual awakening.

This section of the Seven-Point Mind training is also known as an invitation to work with the "Five Forces," which are

1. Being intense and committed.
2. Getting familiar with what you want to do and be.
3. Distinguish between the seeds you choose to plant in your mind.
4. Turning away entirely from ego trips.
5. Devoting the fruits of your efforts to the wellbeing of all.[8]

If we practice these "Five Forces," we will not have any regrets and be prepared for death at any time.[9]

5. The criterion of proficiency in the mind training. This point explains the conditions for assessing our progress in spiritual practice. It focuses on one aim: releasing the sense of self-grasping entirely, as this is the source of all problems.

    Critical considerations at this stage:
    - All teachings are focused on the same ultimate goal.
    - Consider both perspectives, the internal and the external one, and go for the internal.
    - Always maintain a happy frame of mind.
    - Keep on practicing, even when you get distracted.[10]

6. The pledges of the mind training. This step alerts us on a number of behaviors to avoid: dismissal of vows, dangerous situations to practice mind training, and restricting mind-training to good times alone. It calls for moderate behavior, even after spiritual awakening; abstinence of negative speech about—or judgment of others; releasing focus on rewards of any kind; avoiding poisonous food; refraining from self-righteous thinking, malice, sarcasm, mean-spiritedness, overbearing of others, self-flattery, pretense, disrespect of enlightened beings, and thriving on others' misfortune.

    In Thrangu Rinpoche's words, these are the commitments of the Mind Training:

    1. Always observe the three basic principles, which are
        a. Practicing regularly.
        b. Not wasting time on unimportant things.
        c. Refraining from defending and rationalizing our mistakes.[11]
    2. Change your attitude, but keep your authenticity.
    3. Don't judge or discuss others' shortcomings.
    4. Don't infringe on others' affairs.
    5. Work first on your biggest shortcomings.
    6. Don't hope for any results.
    7. Avoid poisonous food.
    8. Don't be excessively consistent.
    9. Don't engage or entertain yourself in spiteful gossip.

Buddhist Business Leaders in Action **159**

10. Don't set traps for others.
11. Don't make matters painful.
12. Don't transfer an ox's burden onto a cow.
13. Don't compete with others.
14. Don't be a snitch (don't be mean toward or tell on others).
15. Don't turn gods into demons (don't make good things go bad).
16. Don't thrive on others' misfortune.[12]

7. The guidelines of the mind training. This point provides ethical guidance in developing strength of purpose and purity such as continued maintenance of *Bodhicitta* (awakened mind); continued practice of Dharma in good and bad times; alertness and swift dismissal of mental afflictions; attaining proper guidance and remaining true to the practice.

The following recommendations are useful:
1. Keep a single focus in all your actions.
2. Treat all adversities in a positive way.
3. Remain committed from beginning to end.
4. Accept good and bad with patience.
5. Guard (be cautious with) both, even at risk of your life.
6. Practice the three difficult points: a) identifying your neurotic tendencies, b) overcoming them, and c) transcending them.
7. Acquire the three primary resources: a) finding a teacher, b) taming the wandering mind, and c) engaging in a lifestyle that enables practicing.
8. Appreciate your teacher, enjoy your practice, and maintain your devotion.
9. Keep your body, mind, and spirit focused on the path.
10. Practice equally in all areas: devoted and continuous practice is critical.
11. Consistently meditate on whatever upsets you.
12. Don't depend on external circumstances.
13. Focus on the most meaningful issues.
14. Don't let your emotions derail you.
15. Be consistent in your practice.
16. Train with your whole heart.
17. Liberate yourself by watching and analyzing.
18. Don't take yourself too seriously.
19. Don't lose your temper.
20. Stay focused.
21. Don't crave any recognition.[13]

Figure 10.2 presents the Seven-Point Mind Training at a glance.

The Seven-Point Mind Training is obviously not something we will perform in one simple sitting. Once devoted to the training, it becomes a way of living, with practices that become our nature, thus determining our behavior from day to day, minute to minute, among others and when alone, and under all circumstances.

160 Buddhist Business Leaders in Action

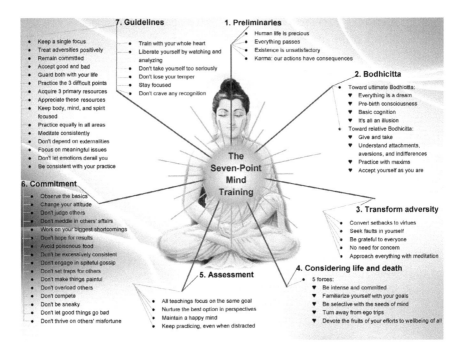

FIGURE 10.2 The Seven-Point Mind Training

Summary

In this chapter we presented:

- Observations of four Buddhist business leaders across three businesses: three American and one Tibetan in India. Each of the leaders worked in a different industry: one president at a major financial consortium, the second, a couple, had founded their own small marketing business, and the third managed a nonprofit organization.
  - *The Finance Expert* explained that his Buddhist background had kept him sober and reasonable throughout the high stress of his work. Thanks to his awareness of some critical Buddhist principles such as interdependence, impermanence, and karma, he could keep himself involved, yet not excessively attached. Dealing with strong senses of ambition and sometimes even greed, he became experienced in positively utilizing constructive conflict, and minimizing destructive conflict.

    Thanks to regular meditation, Buddhist reading, and dialogues with fellow Buddhists, he managed to quickly detect negative emotions, so that he could deal with them properly. Similarly, he had learned to positively deal with fear, engage in constructive relationships with stakeholders,

Buddhist Business Leaders in Action   161

encourage coworkers in joint social projects, and perform fair yet firm in all circumstances.

- *The Marketing Team*, a Buddhist couple, provided their employees the freedom to engage directly with clients, thus handling their project portfolios and gaining an increased sense of ownership. They also created a "revival room" in which employees could retreat through the day for some rest, prayer, or meditation. The effects of this compassionate act were visible in the company's performance. These leaders also invited their workforce to detect social projects in which they could jointly volunteer.

- *The Monk-Manager* performed as director of a nonprofit organization, and regularly involved the unemployed in his area, regardless of background, ethnicity, or religion, in projects. He regularly mingled with employees, customers, and visitors, and made sure his relationships remained constructive. While he did get upset at times, his meditation and reflection had taught him to release mental enemies, such as anger, spite, despair, disappointment, pride, or other mental afflictions, as soon as he discovered them.

- Some common practices among the described business leaders, such as the fact that they were more interested in relationships than the bottom line, focused on collaboration, engaged in social awareness and charity, worked effectively on stress reduction, encouraged responsibility and ownership among their employees, and meditated regularly.

- The fact that Buddhist practices, if applied responsibly, are not an inhibition, but rather an advantage to work related performance, because a Buddhist leader or coworker will regularly reflect and focus on maintaining essential Buddhist principles in their actions.

- The Seven-Point Mind Training, which is an effective and reputable Tibetan-based instrument with high appeal among practitioners of meditative techniques. The training entails the following seven steps:
  1. Training in the preliminaries.
  2. Cultivating ultimate and relative *Bodhicitta*.
  3. Transforming adversity into an aid to spiritual awakening.
  4. A synthesis of practice for one life.
  5. The criterion of proficiency in the mind training.
  6. The pledges of the mind training.
  7. The precepts of the mind training.

Questions

1. In the beginning of the chapter, a number of well-known Buddhists from different backgrounds are mentioned. Select one name from the list, or find another well-known Buddhist practitioner not mentioned, and engage in a brief review of this person's recent actions. Do you feel that they are truly

162 Buddhist Business Leaders in Action

engaging in Buddhist behavior, based on what you have read so far in this book?

2. The finance business leader in this chapter mentioned that he was somewhat concerned about the sense of entitlement of younger employees. Do you agree that this sense of entitlement exists? Please motivate your answer, either with personal reflections or supported with your findings from external reading about the topic?

3. The marketing team leaders mentioned in this chapter created a revival room to give employees the opportunity to regain energy through the busy workday. What is your personal opinion about this room? Would you also create such a room for your employees if you were a business leader? Why or why not?

4. The monk-manager discussed in this chapter discussed our internal emotional states as potential enemies, which can be more destructive than external enemies. Reflect on a negative emotion you recently felt. What was it about? How did you deal with it then? Seeing this negative emotion as an internal enemy now, how would you deal with it now?

5. Consider the Seven-Point Mind Training:

   a. Which sections or points of the training do you already practice? Please explain.

   b. Which sections or points would you like to work on? Please explain.

   c. Which sections or points do you see as most challenging? Please explain.

Notes

1 Wallace, B. A. (1992). *The Seven-Point Mind Training*. Snow Lion Publications, Ithaca, NY.

2 Wallace, B. A. (2001). *Buddhism With an Attitude: The Tibetan Seven-Point Mind Training*. Snow Lion Publications, Ithaca, NY.

3 Tegchok, G. J. (2006). *The Kindness of Others: A Commentary on the Seven-Point Mind Training* (trans. S. Carlier). Lama Yeshe Wisdom Archive, Weston, MA.

4 Wallace, B. A. (2001). *Buddhism With an Attitude: The Tibetan Seven-Point Mind Training*. Snow Lion Publications, Ithaca, NY: p. 50.

5 Wallace, B. A. (2001). *Buddhism with an Attitude: The Tibetan Seven-Point Mind Training*. Snow Lion Publications, Ithaca, NY, p. 65.

6 Thrangu Rinpoche (2004). *The Root Text of the Seven Points of Mind Training*. (transl. M. Martin as, *The Seven Points of Mind Training in the Mahayana*). Retrieved on May 4, 2014 from www.rinpoche.com/teachings/sevenpoints.htm

7 Using Adversity (2014). From *The Tonglen and Mind Training Site, Entailing a Comparison of Lectures on the Seven-Point Mind Training From Buddhist Scholars, Osho, Chogyam Trungpa, Pema Chödron, Jamgon Kongtrul, Alan Wallace, Geshe Rabten, Geshe Dhargyey*, and *Dilgo Khyentse Rinpoche*. Retrieved on May 4, 2014 from http://lojongmindtraining.com/sectionSummary.aspx?sectionID=3

8 Life and Death (2014). From *The Tonglen and Mind Training Site, Entailing a Comparison of Lectures on the Seven-Point Mind Training From Buddhist Scholars, Osho, Chogyam Trungpa, Pema Chödron, Jamgon Kongtrul, Alan Wallace, Geshe Rabten, Geshe Dhargyey*, and *Dilgo Khyentse Rinpoche*. Retrieved on May 4, 2014 from http://lojongmindtraining.com/sectionSummary.aspx?sectionID=4

9 Ibid.

10 Yardsticks (2014) From *The Tonglen and Mind Training Site, Entailing a Comparison of Lectures on the Seven-Point Mind Training From Buddhist Scholars, Osho, Chogyam Trungpa, Pema Chödron, Jamgon Kongtrul, Alan Wallace, Geshe Rabten, Geshe Dhargyey,* and *Dilgo Khyentse Rinpoche.* Retrieved on May 4, 2014 from http://lojongmindtraining.com/sectionSummary.aspx?sectionID=5

11 Commitments (2014). From *The Tonglen and Mind Training Site, Entailing a Comparison of Lectures on the Seven-Point Mind Training From Buddhist scholars, Osho, Chogyam Trungpa, Pema Chödron, Jamgon Kongtrul, Alan Wallace, Geshe Rabten, Geshe Dhargyey,* and *Dilgo Khyentse Rinpoche.* Retrieved on May 4, 2014 from http://lojongmindtraining.com/sectionSummary.aspx?sectionID=6

12 Thrangu Rinpoche (2004). *The Root Text of the Seven Points of Mind Training.* (trans. M. Martin, as *The Seven Points of Mind Training in the Mahayana*). Retrieved on May 4, 2014 from www.rinpoche.com/teachings/sevenpoints.htm

13 Ibid.; Guidelines (2014). From *The Tonglen and Mind Training Site, Entailing a Comparison of Lectures on the Seven-Point Mind Training From Buddhist Scholars, Osho, Chogyam Trungpa, Pema Chödron, Jamgon Kongtrul, Alan Wallace, Geshe Rabten, Geshe Dhargyey,* and *Dilgo Khyentse Rinpoche.* Retrieved on May 4, 2014 from http://lojongmindtraining.com/sectionSummary.aspx?sectionID=7

INDEX

Page numbers in italics refer to information in figures and tables.

Ahimsa (principle of non-harming) 69, 133–5, 142–4
AIDS 23
American Revolution 4–5
Argyris, Chris 35
Arnold, Edwin 71
asbestos 38, 40
Atīśa (eleventh-century Buddhist teacher) 156

baby boom generation 18–23, 26
Barth, Carl 31
Bermudes, Peter 113
Black Tuesday (October 29, 1929) 19, 25
Bodhi (awakening) 137, 157
Bodhi, Bhikkhu 1, 146
Bodhicitta (spirit of awakening) 67–9, 77, 90, 103, 137–9, 143–4, 157–9
Bodhisattva (enlightened being) viii, 67–8, 76–8, 80
BRIC countries (Brazil, Russia, India, and China) 9
Britain *see* Great Britain
Buddha *see* Siddhartha Gautama (the Buddha)
Buddha nature 67–8, 77–8, 98, 104, 116
Buddhism: *Ahimsa* (principle of non-harming) 69, 133–5, 142–4; *Bodhicitta* (spirit of awakening) 67–9, 77, 90,

103, 137–9, 143–4, 157–9; *Bodhisattva* (enlightened being) viii, 67–8, 76–8, 80; challenges for the workplace 131–43; collaboration 122–3, 126, 132, 139, 142, 144, 154; consciousness 96–103; dependent origination 70; detachment 119–21, 124, 126, 132, 135–6, 142, 144; equanimity, principle of 135–6, 138–9, 143–4; impermanence 61, 70, 87, 95, 135, 153–4, 156, 160; karma 70, 117–18, 122, 126, 132, 157; main vehicles 70; Middle Way viii, 65, 130–1; mindfulness 70, 85, 89, 92–3, 102–3, 112, 123–4, 155–6; *Nirvana* 66–7, 70, 77–8, 88–9; no competition, principle of 136–7, 139, 142–4; no-self mindset 70, 78, 120, 123; Noble Eightfold Path 47, 85, 89–95, 102–3, 123, 126, 132, 156; perceived manipulation of 141–2; personal responsibility 117–19, 126, 131–2, 142, 144; as a psychology 55, 62, 65, 74, 80, 112–26, 131–42, 146; religious perspective of 140–1; science and 116–17, 126, 131, 136, 141, 146; self 65, 68–70, 77–9, 88–9, 96–102, 119–23, 126, 156–9; suffering 70, 78, 80, 85–93, 102–3, 105n3, 119–20, 138–9, 141–2; Three Gems (Buddha, *Dhamma/Dharma*, *Sangha*) 69, 78; in the United States

166 Index

70–5, 147–53; Vajrayana (Tibetan) Buddhism 67, 72, 75–7, 79–80, 96; values in the workplace *117*; wholesome view 123–5, 132–3; *see also* Four Noble Truths; Mahayana Buddhism; Theravada Buddhism
Buddhist business leaders: common practices 154–6, 161; finance expert 147–51, 160–1; marketing team 151–2, 161; monk-manager 153–4, 161; Seven-Point Mind Training 156–9, *160*, 161
Bush, George H. W. 24
business: Buddhism's appropriateness for 112–14, 126; change/discontentment and 109–11, *111*, 125–6; collaboration 122–3; corporations 3–6, 12; change, growth, and development 37–40; healthy detachment and 119–21; history of trade 1–3, 12; Industrial Revolution 6–9, 13–14; mercantilism 3, 12; personal responsibility 117–19; reputation of 39; in the twentieth century 9–13; useful Buddhist practices for 114–17, 126; wholesome view and 123–5; *see also* Buddhist business leaders; management

capitalism: Buddhism and 112–13, 126; entrepreneurs and 2; Great Depression and 19; Industrial Revolution and 8; management trends and 11, 14
child labor 17–18, 25
China 2, 9, 67, 69, 114, 116; immigrants from 71, 73, 78, 112; invasion of Tibet 72, 75–6, 153–4; Japan's invasion of 20
Christianity 4, 71, 101, 104
civil rights movement 22, 26
Coca-Cola Company 50
colonialism 9, 13–14
Common Market 3
compassion: *Bodhicitta* and 69, 157; consciousness and 97; Dalai Lama and 76–7, 113; leadership and 46, 51–2; Mahayana Buddhism and 67–9, 78; social involvement and 153; in the workplace *115*, 120, 122–4, 132, 138–9, 142–3, 151, 161
Complete Economic Integration 3
consciousness 66, 96, 112, 138–9, 143–4; Buddha's perspective on 96–8, 104; *citta* 97–8, 104, 137, 157; Dalai Lama's perspective on 98–9, 104; higher 138–9, 143–4; levels of 99–101, 104; religions and 101, 104–5; Vipassana meditation

and 93; Western perspective on 99–101, 103–4
Constitution, U.S. 5
Cooke, Morris 31
corporate scandals 43, 45, 51
corporations 3–6, 12; multinational 24, 38, 45
crime 22–3

Dalai Lama, His Holiness Tenzin Gyatso: on altruism and compassion 76–7, 113; on *Bodhicitta* 138; on consciousness 98–9, 104; on early Buddhist traditions 66; exile of 72, 75–6, 153; as leader of Tibetan Buddhism 75–6, 79–80; on non-harming 43, 134; popularity of 74, 76, 114, 116; public appearances of 146; on reinvention of Buddhism 75, 79, 141; on science 116–17, 126, 136; on sexual misconduct 75
Deming, W. Edwards 11
desire 88–90, 102–3, 105, 109, 120–1
detachment 119–21, 124, 126, 132, 135–6, 142, 144
Dhamma (Dharma) 60, 69, 78, 84, 105n2, 159

education 18; consciousness and 100; Dalai Lama's encouragement of 117, 136; GI Bill 20, 26; happiness and 110; Industrial Revolution and 7; racial segregation and 16–17; women and 109
entrepreneurs 37, 113, 131, 139
equanimity, principle of 135–6, 138–9, 143–4
Eye of the I, The (Hawkins) 100–1

family, historical perception of 3–4
Favier, Jean 14
Fayol, Henri 32–3, 39
Fields, Rick 74
Fiscal Union 3
Five Forces 158
Follett, Mary Parker 11, 34, 40
Four Noble Truths 84–5, 155–6; Buddhist schools and 70, 78; cautionary side of 131–2, 142; First Noble Truth (suffering exists) 85–7, 102; Noble Eightfold Path (Fourth Noble Truth) 85, 89–95, 102–3, 123, 126, 132, 156; Second Noble Truth (suffering has a cause) 87–8, 102; soft skills and 47; Third Noble Truth (suffering can be ended) 88–9, 103
Fourteenth Amendment 5

Index **167**

Gandhi, Mahatma 99–100, 139
Gantt, Henry 31
Gautama Buddha *see* Siddhartha Gautama (the Buddha)
General Motors 11
GI Bill 20, 26
Gilbreth, Frank 31–2
Gilbreth, Lilian 31
Gold & Spices: The Rise of Commerce in the Middle Ages (Favier) 3
Great Britain 5, 7, 9, 13–14
Great Depression 19–20, 26, 34
Gulick, Luther 33

hard skills 44, 47–8, 50–2; *see also* soft skills
Hathaway, Horace 31
Hawkins, David 99–101, 104
"Hawthorne effect" 34
Hawthorne Experiments 11, 34
health: Buddhism and 65, 69, 77, 80; hazards 17–18, 38, 40, 124, 134; workplace conditions and 18, 25, 136
health care 20–1, 24
healthy detachment 119–21, 124, 126, 132, 135–6, 142, 144
Herzberg, Frederick 35, 41
Hewlett, Bill 11
hierarchy of needs (Maslow) 35, 41
Hoover, Herbert 19
Hugo, Victor 130

immigration 17, 20, 23, 25–6; Buddhist 71–3, 78–9, 112; laws 18, 21, 23, 26
Industrial Revolution 6–9, 13–14, 30, 44, 71, 110
Inquiry into the Nature and Causes of the Wealth of Nations, An (Smith) 3
internet 22, 24–5, 27, 110, 136
inventions 2, 17; 1900s 17; 1910s 18; 1920s 18–19; 1930s 20; 1940s 20; 1950s 21; 1960s 22; 1970s 23; 1980s 24, 1990s 24–5

Japan 11; Buddhism and 67, 71, 78–9, 112, 141; Deming's management theory and 11; invasion of China by 20; in World War II 20
Johns-Manville Corporation 38, 40

Kennedy, John F. 22
Kennedy, Robert 22
King, Martin Luther, Jr. 22
Kornfield, Jack 74, 146

leadership: Authentic Leadership 46, 52; Awakened Leadership 46, 52; Engaged Leadership 46, 52; Respectful Leadership 46, 51; soft skills and 43–4, 46–7, 51–2; Transformational Leadership 46, 52
Light of Asia, The (Arnold) 71
living standards 7–8, 36–7

McGregor, Douglas 35
Mahayana Buddhism 67–8, 77–8, 156; *Bodhisattva* (enlightened being) viii, 67–8, 76–8, 80; consciousness and 101, 105; Theravada Buddhism and viii, 68–70, 78; Tibetan Buddhism and 75–7, 79–80, 116
Malcolm X 22
management: administrative theory 11, 32–3, 36, 39; behavioral theory 34–6, 39–40; bureaucratic theory 11, 33, 36, 39; human relations theory 11, 35–6, 39–40; human resources theory 11, 35–6; Motivation–Hygiene Theory (Herzberg) 35, 41; Motivation Theory (Maslow) 35, 41; POLC (Planning, Organizing, Leading, and Controlling) 32–3, 39; scientific management 11, 14, 30–2, 36, 39; twentieth-century theories *36*
Management by Wandering Around (MBWA) 11, 153
manufacturing 5–9, 13, 16–17, 30–1, 48–9
Maslow, Abraham 35, 41
Mayo, Elton 34, 40
meditation 118, 135, 141–2, 147–8, 153, 156–7, 160–1; Buddha and 59–60, 62; mindfulness 70, 85, 89, 92–3, 102–3, 112, 123–4, 155–6; Transcendental 22, 26–7; Vipassana viii, 60, 62, 93–4, 103, 105, 156
mercantilism 3, 12
Monetary Union 3
Monsanto Corporation 38–40

Naropa Institute 72, 79
Niger Delta ethnic conflict 38, 40
Nirvana 66–7, 70, 77–8, 88–9
Noble Eightfold Path 47, 85, 89, *95*, 123, 126, 132, 156; Right Action 91, 103, 123–4; Right Concentration 94–5, 103, 124; Right Effort 92, 103, 124; Right Intention 90–1, 103, 123; Right Livelihood 92, 103, 124; Right Mindfulness 92–4, 103, 124; Right Speech 91, 103, 123; Right View 89–90, 103, 123

168 Index

no competition, principle of 136–7, 139, 142–4
no-self mindset 70, 78, 120, 123

Packard, David 11
Parks, Rosa 21, 26–7
personal responsibility 117–19, 126, 131–2, 142, 144
Philadelphia (film) 23
POLC (Planning, Organizing, Leading, and Controlling) 32–3, 39
Power vs. Force (Hawkins) 99–101
Preferential Trading Agreements (PTAs) 3, 14
psychology, Buddhism as 55, 62, 65, 74, 80, 112–26, 131–42

racial segregation 16–17, 21, 23, 25
Reagan, Ronald 23
Revival Room 152, 154, 161–2
Right Action 91, 103, 123–4
Right Concentration 94–5, 103, 124
Right Effort 92, 103, 124
Right Intention 90–1, 103, 123
Right Livelihood 92, 103, 124
Right Mindfulness 92–4, 103, 124
Right Speech 91, 103, 123
Right View 89–90, 103, 123
Roosevelt, Franklin Delano 19–20, 26

Salk, Jonas 21
science, Buddhism and 116–17, 126, 131, 136, 141, 146
science, technology, engineering, and math (STEM) 48–9
scientific management 11, 14, 30–2, 36, 39
Serlingpa (tenth century Buddhist teacher) 156
Seven-Point Mind Training 156–9, *160*, 161
Shambhala training 72
Siddhartha Gautama (the Buddha) viii, 65–6, 84; American Buddhism and 75; ascetic years of 58–9, 62; becoming Buddha 59–60, 62; on consciousness 96–7; early years and family of 55–8, 60–2; and Gopa (wife) 56–7, 62; on happiness 132, 146; influence on his family 60–2; lessons learned by 60–1, *61*; lifestyle of viii, 58–9, 62–3; Mahayana Buddhism and 67–9, 77–8; marriage(s) of 56–8, 62; and Rahula (son) 57–63; as teacher rather than god 65, 77; Theravada Buddhism and viii, 66, 68–9,

77–8; on victimized thinking 131; Vipassana meditation and viii, 60, 62, 93–4, 103; and Yasodhara (wife) 57–8, 60, 62; *see also* Buddhism
Sloan, Alfred 11
Smith, Adam 3, 12
soft skills viii: defined 44–5, 51; diversity and 49–52; empathy 44, 51; impact on organizational success *50*; leadership and 43–4, 46–7, 51–2; motivation 44, 49, 51; mistaken mindsets concerning 47–8; rise of 45, 51; self-regulation 44, 51; social skills 44, 51; stakeholder inclusion and 48–9, 52; in today's workforce 47–51; trust 45–9, 51–2
Sogyal Rinpoche 130
spirituality at work 112, 114, 126–7, 140–1
stakeholders viii, 45–50, 52, 118, 126, 134–5, 148–9
suffering: cause of 87–8; end of 88–9; existence of 85–7; misperceptions about 142; Noble Eightfold Path and 89–95; types of 85–7
Supreme Court, U.S. 5, 21, 23, 27
Suzuki, D. T. 16
Suzuki, Shunryu 55

Taylor, Frederic Winslow 11, 31–3, 39
Taylorism 11; *see also* scientific management
Tegchok, Geshe Jampa 156; *see also* Seven-Point Mind Training
Templeton, David 113
Theosophical Society 71
Theravada Buddhism 66–7, 77, 80; consciousness and 101, 105; Mahayana Buddhism and viii, 68–70, 78; Tibetan Buddhism and 75, 79, 93
Thich Nhat Hanh 30, 74, 79, 89–90, 97, 104, 146
Thompson, Sanford 31
Thrangu Rinpoche 157–8
Three Gems (Buddha, *Dhamma/Dharma*, *Sangha*) 69, 78
Thurman, Robert 76, 146
Tibet, Chinese invasion of 72, 75–6, 153–4
Tibetan (Vajrayana) Buddhism 67, 72, 75–7, 79–80, 96
trade: agreements 3, 10; development 9–10, *10*; family ownership 9; history of 1–3, 9–10, 12
Transcendental Meditation 22, 26–7

Transcending the Levels of Consciousness (Hawkins) 101
Truman, Harry 20–1
Trungpa, Chogyam (Trungpa Rinpoche) 79
Twain, Mark 130

unemployment 18–24, 26–7
United Kingdom 9, 13–14; *see also* Great Britain
United States: booming years (1920–1929) 18–19, 25; Buddhism in 70–5, 147–53; economic struggles (1910–1919) 17–18, 25; family values revived (1950–59) 21, 26; global communication (1990–1999) 24–5, 27; Great Depression 19–20, 26; manufacturing era (1900–1909) 16–17, 25; population 17–18, 20–4; post-World War II and baby boom 20, 26; radical changes (1960–1969) 21–2, 26; religion in 140–1; rights and racial integration (1970–1979) 22–3, 26; Tibetan Buddhism in 72; in the twentieth century *25*; wealth accumulation and consumerism (1980–1989) 23–4, 26–7; World War I 17–18, 25; World War II 19–20, 26
Urwick, Lyndall 33–4

Vajrayana (Tibetan) Buddhism 67, 72, 75–7, 79–80, 96
Vietnam War 22–3, 26
Vipassana meditation viii, 60, 62, 93–4, 103, 105, 156
Vroom, Victor 35

Wallace, Alan 76, 96, 104, 156; *see also* Seven-Point Mind Training
Wal-Mart 6, 50
Weber, Max 33, 39
work *see* business
workplace spirituality 112, 114, 126–7, 140–1
Works Progress Administration (WPA) 20, 26
World War I 18, 25, 31
World War II 19–21, 26, 71
World Wide Web 24–5, 27; *see also* internet
Wright, Karen 96, 103

Zappos 48–9
Zen Buddhism: consciousness and 101, 105; growth and popularity of 22, 26, 71, 79; Mahayana Buddhism and 67; modest environment of 73; Steve Jobs and 146
Zentrepreneurism (Holender) 113

An environmentally friendly book printed and bound in England by www.printondemand-worldwide.com

This book is made of chain-of-custody materials; FSC materials for the cover and PEFC materials for the text pages.